Getaway

Cape to Cairo

MIKE COPELAND

SUNBIRD
PUBLISHING

First published in 2003
2 4 6 8 10 9 7 5 3 1

Sunbird Publishing (Pty) Ltd,
34 Sunset Avenue, Llandudno, South Africa
Registration number: 4850177827

Publisher Dick Wilkins
Design and maps Marcelle de Villiers-Louw
Editor Marion Boddy-Evans
Proofreader Margy Beves-Gibson
Editorial adviser David Bristow

Reproduction by Unifoto (Pty) Ltd, Cape Town
Printed and bound by Tien Wah Press (Pte) Ltd, Singapore

ISBN 1919938079

Front cover (main photo): The author studies the map on the road between Addis Ababa and Bahir
Dar, Ethiopioa. Title page: The Blue Nile Falls near to the source at Lake Tana, Ethiopia. Page 190: On
the road near Sesriem, Namibia.

It is with warm affection that I acknowledge and thank my wife and children who have accompanied me on so many wonderful journeys in Africa and beyond. And, to my dear friend Rennie Orton in Addis Ababa, always so hospitable, I say: "*Betam ameseghinalehu*." Thanks too to Keith and Colleen Begg who helped me with up-to-date information on Mozambique.

The creation of this guidebook owes so much to the vision and input of David and his team at *Getway*, particularly the considerable talents of Marion, my editor, and Marcelle, who created the beautiful layouts and artwork.

I dedicate this book to my parents, George and Jean, who nurtured my appetite for travel and taught me to love this great continent of ours, Africa.

God bless Africa
guard her people
guide her leaders
and give her peace

Contents

REGIONAL MAPS

STRIP MAPS

KEY TO STRIP MAPS

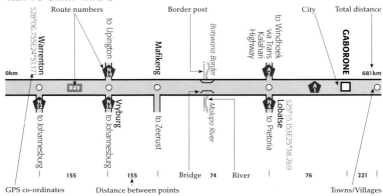

HOW TO USE THIS BOOK

The first 10 chapters offer advice on deciding what route to take, what vehicle to use and the equipment you will need. Tips are given on food and acommodation, medical precautions and dealing with road conditions and situations. Useful local phrases are listed and there is a chapter on the availability and use of public transport to travel through Africa. The second part devotes a chapter to each of 12 different routes, described in detail with stripmaps, GPS co-ordinates, sights to see, and food and fuel availability.

As routes are described from south to north, Cape Town contacts are listed in the initial chapters on organising and fitting out the trip. If you're starting from another centre, use the information listed under the relevant city. Starting from the north, you will have to do your planning from home, as there is not much information or equipment available in North Africa.

The website of *Getaway* magazine, www.getawaytoafrica.com, is also an excellent source of information on Africa.

Prices in this book are quoted in United States dollars, telephone numbers are listed as you would dial them within the country (including the city code).

Introduction

We are all nomads at heart and Africa is the ideal place to follow your travelling instincts. It is still possible to lose yourself, literally and figuratively, in the wilderness and cultures of this vast continent.

If it is adventure and danger you crave, then it's here in truckloads. The mountains, jungles and deserts will fill you with awe. The ancient civilisations, cuisines and lifestyles will beg more time for appreciation. Wild animals roam the open spaces like bit players in a timeless saga, while in the ever-changing modern cities, politicians and bureaucrats overact their parts to a soundtrack of loud, throbbing music and traffic. In Africa you have to look alive, or you could be dead!

Archaeological discoveries suggest that all of humanity has its origins in Africa, which means that the first human explorers were actually venturing out of this continent, not into it.

Over millenia, interaction has taken place between the northern continents and Africa. The Romans sent chariots to trade in the Sahara, the Greeks rowed their galleons down the Red Sea, and the Arabs and Indians used the dependable monsoon winds to make regular journeys up and down the east coast.

Latter-day 'discoverers' pinpointed Africa's treasures and publicised them in Europe, but Bruce, Burton, Speke and Livingstone were only following in others' intrepid footsteps.

The colonial period that followed allowed for relatively safe, free travel throughout the continent. Roads and railways were built and routes forged. These days, we may have stronger vehicles, air travel and guide books, but the adventure has crept back into African travel and the overlander can again feel a sense of achievement making their way across the continent.

I was born in Africa and it has made me who I am. I have loved my travels and hope I can impart the knowledge and infuse my love of this vast mass of land and humanity. However, in Africa nothing stays the same for too long; routes and situations change all the time. Mainly for political reasons, roads can become too dangerous or visas unobtainable, and so the routes and advice described in this book are only your best current options. Always obtain up-to-date information locally before setting out along a particular route.

If it's been a long-held ambition to travel through Africa, but you keep on putting it off, remember the accusing words in the Rodrigues song about people who lose their dreams and later say they were stolen.

1 Route planning

The traditional Cape to Cairo route was essentially a British one. It linked all the British colonies and protectorates – the pink bits on the map – and traversed South Africa, the Rhodesias, Tanganyika, Kenya, the Sudan and into Egypt. Simple then, but when wars in the Sudan, Ethiopia and Eritria dragged on for decades, north to south travellers swung west towards the predominantly French route through Algeria, Niger, Central African Republic and the Congo.

Now civil war in West Africa and kidnappings in Algeria have swung the pendulum back east and travellers are advised to avoid Central Africa and travel through three very definite way-points. These are:

Above: The road to the mountain-top monastery of Debre Damo in Ethiopia. Left: Delivering thatch on Lake Malawi.

• **Mbeya**, between Zambia and Tanzania. Although there is limited vehicular access across the Ruvuma River in the north of Mozambique and access west of Mbeya is possible along Lake Tanganyika, Angola and the Congo are still too chaotic to recommend. This funnels almost all vehicular traffic through Mbeya.

• **Moyale**, on the border between northern Kenya and Ethiopia. To the west, southern Sudan suffers a seemingly neverending civil war which denies safe access, while in the east the fighting Somali clans make it too dangerous.

• **Wadi Halfa**, between the Sudan and Egypt. The Libyan Desert and the red tape of Chad in the west and the inhospitable troops and terrain up the Red Sea coast make this way-point a must.

There are many tempting alternative routes in Southern Africa up as far as the border into Tanzania. The roads through Namibia, Botswana, Malawi and Mozambique are all passable and take one through beautiful and interesting parts of Africa. East Africa also offers alternative routes and a lot to see – the shortest route is not necessarily the best. The historic sights of Ethiopia will also draw any traveller off the direct route and into the mountains of this fascinating country. Even the dry desert regions of Sudan and Egypt offer alternative routes. At the time of writing Angola was opening up, the cease-fire between Ethiopia and Eritrea was holding up and there was talk of an end to hostilities in southern Sudan, so keep an eye on the situation and plan accordingly.

Choose your route north or south

The shortest, easiest and most sensible route is:
Cape Town, Bloemfontein, Johannesburg, Beitbridge, Harare, Chirundu, Lusaka, Kapiri Mposhi, Mbeya, Dar es Salaam, Arusha, Nairobi, Marsabit, Moyale, Sheshemane, Addis Ababa, Bahir Dar, Metema, Gedarif, Khartoum, Dongola, Wadi Halfa, Aswan, Luxor, Cairo.

This route has the benefit of traversing some of the most historically interesting countries of Africa as well as being scenically beautiful. From the hedonistic pleasures of Cape Town's beaches and nightlife, to ancient religious relics on remote Ethiopian mountain tops, this route has it all.

according to what you prefer: tropical beaches, hustle and bustle of big towns, bird-watching, game parks, the desert. The Southern African region offers a selection of circle routes as does East Africa, and vehicles can be hired to explore these areas. An alternative is to use public transport to get around.

When to go

The routes described take the traveller through mostly mild and temperate regions, with the exception of the dry heat of the Sudan and Egypt. The main climatic problem, however, is rain and what it does to the unpaved roads.

In the South, around Cape Town, the climate is pleasantly Mediterranean with warm, dry summers and cool, wet winters. As one heads north, it becomes

You can't plan without good maps.

in fact the whole of Ethiopia) receives rain twice annually. The 'big rains' fall from June until mid-September and the 'small rains' from late January to early March. Time your trip to pass this way during the rain-free months.

Although the main road system inside Ethiopia is fairly good, the country is very mountainous and has some unavoidable unpaved routes. Beyond Khartoum the weather does not affect the roads, but it is wise to avoid the debilitating heat of the summer months. It is also a good idea to try to avoid the month of Ramadan in the Islamic countries of the Sudan and Egypt as business virtually comes to a standstill and it is difficult to find food during daylight hours.

Ramadan should fall between 26 October and 25 November in 2004 and, as the dates are set by the Justinian calendar, will be about 11 days earlier each subsequent year.

How long will it take?

Well, that's like asking what time the bus leaves in Africa. I think three months is about right. It allows you enough time to see all the interesting and important sights along the way, without dawdling and settling down for too long in one place.

If you summarise all the above, it means aiming for Marsabit/Moyale and Metema in April/May or November/December. So, if you're planning on taking three months, then leave Cape Town in late February, to pass Marsabit, then through Ethiopia and Gallabat before the end of May. Or, late September to get through before the end of December.

Dead simple ... good luck!

drier and changes to summer rainfall.

The mild temperatures and predictable thundershowers make for fairly trouble-free driving along vast open stretches crisscrossed with good surfaced roads.

North of Zimbabwe and into East Africa, the roads deteriorate, but are still passable and, with a mild climate and topography, driving is still quite easy.

Heading north out of Kenya, however conditions change quite drastically, and the driving becomes a glorious challenge. The road from Isiola to Marsabit and Moyale, on the Ethiopian border, sometimes becomes impassable during the rains. The thick, gluey, slippery mud of the black cotton soil causes whole convoys of trucks to bog down and block the road completely. To complicate matters, the region (and

How to travel

2

One of the first decisions you will need to make is how to travel: will you take your own vehicle, hire a fully equipped 4x4, join a tour group, or use public transport? Each has their own appeal and hassles. You don't need to take your own vehicle, but it does give you the freedom to come and go as you please. You will be independent of all others and able to ignore public transport time tables. You can carry more luggage and equipment and your vehicle can be your mobile home, serving as bedroom and kitchen. It can be your refuge and can protect you. It will take you quickly from place to place and to destinations where public transport doesn't go.

The MV *Ilala* on Lake Malawi services some small lakeside villages that are inaccessible by road.

Buy or hire?

To go the whole way, you will need your own vehicle. But if your time is limited or you don't want to go all the way, it makes sense to hire a vehicle, though it does mean you'll have to do a round trip back to a major city. Well maintained and even fully equipped vehicles can be hired in South Africa and Namibia. In the rest of Africa it's really possible only in Nairobi.

Bring or buy locally?

All overlanders encounter the problem of having to ship their vehicle sooner or later and it is usually very expensive. If you're a South African who's driven north to Cairo, what do you do with your vehicle when you get there? Cairo isn't an easy place for a foreigner to do business in, so consider shipping your vehicle across the Mediterranean and driving it further into Europe before selling it or shipping it home. Another

> **Look in the classified ads** of local papers for private vehicle sales and check out the notice boards at backpackers lodges for foreign-registered vehicles being sold rather than shipped home.

option is to fly to Europe, buy and equip a vehicle there and drive it south. The easiest option for travellers from Europe is to fly to Cape Town, buy a vehicle locally (new or used), equip it, and drive it home.

Shipping costs

Safmarine quoted the following prices to ship a 20-foot, general-purpose container, suitable for a vehicle. These prices are subject to changes in original terminal handling charges; destination terminal handling charges; additional bunker surcharges and war risk sur-

---

CAR HIRE COMPANIES SPECIALISING IN 4X4S

Avis Van Rental, Manchester Road, Airport Industria, Cape Town, tel: 021-386-6670, fax: 021-386-6654, E-mail avis@adept.co.za, website: www.avissainbound.co.za

National Car Rental, Cape Town International Airport, tel: 021-934 7499, fax: 021-934-7499, e-mail: nationalcar@cmh.co.za

Sani Rentals, Michigan Street, Airport Industria, Cape Town, tel: 021-386-2111, fax: 021-386-2323, e-mail: mail@sanirentals.co.za, website: www.sani.co.za

Kenings Bakkie and Car Hire, 323 Koeberg Road, Milnerton, Cape Town, tel: 021-511-1238, fax: 021-511-8460, e-mail: kenings@satis.co.za, website: www.kenings.co.za

Universal 4x4 Hire, 75 Keurboom Road, Rondebosch, Cape Town, tel: 021-683-1590, fax: 021-683-6861, website: www.universal4x4.co.za

Just Done It 4x4 Rentals, 112 De Waal Road, Diep River, Cape Town, tel: 021-706-8131, fax: 021-706-8161, e-mail: justdone@iafrica.com, website: www.4x4hire.co.za

---

CAPE TOWN 4X4 DEALERS: (SEE PAGE 65 FOR JOBURG DEALERS)

Forsdicks Land Rover, (new and used), 10 Kloof Street, Gardens, Cape Town, tel: 021-426-2806. fax: 021-426-2859, e-mail peterg@cmh.co.za, website: www.landrover.co.za

Market Toyota, (new and used), Culemborg Motor City, Foreshore, Cape Town, tel: 021-410-9300, fax: 021-410-9328, e-mail: etoyota@culemborg.co.za, website: www.toyota.co.za

Schus Nissan, (new and used), 396 Voortrekker Road, Parow, Cape Town, tel: 021-930-3333, fax: 021-930-3390, e-mail nicholass@imperialnissan.co.za, website: www.nissan.co.za

McCarthy Motors Jeep, Culemborg Motor City, Foreshore, Cape Town, tel: 021-419-7100, fax: 021-419-0309

Reeds Isuzu, (new and used), Main Road, Observatory, Cape Town, tel: 021-448-4464, fax: 021-447-9668

L R Sales, (used Land Rovers), 201 Victoria Rd, Southfield,Cape Town, tel: 021-705-0474

Orbit Motors Mitsubishi, (new and used), N1 City, Goodwood, Cape Town, tel: 021-595-8100, fax: 021-595-8111, e-mail orbit@orbit.co.za, website: www.mitsubishi-motors.co.za

Table Bay Motors, (new and used 4x4s), 28 Marine Drive, Paarden Eiland, Cape Town, tel: 021-510-3289, fax: 021-510-3074

Symonds Autos, (used 4x4s), 72 Durban Road, Mowbray, Cape Town, tel: 021-689-9576

---

charges: Cape Town to Alexandria $1 000, Cape Town to Port Sudan $1 300, Cape Town to Mombassa $700, Port Sudan to Cape Town $2 000, Port Sudan to Gio Taura (Italy) $1 100, Alexandria to Gio Taura (Italy) $250, Alexandria to Cape Town $1 550, Gio Taura (Italy) to Cape Town $1 300, Mombassa to Cape Town $500.

SAFMARINE CONTACTS:
South Africa: Paul Zunckel, tel: 021-408-6911, e-mail: safsclmkt@za.safmarine.com.
Kenya: Janet Anota, tel: 02-21-6206, e-mail: kensclsal@ke.safmarine.com.
Sudan: Abhijit Gokhale, tel: 031-20-558, e-mail: wcasclcom@sd.safmarine.com.

Egypt: Koen de Bakke, tel: 02-418-1710, e-mail: egysclmng@eg.safmarine.com.
Italy: Craig Coffey, Tel 010-5319-1408, e-mail: itascltop@it.safmarine.com.

Taking public transport

Many travellers prefer the footloose and unencumbered style of public transport (hitching or getting free rides is not really an option in Africa). They like to be unencumbered by a vehicle and all the extra baggage, and free of the responsibility of securing and maintaining one.

The more baggage you travel with, the more you become an obvious target for theft and rip-offs and are regarded as rich enough to be overcharged.

Some routes and rivers can't be traversed by any vehicle, making it better to be without one. You don't have to worry about what to do with your vehicle in the event of a serious accident, breakdown or at the end of your trip. You just hop a plane and go. Borders are easier and less expensive to cross.

Nothing beats public transport for bringing you into contact with people, you're not isolated in your vehicle from the local people in the countries you travel through. You're accepted with courtesy and respect as a fellow traveller and you will make the most wonderful friends and have the most rewarding experiences.

Joining a tour group

A third option is to join a tour group. These range from a crowded bus on a tour of city sights to an exclusive safari into one of Africa's great game parks with your own driver and game tracker. Huge 4x4 trucks also travel some of the routes covered in this book. Travelling in a group has its obvious pro's and con's but, ultimately, the choice is yours.

Travelling partners

Another choice you will have to make is whether to travel alone, with a companion (for all or part of the way), in a group or in convoy with others. This is also a very personal decision.

The purist loves to immerse themself in the various cultures of foreign

"Rather a live donkey than a dead lion" – Shackleton when aborting his South Pole attempt.

BUS/TRAIN COMPANIES THAT RUN ROUND SOUTH AFRICA AND NEIGHBOURING COUNTRIES

Greyhound, tel: 021-505 6363,
fax: 021-505 6380,
e-mail: enquiries@greyhound.co.za,
website: www.greyhound.co.za

Intercape Mainliner,
tel: 021-380-4400, fax: 021-386-2488, e-mail: info@intercape.co.za
website: www.intercape.co.za

Translux, tel: 021-449-3333,
fax: 021-449-2545,
e-mail: translux@apx.co.za,
website: www.translux.co.za

The Baz Bus, (aimed at backpackers and runs from hostel to hostel around South Africa),
tel: 021-439-2323,
fax: 021-439-2343,
e-mail: info@bazbus.com,
website: www.bazbus.com

Spoornet
(the South African railway service)
tel: 086-000-8888,
fax: 011 359 2206,
e-mail: bluetrain@spoornet.co.za,
website: www.spoornet.com

---

countries. If you're travelling alone and on public transport, nothing will dilute this experience or comes between you and the locals. Other more gregarious travellers like the companionship, fun and security of groups or convoys.

Make up your own mind, but don't be afraid to try anything new. Pick your companions carefully – you will be spending a lot of time with them.

An excursion on the refurbished Union Express is one way of getting around South Africa.

OVERLAND COMPANIES THAT GO 'ALL THE WAY' OR OFFER TRIPS THROUGH SOUTHERN AND EAST AFRICA

South Africa based companies

Karibu Safari
tel: 031-563-9774, fax: 031-563-1957,
e-mail: karibu@karibu.co.za,
website: www.karibu.co.za

Wild Frontiers
tel: 011-702-2035, fax: 011-468-1655,
e-mail: wildfront@icon.co.za,
website: www.wildfrontiers.com

African Routes
tel: 031-563-5080, fax: 031-563-5541,
e-mail: aroutes@iafrica.com,
website: www.africanroutes.co.za

Drifters
tel: 011-888-1160, fax: 011-888-1020,
E-mail drifters@drifters.co.za,
website: www.drifters.com

UK based companies

Africa Overland Club
tel: 01740-62-3633, fax: 01728-86-1127,
e-mail: ron@africa-overland.com,
website: www.africa-overland.com

Dragoman
tel: 01728-86-1133, fax: 01728-86-1127,
e-mail: info@dragoman.co.uk,
website: www.dragoman.com

Encounter Overland
tel: 020-7370-6951, fax: 020-7244-9737,
e-mail: adventure@encounter.co.uk,
website: www.encounter-overland.com

Truck Africa
tel: 020-7731-6142, fax: 020-7731-7445,
e-mail: sales@truckafrica.com,
website: www.truckafrica.com

3 What vehicle?

Assuming that you have decided to drive yourself through Africa, you will need a vehicle. The most important attribute of a vehicle for Africa is strength. It must be tough. An old, robust 4x2 pickup will get you further than some new, fancy 4x4s. Ideally you need a strong and mechanically simple vehicle with good fuel economy, easily available parts availability, high ground clearance and enough space to carry a fairly heavy load. Phew!

There is, of course, no perfect vehicle. Personal needs and preferences play a large role and you may already have what you consider to be the ideal transport. If not, here are some questions to ask yourself.

Well-equipped Land Cruisers in convoy or alone on a motorbike with the bare essentials? The choice is yours.

How big?

Two people, travelling light, would be safe and comfortable in a Japanese pickup with a canopy; more people wanting more luxury and luggage might choose a large five-door station wagon. Just remember that the more you take, the more effort you have to expend on carrying, maintaining and protecting your possessions, although it's also true that a vehicle with a big engine and large diameter wheels is less likely to get into trouble.

How old?

Rather 'tried and tested' than 'new and shiny'. A well-maintained, older vehicle may well be tougher and more reliable than a brand new one, as newer vehicles contain parts that must be replaced rather than repaired, such as sophisticated computer systems or plastic components.

What spares are available?

Land Rover and Toyota spares are probably easier than most to find along the Cape to Cairo route, but don't bet on it. Fortunately, African mechanics are great 'fixers' rather than mere 'parts replacers' and their ability to repair will always surprise you.

Petrol or diesel?

In the more populated regions of Southern and East Africa both petrol and diesel are widely available but, as you get farther off the beaten track, petrol is more difficult to find. Diesel is also cheaper than petrol in most countries. Diesel vehicles should be more fuel efficient and perhaps less likely to break down but, more trouble when they do.

> Personal preference
> and your knowledge of and ability to
> repair a certain model of vehicle
> play a role too. The most important
> words regarding a vehicle are:
> tough and reliable.

Preparation and maintenance

Now that you have a vehicle, you're going to need a toolkit and spares. This could be a very heavy and bulky collection and depends very much on the vehicle, your own mechanical ability and the space available. But remember, a good tool set and the necessary replacement part are worth their weight in gold in an emergency.

Essential vehicle equipment

Tyres: The best all-round tyres for load, speed and reliability are new, (no retreads), heavy-duty, truck tyres – radial or cross-ply. Find the highest ply rating you can, especially for the sidewalls, and rather choose a high profile than a wide, low profile tyre, as the best footprint for sand is long rather than wide. You will also have better ground clearance. The standard tyres and rims for the vehicle are usually best, and if tubeless, take plugs, gaiters and tubes for when you get punctures.

Fuel: A built-in, long-range fuel tank is a must for serious overlanding, otherwise steel jerry cans should be carried, best low down on bumper racks.

Water: Having a built-in water tank with tap is very useful, but a 25 litre plastic can is quite acceptable.

Battery: An extra 12 volt battery with switch to charge it separately.

Other: Polyurethane bushes for the suspension are also good accessories to have, but guard against loading yourself down with unsuitable and seldom needed junk.

Cape Town has well-stocked 4x4 spares and accessories shops, but the best suppliers of safari gear on the continent are in Joburg (see page 66–67):

4x4 Mega World, (branches countrywide), 52 Marine Drive, Paarden Island, Cape Town,
tel: 021-511-3311, fax: 021-511-3350,

e-mail: megaworld@oldmanemu.co.za,
website: www.oldmanemu.co.za

Just Done It, 112 De Waal Drive, Diep River, Cape Town,
tel: 021-706-8131, fax: 021-706-8161
website: www.4x4hire.co.za
e-mail: justdone@iafrica.co.za

Safari Centre, (branches countrywide) N1 Motor City, Goodwood, Cape Town,
tel: 021-595-3910, fax: 021-794-1675,
e-mail: sales@safarict.co.za,
website: www.safaricentre.co.za

ESSENTIAL TOOLS AND SPARES

- Workshop manual for vehicle.
- Full set of socket, ring and open spanners (compatible with your vehicle)
- Selection of screwdrivers (large and small, philips and flat)
- Pliers and locking pliers
- Shifting spanner and monkey wrench
- Hammer and spade
- Hacksaw and file
- Wheel spanner and 2 jacks (one hi-lift)
- Tyre levers (long and strong)
- Puncture repair kit (including patches of assorted sizes, gaiters, plugs and solution)
- Tyre pump or on-board compressor
- Pressure gauge and valve tool
- Two spare tyres and tubes
- Battery jumper cables
- Fan belts (one universal)
- Engine oil, gearbox oil and brake fluid

- Towrope
- Siphon pump for water or fuel
- Selection of nuts, bolts and self-tapping screws
- Assortment of rope, string and wire
- A selection of plastic pull-ties
- Electric wire, fuses, connectors and light bulbs
- Set of spark plugs, points and condenser (petrol only)
- Set of fuel, air and oil filters
- Spare radiator hoses and clamps
- Insulation, masking and filament tape
- Warning hazard triangles (legal requirement in some countries)
- Fire extinguisher (good one, no toys)
- Spare set of keys, hidden somewhere on outside of vehicle

If vehicle has a particular weakness that you know of, then carry the appropriate replacement parts

What about a motorbike?

Biking can give you the best of both worlds. You have freedom of movement without being encumbered with a large vehicle and all the responsibility and expense. And, if the manure hits the air conditioner, you can truck the bike out or even have it flown out.

You must, of course, be an experienced rider or you will probably end up injuring yourself. Take more care on a bike than you would when driving a 4x4. Anything can happen on an African road, and when it does, you're not protected by a vehicle's bodywork – you get hurt.

Like a 4x4, you will want a good, solid and simple model with the ability to carry a load. Honda's Africa Twin, Yamaha's Teneres and BMW's GS models are all pretty ideal.

Your bike should have a good double-sized fuel tank, heavy duty spokes and a strong luggage rack or panniers. Trail pattern tyres are good all rounders although a strong road tyre is probably adequate. A fairing will add to your

Driving in this sort of sand requires special equipment and off-road skills.

> **ESSENTIAL EQUIPMENT FOR MOTORBIKING**
>
> Start with the lists for 4x4s, strip them down to the bare minimum, and add:
> - Riding boots and gloves
> - Riding trousers and jacket
> - Crash helmet and goggles
> - Kidney belt
> - Spare universal control cable
> - Spoke key
> - G-clamp to break tyre bead

ride comfort and safety. Shaft-drives are virtually maintenance free.

Useful contacts in Cape Town:
Trefco BMW, 8 Northumberland Street, Bellville, tel: 021-925-2490, fax: 021-945-4528, e-mail: don.fullard@bmwdealer.co.za

Linex Yamaha, Roeland Street, Cape Town, tel: 021-461 5125, fax: 021-461-5191, e-mail: linexcta@iafrica.com, website: www.linexyamaha.co.za

Mekor Honda, Cnr Buitengraght and Strand Street, Cape Town, tel: 021-487-5000, fax: 021-487-5001, e-mail: dawiek@mekor.co.za, website: www.honda.co.za

A good contact for motorbike hire and tours is the very experienced:
Rolf van der Venn, 5 Scholtz Road, Three Anchor Bay, Cape Town, tel: 021-434-0968, fax: 021-439-4128, e-mail: tours@capetown.to, website: www.capetown.to/moto/

Left: Village stores, this one in northern Zambia, stock almost all the groceries you'll need, so don't carry too much. Below: A roof rack is useful for messy, bulky stuff and, of course, a roof-top tent.

4 What to pack

It's very important to take what you need. This sounds like an obvious statement, but it also implies that you don't take what you don't need. Don't carry an un-used camping bath with you all the way, but wonder why you forgot a flashlight. The best advice I've heard is to make two piles: one small one with money and other absolute necessities and another bigger one with the rest, then double the money pile and half the other one. You'll have a great trip!

Before you pack anything, get your documents in order. Africa is a Third World continent, which often means a strong belief in restricting the free move-ment of people without lots of documentation.

Travel in too many African countries is not regarded as a right, but a favour and only grudgingly granted. Bribery and corruption also occurs, although not as often as is generally thought. If you have the correct documentation, stand up for your rights and don't let officialdom bother you unfairly. Travellers of the world unite!

Passport: Make sure it is valid for at least three months after you expect to use it and that it has at least two blank pages for each country for visas and eager immigration officials. Try not to let it out of your sight. Rather pay in advance than giving it to hotel staff and when handing it over to officials, make sure they are entitled to ask for it.

Visas: Try to obtain as many of the required visas in your home country before you leave, or in South Africa, but check that their validity expires well after you need them. Harare, Nairobi and Addis Ababa are quite good for acquiring neighbouring countries' visas and some can be obtained at the borders, but make very sure as it can be a long trek back to get one.

For the latest details on visa requirements, visit www.the-gsa.co.za.

Visa requirements

South Africa:
Not required for most nationals. Not available at borders.

Namibia: Not required for most nationals. Not available at borders. Cost $16.
Consular Office, 197 Blackwood Street, Arcadia, Pretoria, tel: 012-481-9100, fax: 012-343-7294. The Namibian Tourism Offices inCape Town (tel 021-419-3190) and Johannesburg (tel 011-784-8024) are also authorised to issue tourist visas.

Botswana: Not required for nationals of USA, UK, Germany, Holland and most Commonwealth countries. Not available at borders. Cost of visa: $5.
Consulate-General, PO Box 3288, Cape Town, tel: 021-421-1045, fax: 021-421-1046

Zimbabwe: Available free at port of entry for South Africans. Required for most other nationals, available at border. Cost $32.
Consulate, 30 Anderson Street, Johannesburg, tel: 011-838-2156, fax: 011-838-5620.

Mozambique: Required for all. Not available at borders. Cost of visa: $10.
Consulate, 8 Burg Street, Cape Town, tel: 021-426-2944, fax: 021-426-2946

Zambia: Not required for Commonwealth nationals except British and Irish. Required for all other nationals. Available at borders. Cost: $25.
High Commission, 1159 Ziervogel Street, Arcadia, Pretoria, tel: 012-326-1847, fax: 012-326-0263

Tanzania: Required for all. Not available at borders. Cost: $50.
High Commission, 822 George Avenue, Arcadia, Pretoria, tel: 012-342-4393, fax: 012-430-4383

Kenya: Required for all except South Africans. Available locally only if arriving by air at Jomo Kenyatta Airport in Nairobi. Cost: $50.

High Commission, 302 Brooks Street,
Menlo Park, Pretoria, tel: 012-362-2249,
fax: 012-362-2252

Ethiopia: Required for all. Not available at borders. Cost: $20.
Embassy, 47 Charles Street,
Brooklyn, Pretoria, tel: 012-346-3542,
fax: 012-346-3867,
e-mail: ethemb@mweb.co.za

Sudan: Required for all. Not available at borders. Cost: $50.
Embassy, 1203 Pretorius Street,
Hatfield, Pretoria,
tel: 012-342-4538, fax: 012-342-4539

Egypt: Required for all. Available locally only at Cairo Airport. Cost: $40.
Embassy, 270 Bourke Street,
Muckleneuk, Pretoria,
tel: 012-343-1590, fax: 012-343-1082

Visa courier services
As the requirements and costs change regularly, I find it best to make use of a visa courier services for advice and procuring my visas. There are two in Cape Town:
The Visa Service, 901 Strand Towers,
66 Strand Street, Cape Town,
tel: 021-421-7826, fax: 021-419-4836,
e-mail: visacape@mweb.co.za

The Visa Shop, Thibault House,
Hans Strydom Avenue, Cape Town,
tel: 021-421-1059, fax: 021-421-1065

International driver's licences
There are two international conventions on driver's licenses covering different countries. Get both international licences and carry your original one too. Your local automobile organisation will

> Make copies of all your documentation and keep them separate from your originals. Take at least a dozen spare visa photos.

issue them for you. The **Automobile Association of South Africa** (tel: 0861-11-1994, e-mail: aasa@aasa.co.za, website: www.aasa.co.za) has branches in all major centres. **The Cape Town branch is in the Picbel Arcade, Strand Street, tel 021-419-6914, fax: 021-421-1343.**

Yellow International Certificate of Vaccination
This is important. Don't let doctors tell you that some inoculations are not necessary or old fashioned and don't work. Carry your yellow card for at least yellow fever, cholera and typhoid. It's a lot safer than being jabbed at a border. In Cape Town visit:
The British Airways Travel Clinic,
Fountains Medical Centre, Adderley
Street, Cape Town. tel: 021-4193172.

Vehicle documentation
Carry proof of ownership, registration certificate, licence, road tax and, if the vehicle is not registered in your name, an official letter on a letterhead giving you permission to drive the vehicle.

Insurance

It's not easy to obtain insurance for a vehicle travelling through Africa and you might have to 'self-insure'. At the very least you should take out medical and theft insurance though.

Three knowledgeable insurance companies that can help are:

Ream Insurance Brokers (Tuffstuff),
tel: 0861-44-4400,
e-mail: info@tuffstuff.co.za,
website: www.tuffstuff.co.za

Outsurance, tel: 0860-06-0000,
e-mail: info@out.co.za,
website: www.outsurance.com

The Automobile Association of South Africa has a new Third Party Policy that covers Zambia, Malawi, Tanzania, Uganda and Kenya. See above for contact details.

Carnet de passage

A very necessary document which must be obtained through the automobile organisation of your home country. You lodge a sum of money with the issuer and are then guaranteed for the possible payment of import duties on the vehicle. It eases your vehicle's passage through borders.

Very importantly, some countries require the driver's name on the carnet, not just the owner's.

Maps and guidebooks

Without good guidebooks and maps you could miss so much of a country you'd come so far to see, but don't expect to buy them along the way. In Africa, only South Africa has a selection of good bookstores which stock guidebooks and maps for all countries. You may have your favourites; Lonely Planet, Bradt, Spectrum and Rough Guides are all good.

Michelin map no 953 covers North and West Africa, no 954 the North and East and no 955 covers Central and Southern Africa, all on a scale of 1 in 4 000 000. Buy them before you come to Africa or in South Africa where you can also buy the excellent road atlases compiled by MapStudio. The South African Automobile Association publishes comprehensive maps of all the neighbouring countries.

Always check the accuracy of maps with local information, as roads which look impressive on paper might be old, overgrown tracks or recently washed away in floods. Conversely, new roads might have been built or upgraded since the publication of the maps.

Take books or magazines to read on the trip, as these are sometimes difficult to find. Do read local newspapers along the way, it'll put you in touch with what's happening in the region.

If you're interested in birds or other fauna and flora, make sure you have the relevant field guides and a pair of good binoculars.

GPS and navigation

A small, handheld GPS is a navigational aid which uses satellite signals to pinpoint your position anywhere on earth to within 10 metres. It can also calculate your speed and heading or plot a course for you. I have included

If you're worried about ruining precious books and maps, make copies of relevant sections for everyday use.

GPS co-ordinates on all the main routes as it's reassuring to have confirmation of where you are, and to alert you to important crossroads and turnoffs. A simple, recreational GPS unit will suffice; an external antenna, mounted on the vehicle's roof, will improve your signal. You should also have a power adapter to run it off the vehicle's battery.

Take note of distances travelled between points by zeroing your vehicle's tripmeter. If you doubt your direction or the road, then stop and try to make sure of your position. If you feel lost, retrace your route back to where you're certain of your position, rather than blundering farther into trouble. Remember that often a track looks well used only because it has been used twice by everybody – once going out and once again returning when they realise they are lost.

> A GPS is very useful, but it does
> ## not replace good maps
> and the ability to use them.

Keeping the simple things in mind when driving, such as what side of the vehicle the sun is shining into, will help, as will using a distant landmark as a point of bearing. A compass can be useful in these circumstances, but remember to keep well away from metallic influences when using it. Asking the way from locals can be useful, but not always accurate. Ask "Where does this road go to?" rather than "Is this the way to…?" as often the answer will be an automatic "yes". Fuel pump attendants at garages are usually the best people to ask.

If travelling in convoy, stay close together. It's surprisingly easy to lose someone – especially if one in the convoy takes the wrong turn. Have an agreement to stop and regroup at each town or every so-many kilometres. Radio contact between vehicles is not always feasible, as two-way radios are illegal in some African countries, and in others you could be mistrusted and even suspected of spying.

Clothing

What you pack in the way of clothing and gear is a very personal choice and depends on how you are travelling. If you plan to be backpacking, pack as lightly as you can. For travelling on public transport, eating the local food and sleeping in guest houses and small hotels, I would suggest little more than the bare necessities. If driving your own vehicle, add to the clothing and include optional items, but remember

---

GOOD BOOK AND MAP STORES

Sunbird Publishing produces touring maps and atlases of Southern Africa. For nearest stockist, tel 011-622-2900.

Mapstudio, Freeway Park, Maitland, Cape Town, tel: 021-510-4311, fax: 021-510 4766, e-mail: ginam@mapstudio.co.za, website: www.mapstudio.co.za

Exclusive Books, 225 Victoria Wharf, Waterfront, Cape Town, tel: 021-419-0905, fax: 021-419-0909, e-mail: waterfront@exclusivebooks.co.za, website: www.exclusivebooks.co.za

Traveller's Bookshop, 2 Kings Warehouse, Waterfront, Cape Town, tel: 021-425-6880, fax: 021-425-6811

CLOTHES

- 1 pair of boots or walking shoes (well worn in)
- 3 pairs of socks (soft and adsorbent)
- 1 pair of lightweight long pants or skirt (easy to wash and dry)
- 1 pair shorts
- 3 shirts (lightweight, cotton)
- 1 lightweight sweater or jersey
- 3 sets of underwear
- 1 set of sleepwear (cool cotton)
- Cap or hat
- Towel

Optional

- Bathing costume
- Lightweight jacket or windbreaker
- Kikoi (go local)
- Sandals or strops

GEAR

- Backpack (ideally a very strong one that has a zipped flap to cover the straps and turn it into a carry bag)
- Small daypack
- Water bottle
- Length of strong cord and wash pegs
- Multi-purpose tool or penknife
- Torch and spare batteries
- Matches or lighter
- Candles
- Notebook and pen
- Travel guide books and maps
- Watch with built-in alarm
- Filament tape

Optional

- Reading matter
- Small padlock
- Pocket calculator (how good is your mental arithmetic?)
- Earplugs and eyeshades
- Sewing kit with scissors
- Plugs and adapters to run or recharge electrical gear
- Shortwave radio (or built into vehicle)
- Music tapes

TOILETRIES

- Soap, shampoo and toothbrush
- Hairbrush or comb
- Toilet paper
- Sunglasses
- Sanitary towels
- Condoms

Optional

- Nail clippers
- Contact lens cleaner
- Reading glasses and spare spectacles
- Shaving kit

PHOTOGRAPHY

- Camera (a 28–90 mm or similar lens is ideal)
- Film (take all you need, 100 ASA is good for all round work)
- Spare batteries

Optional

- Camera bag and tripod
- Extra lenses and filters

that you will be able to buy and replenish supplies along the way.

Keeping in mind that most of Africa is in the tropics or subtropics, light, cool, loose clothing made from natural fibres should be selected. Your clothing should blend in and not offend local customs and religions – keep it informal, never outrageous and in subdued colours. Try and choose garments that don't show the dirt and that wash and dry easily. Don't skimp on personal gear, which is usually small and light – having all your usual goodies makes life a lot easier.

Shops that stock good outdoor clothing and camping gear:

Cape Union Mart (branches throughout South Africa), tel: 0800-03-4000, e-mail: info@capeunionmart.co.za, website: www.capeunionmart.co.za

Outdoor Warehouse, (branches countrywide), Raglan Street, Bellville, tel: 021-948-6221, fax: 021-462-2161, website: www.outdoorwarehouse.co.za

Tips on African photography

There is a greater variety of subjects to photograph in Africa than anywhere else in the world. The colourful people, natural wonders and exotic wildlife cry out to be photographed and you will take more than normal, so take plenty of film. Unless you're a professional photographer, don't take too much equipment. Travel light and be ready for anything, anytime.

Try and take your photographs in the early morning and late afternoon – the strong African sun washes out colour in the middle of the day and will give you very bland photographs. If possible, take your time. Get in close – so many shots have their main subject too small and far away. Stand so that the light source is behind you and selectively expose and focus for the darkest part of your main subject. Then compose your shot, imagining how it will look on the cover of a magazine.

Always make sure people are comfortable with you photographing them. Try to engage them in conversation first, then motion with the camera that you want to take a shot of them and gauge their reaction. Usually, if you have just bought something from them in a market, or if they are showing off something they are proud of, you will not have a problem. Although you might want to give sweets or pens to the people you photograph, you will also be asked for money. Resist this, as it creates the impression that travellers are an easy source of money. And don't promise to send them a copy of the shot unless you honestly intend doing so.

Be very wary of photographing anything that might be considered of military importance, and show sensitivity at religious sites. Develop an eye for colourful detail – the intricate jewellery worn by women or unusual items for sale at a market often make better photographs than the overall shot.

For good close-ups of animals, you will need a powerful telephoto lens. Get as close as possible in your vehicle, without leaving the road or disturbing the animal, switch off the engine so as not to cause camera vibrations and sit patiently waiting for something interesting to happen.

If you are hoping to sell your photographs, remember that most publications prefer slides. Otherwise digital or print film is fine.

Rather wait until you get home to have your film developed and, even then, choose the most professional outfit you can find – these are your precious memories.

Two good photographic shops:
Orms, Roeland Square, Roeland Street, Cape Town, tel: 021-465-3573, fax: 021-465-2928

Fotostaa, Street Georges Mall, Shortmarket Street, Cape Town, tel: 021-424-1979, fax: 021-424-1979

Fitting it all in

Compromising on what to take and what to leave is very important. You can't take it all. You will arrive at your destination with some things unused, and wished you'd taken other items that were needed along the way.

Relax, it happens to all of us. Remember, you can buy a lot of what you need along the way and also benefit the local economy.

If travelling in your own vehicle, tightly pack all the heavy items flat on the floor or strap them down to avoid shifting and breakage.

Plastic crates with sealable lids are ideal for the foodstuff; steel trunks can carry the heavier items. Gas tanks and fuel cans are safe only if stored outside the vehicle. Snack food should be in the front cab and an overnight bag handy in the back.

Roof racks are sometimes a necessary evil. Although they make your vehicle top heavy and create wind resistance, they do afford extra luggage space when you simply cannot fit everything inside. You can also sleep on them and they make great game-viewing platforms.

Use a **trailer** only as a last resort and then the strongest purpose-built, off-road type you can find. If you're doing a short, regional trip with a vehicle full of people, then a trailer might be your only solution, but driving a vehicle through Africa is tough enough without making it more so with a trailer.

Camping equipment & trailer suppliers:
Leisureland Campworld, (branches countrywide), Durban Road, Bellville, tel: 021-919-4974, fax: 021-919-9764, e-mail lland@mweb.co.za, website: www.campworld.co.za

Cristy Sports, 35 Kendall Road, Diep River, Cape Town, tel: 021-712-5078, fax: 021-712-5785, e-mail: cristys@mweb.co.za, website: www.cristys.co.za

Safari Centre, (branches countrywide), N1 Motor City, Goodwood, tel: 021-595-3910, fax: 021-794-1675, e-mail sales@safarict.co.za,

Use and test everything you intend taking before you leave. That way you will know it works, and also how it works.

5 Eating & sleeping

Will you cook for yourself or eat in restaurants? The answer is, of course, both. How boring it would be, and how much you would miss of the delightful and diverse local cuisine, if you cooked for yourself all the time. On the other hand, what a pleasure to be able to stop anywhere you fancy and be totally independent of restaurants.

There are not many supermarkets outside of the major cities and shopping for ingredients is sometimes more difficult and expensive than buying a meal. Don't assume that all local food is unhealthy or unclean. It's not. I recommend a cautious but adventurous approach to eating out in Africa.

Above: With good equipment, there is no need for an elaborate camp site. Below: This market beside the Luangwa River near Feira in Zambia is a treasure trove of crafts and essentials.

Local restaurants and foodstalls have a simple but healthy system of buying and preparing small quantities of ingredients at a time, thereby assuring fresh food most of the time. Beware, however, of some hotels and tourist restaurants that have refrigeration and think that food can be stored for too long. The best is to eat in a place full of locals.

Water is purified and chlorinated in most large towns and cities, and is safe to drink. However, some travellers prefer to drink only bottled water.

You know your stomach, you make the choice!

Regional cuisine

South Africa is a cosmopolitan country and has food to match, from barbeque to *nouvelle cuisine* and everything in-between. I suppose the local speciality would have to be a braaivleis, which is a barbecue in its most natural and original form. A true *braai* is cooked outdoors over a real fire and consists of meat, meat and more meat. Lamb chops, *boerewors* (spiced sausage made with beef and pork), steak and *sosaties* (kebabs) will be grilled to perfection and enjoyed with *stywepap* (stiff maize meal porridge) and a variety of

---

ESSENTIAL COOKING INGREDIENTS

Durables

- A selection of canned meats, fish and vegetables (not too many, they're heavy)
- A selection of dehydrated foodstuffs (beware of grotty 'instant meals', rather stock up on vegetables and soups)
- Breakfast cereal or muesli mix
- Sugar
- Powdered milk
- Tea and coffee
- Crisp bread and crackers
- Biscuits and rusks
- Flour and baking powder (yes, you can bake bread over a fire)
- Salt, pepper, herbs and spices (all in one sealable box)
- Dried fruit and nuts
- Rice and pasta
- Powdered eggmix

- Cooking and salad oil
- Honey and jam
- Peanut butter and Bovril
- Wine, beer (buy beer locally in every country except Sudan)

Semi-durables

- Potatoes, onions, cabbage and carrots
- Apples and oranges
- Cheese
- Margarine (butter melts too easily)
- Bacon and salami

Perishable (buy along the way and store in ice box or fridge)

- Meat
- Eggs
- Salad
- Tomatoes
- Soft fruit

salads. Sometimes a heavy cast iron pot will be suspended over the coals to cook *potjiekos* (pot food) or *potbrood* (pot bread). All this should be washed down with copious quantities of the wonderful Cape wines. The Western Cape also boasts the unique Cape Malay style of cooking which was brought over from the East by slaves from that region.

Namibia's colonial past has left it with the best German-styled cured meats and beer on the continent, while the huge cattle ranches of **Botswana**

and **Zimbabwe** ensure some of the best steak in the world. **Mozambique's** seafood, particularly it's prawns in *peri-peri* sauce, is legendary, and the grilled lake fish in **Malawi** is good too.

Zambia has *sadza nyama* (a meat and maize meal dish) and **Tanzanians** like omelettes and lots of delicious *chipatis* (fried pancakes). **Zanzibar** lives up to its title of The Spice Island in its tasty *pilaus* (seafood or duck and rice dishes), although you might struggle to find a beer to wash it down with in some traditional Muslim areas. **Kenya** is the home of tasty, cheap and plentiful Tusker beer which goes so well with the ubiquitous *chipatis*. Also good curries and lots of fresh fruit will make sure you get a balanced diet.

The most unique and unusual cuisine is in **Ethiopia**. The basis for every meal is *njera*, a large, grey, sponge-like pancake made from fermented teff. Definitely an acquired taste, but the ideal counter to the very hot, spicy stews and sauces called *wat*. Raw minced beef is another dish for the adventurous diner. But, one doesn't have to be adventurous to enjoy the fine coffee in this, it's country of origin. After coffee, beer is the national drink, which is inexpensive and available everywhere in draft or bottled form.

Get your fill of beer before you enter tea-totalling **Sudan**, as *chai saada* (sweet tea) is the national beverage there. Middle Eastern dishes such as

ESSENTIAL COOKING EQUIPMENT

Sitting around a camp fire, cooking under the stars is one of life's great pleasures and the well equipped camper should have the following:

- Cooker and fuel (gas or paraffin)
- Ice-box or small fridge (compressor type only)
- Barbecue grid and bag of wood or charcoal
- Firelighters and matches
- Pot (a traditional black, cast-iron potjie is best)
- Frying pan and kettle
- Plates and bowls
- Chopping board and sharp knife
- Jug for mixing powdered milk
- Mugs and glasses
- Cutlery and can opener
- Washing bowl, soap and cloth
- Water supply in containers
- Paper towels

schwarma and *baklava* as well as the most refreshing fruit juices imaginable start to appear in foodstalls and desert truckstops. **Egypt** is paradise for lovers of Middle Eastern dishes such as *kosharia, felafel* and *schwarmas* – although *fuul* (stewed beans) is not the most appetising of meals.

So you see, Africa is not just a feast for the eyes. Be careful not to put on too much weight like I usually do!

What food and cooking equipment should you take?

For the initial stocking up, South Africa's supermarkets have everything you will need, but, don't take too much. Replenish along the way. That way you will be cooking with fresh ingredients and supporting the local economies. To be safe rather than sorry, wash, peel or cook all fresh produce.

Don't carry soft fruit and vegetables such as peaches and tomatoes for too long – they will just turn to pulp on the rough roads. All containers must be sturdy and seal well. Pack all your foodstuff in a lockable steel trunk. The monkeys and baboons at some camp sites are masters at opening anything not padlocked!

Getting a good night's sleep

If you're properly equipped for camping and the camp site is secure, this can be very pleasant and indeed the best way to experience the wild solitude of the continent. Good commercially run camp sites are plentiful in South Africa, Namibia, Botswana and Zimbabwe, less so in Zambia, Malawi, Mozambique, Tanzania and Kenya and almost

One of the pleasures of travelling is experiencing local food and customs, such as this coffee ceremony in Axum, Ethiopia.

non-existent in Ethiopia, Eritrea, Sudan and Egypt. National parks usually have good camp sites and some hotels allow you to camp in their grounds, but be careful when 'free-camping' in Africa, you are likely to be hassled, or worse, by the locals.

Setting up camp and etiquette

Always sleep in a tent or vehicle, not in the open, especially in game parks, where you must also avoid blocking game paths with your camp. Choose a level and smooth site, preferably under

A guesthouse and grocery store side by side in Zambia. What more could you ask for?

a tree for shade. Place the back of your tent into the prevailing wind and try to give yourself a nice view if possible. Have enough space in front of your tent to set up a table and chairs and to light a fire or set up your stove. For security, park your vehicle close to the tent. You can then use it as pantry and wardrobe as well as take a lead from the battery for light. If in a group, you may want to pitch the tents in a semi-circle and socialise and cook together.

Don't crowd or disturb the other campers. If there is no appropriate place to dispose of your rubbish, carry it with you until there is. Act fairly and responsibly towards the local people, so that fellow travellers will be welcome in the future.

Most national parks and some public camp sites have huts or bungalows to hire, which is also nice and outdoorsy. However, in some towns and cities, especially in the northern countries, you're going to have to stay in hotels, guest houses or backpackers lodges. Recommendations are made in the appropriate route sections, but here are a few tips.

Some of the best value for money places will be in the centre of town, especially around the bus stations. Private bathrooms are all very well, but in cheap hotels they're never properly maintained and usually don't work,

whereas the shared ablutions have to function well to satisfy the local travellers. It pays to shop around – look at different rooms in various hotels before making your final choice.

Try to get a room with a fan and/or mosquito net and, most importantly, never take a room near the bar. Late at night, when you're trying desperately to sleep, the thumping music will just keep getting louder!

ESSENTIAL CAMPING EQUIPMENT

- Tent (simple, strong and easy to erect, with built-in mosquito net). Roof tents that fit on a vehicle's roof rack are comfortable, safe and popular
- Camp stretchers and/or foam mattresses. (make sure you are really comfortable)
- Folding/light camp chairs and table
- Lamp (best is fluorescent type that works off vehicle's battery)

Mike's never-flop recipes

Not being a great cook, and usually prefering to eat 'local', I'm offering only one simple recipe each for breakfast, lunch and supper. Though nothing beats a thick steak grilled over a thorn-wood fire with potatoes, onions and butternut cooked in aluminium foil in the same coals.

BULLY BEEF HOTPOT

1 tin bully beef

4 tablespoons powdered milk

1 $\frac{1}{2}$ cups dehydrated potato flakes

Mix powdered milk into a paste with a little water, add 2 $\frac{1}{2}$ cups of water and bring to the boil. Stir in chopped-up bully beef and potato flakes to the desired consistency. Season to taste with herbs and/or curry. Serve with vegetables or salad.

I just had to add this, it's so easy

POTJIE BREAD
(bread baked in a cast iron pot)

500 g self-raising flour

1 beer

1 teaspoon salt

Mix ingredients and place in a greased potjie (flat or round). Place over mild coals and pile other coals on top (it must cook slowly). A skewer poked into the bread will not stick when it is cooked. Add cheese, onion, seeds or nuts as you like.

HOMEMADE MUESLI
(Make up and store)

2 cups rolled oats (roasted are best)

4 more cups of a mixture of rolled wheat, wheatgerm and/or bran

$\frac{1}{2}$ cup each of peanuts, sunflower seeds, raisins, dried fruit

Powdered milk and sugar to taste

Serve with hot or cold water and fresh fruit for a quick, tasty and healthy breakfast (or anytime).

CHEESE OMELETTE

6 tablespoons powdered eggmix

4 tablespoons powdered milk

generous pinch of salt

handful of grated cheese

Mix all except cheese with 1 cup water, let stand for 2 minutes and then whisk with fork. Cook in pan with oil and sprinkle cheese on top.

6 Staying alive

Africa is a minefield of diseases, germs and nasty bugs, but don't let worrying about them spoil your trip. With a bit of preparation and care, you should be able to dodge most of them. Of course, Africa has real minefields too and nasty bugs of the human kind, but these too can be avoided.

At least six weeks before leaving, see your doctor or if they're not clued up on African conditions, then visit a travel clinic for advice and shots. Have a good medical and dental check-up before you go and stock up on any special medication you might need. If you wear glasses or contact lenses take spares and sufficient cleaning solution.

Eating local food (left) is usually safe, but if you need medical assistance, more modern service than a sangoma (above) is available.

Doctors in Africa are very experienced and resourceful, and have good knowledge of local diseases, even though they usually lack effective drugs and equipment. Medical facilities are best in South Africa, so if possible, get there for treatment. And remember to inform your doctor where you have been and what you've done.

Immunisation

A yellow fever vaccination is a legal requirement for entry into some countries and is valid for 10 years. Tetanus is a serious wound infection, so it's vaccination is a must too. Discuss cholera, hepatitis, typhoid, polio, tuberculosis, meningitis and rabies. The list is scary and you will probably not encounter any of them, but let your doctor guide you in what you need.

Medical insurance

Don't leave home without adequate medical insurance, the type that evacuates you if necessary. Your existing medical aid might cover you, otherwise see a travel agent (check the policy exclusions). For good cover in Africa:
Netcare 911, Cape Town,
tel: 021-592-2663, fax: 021-592-2661,
e-mail: traumalink6@worldonline.co.za ,
website: www.netcare911.co za

Europ Assist,
tel: 011-254-1000, fax: 011-254-1110,
e-mail: assist@europ-assistance.co.za,
website: www.europ-assistance.co.za

Along the way

Sensible eating, drinking and personal hygiene will determine your general well-being during the trip. You should be in tune with your body and know how far you can push it and how much dirt and infection it can fight off.

Travellers living in Africa have a stronger immunity against local germs, and can usually eat and drink almost anything. Visiters from outside the continent however, must take more care with what they eat and drink and might have to stick to bottled water and well cooked food. They should remember to "peel it or boil it".

African towns and villages have a good, healthy system of slaughtering their meat and picking their fruit and vegetables early each morning. This is then all sold and consumed by mid-afternoon, which allows little time for food to go off.

However, beware of hotels and restaurants where food that has been specially prepared for the tourist trade is often stored and reheated. On my travels, I have felt more at risk of infection on airlines and at fancy hotels, than while eating at market foodstalls where I can see the food being prepared in front of me.

The tap water in large towns and cities can usually be safely drunk and in small towns and villages it can be filtered with a portable filter, treated with chlorine tablets or iodine, or boiled. Bottled water, or even soft drinks are a safe alternative (but local beer is best!)

Have a cholera vaccination too, even though some health officials will tell you it's not necessary – it's easier and safer than being forced to have one at some obscure border post.

Diarrhoea

Hopefully diarrhoea will be the only ailment you suffer from on your travels.

Most of us eat or drink something that does not agree with us, or is contaminated with bacteria, at some time or another. The best thing to do is to rest up somewhere comfortable and safe, stop eating, avoid any alcohol and drink plenty of clean, clear fluids.

If you have it bad, then you will need an oral rehydration fluid. This sounds very impressive, but is really just sugar, salt and water – so a flat Coke with some salt in it, or a Bovril drink with sugar, will do the trick.

Use blockers such as Imodium or Lomotil only as an absolute last resort as they simply stop the body from excreting the bacteria that is causing your discomfort.

Malaria

This disease is endemic to such a large part of Africa that it's safest to take precautions wherever you are going to be. Your first defence against malaria is to avoid being bitten by mosquitoes between dusk and dawn. Wear long pants, long sleeved shirts and socks, use insect repellent and try to sleep under a net. With malaria, prevention is

---

WHAT TO PACK IN A FIRST-AID KIT

Prepare and take a basic but good medical kit – South African cities all have well-stocked pharmacies. In addition to any special medication your doctor might prescribe, it should contain the following:

◆ Medical first aid book

◆ Malaria prophylactic tablets

◆ Aspirin or paracetamol (for fever and pain and also to gargle with for a sore throat)

◆ Antiseptic for disinfecting cuts and abrasions

◆ Adhesive bandages (strips and roll)

◆ Gauze bandages and cotton wool

◆ Calamine cream for bites and stings.

◆ Thermometer (standard body temperature is 37°C)

◆ Insect repellent

◆ Analgesic eye drops

◆ Analgesic ear drops

◆ Scissors and tweezers (on pocket-knife?)

◆ Safety pins

◆ Water purification tablets (a few drops of iodine works too)

◆ A couple of syringes and needles (just in case)

◆ Sunblock and burn gel

◆ Throat lozenges and flu remedy

Other items you might want to take

◆ Malaria cure

◆ Antibiotics (dangerous if taken without medical advice)

◆ Vitamin tablets

◆ Diarrhoea tablets (rather let it out)

◆ Rehydration mixture (to make your own rehydration drink, dissolve eight teaspoons of sugar and half a teaspoon of salt in one litre of water)

> Beware of fruit, vegetables (and salad) that can't be peeled or washed and undercooked meat and fish.

definitely better than cure. It's also advisable to take prophylactic drugs. The malaria-carrying mosquito has built up immunity to so many drugs that have been thrown at it that it's best to consult your doctor or a travel clinic for the latest recommendations.

After taking all the precautions, you could still contract malaria, and remember that the incubation period can be up to a year. If you experience shivering, shaking, perspiring and general flu-like aches and pains, see a doctor. The local doctors in Africa will recognise malaria and know what to do, but if you've returned home to somewhere where your GP might not, alert them to the likelihood of malaria.

Bilharzia

Just visible to the naked eye, the bilharzia worm infests freshwater snails in the lakes and streams of most of Africa. If you entered the water or washed in it, the worm could decide that you were a better host and bore into your skin to multiply there. Running water is safest, also dry yourself well after bathing. Symptoms are a high fever and blood in the urine. Bilharzia sounds scary, but there is an effective cure.

Aids

The list of bugs and diseases common to Africa seems endless and unpronouncable, but don't let worrying about them spoil your trip, most will never be encountered. However, there is one more that needs special mention – Aids. If you're not careful in Africa, you will contract it and it will kill you. So, no unprotected sex, no dodgy blood transfusions and no using non-sterile needles.

Personal safety

It must be admitted that Africa can be a very dangerous place. Border wars, civil wars and clan wars must be identified and avoided. Areas of banditry should be travelled through only in the company of safe convoys. Robbery of or from your vehicle is another problem which can be avoided by never leaving it unattended. Park it in a hotel's grounds or other safe, guarded site and have some hidden fuel cut-out or immobiliser. Keep out of areas notorious for thieves and pickpockets and carry your valuables as close to your body as possible.

Contrary to what most other guide-books will tell you, I would suggest that you resist an attack as much as safely possible, thieves are used to and prefer soft, easy targets.

Rather don't carry a weapon and definitely not a gun – they're far too dangerous and very illegal. And always remember that your personal safety is more important than hanging on to any of your possessions.

You'll be safe from wild animals if you stay in your car in game reserves and sleep indoors (or a tent).

Travelling in Africa is like walking the high wire without a safety net – if you slip you're going to fall hard. Good common sense and staying alert is important. The upside is that you'll feel so much more vibrant and alive.

7

What it will cost

Most African currencies are weak; so First World, hard currencies will buy you a lot of the local money. This means that Africa is a pretty cheap place to travel through, as long as you don't buy too many imported products. It also means that prices go up all the time as the local currencies devalue at an alarming rate, which makes it difficult for me to quote prices. For ease and accuracy therefore, I have quoted prices in the most widely accepted foreign currency, the US dollar. It's also the easily changed foreign currency in the countries you will be travelling through. Notes are best, but avoid $100 bills, as there are so many counterfeits around and locals won't touch them.

Buying locally will keep costs down, such as negotiating for fresh fish on the beach in Bagamoya.

Sometimes even banks won't touch them. If you like traveller's cheques, the most acceptable are American Express and Thomas Cook, but they are exchangeable only at banks and tourist venues in the big cities. Remember to keep an up-to-date record of numbers in case of theft and the need to claim a refund.

For both cash and traveller's cheques, take small denominations. Too often you need to change money at the last moment or need only a small amount and don't want to sit holding unwanted local currency.

The credit cards that work best are Visa, MasterCard and Amex, but treat them as a stand-by only as they are not widely accepted in all countries. They're good to carry as insurance against sudden large unplanned expenses and will also convince immigration officials that you have sufficient funds. Always make sure you have enough local currency with you and change your foreign currency at the best (and safest) rate.

Changing money on the black market

You cannot travel through Africa and avoid the black-market moneychangers. Who in their right mind is going to accept the official rate of 400 metacais from the bank in Mozambique when the shopkeeper across the street will give you 4 000?

Everyone uses the black market, but do try and avoid the risks. Easy to say, but it means that you try to change with people who have a fixed address and are taking a risk themselves, such as in the privacy of a shop or office.

Stay away from sharply dressed guys on street corners who offer you a better rate than anyone else. It's so easy to get ripped off and, remember, it is breaking the law.

Hiding your valuables

Carry your valuables as close to your body as is comfortable. A wallet or purse in a deep pocket should carry no more money than what you need for the day. Wear a money belt around your waist or pouch around your neck for large amounts, but always under your clothing. Another trick is to have a secret inside pocket sewn into your favourite pants or skirt. A strong, lockable steel box can be securely fixed in some hidden spot of your vehicle, or if you're backpacking, you may want to hide a small emergency fund in the seams of your pack. The more you spread it around, the less likely you are of having it all lost or stolen.

Remember to bargain

Except in the shops of the large cities, nothing in Africa has a fixed price (not even hotels), and it's up to you to bargain, or be overcharged. The rate of 'over-ask' is proportionate to the degree of touristic importance of the area and the number of tourists around. Greed, desperation and plain foolishness also play a role, so it's often difficult to reach a fair price.

Enquire about rates and prices from fellow travellers or try to spot what the locals are paying, but never be mean and don't bargain if you're not interested in buying.

Another good tip is to obtain and use an international student card (remember, even old-timers can be teachers). In some countries, especially

A selection of dishes (and freshly squeezed sugar cane and pineapple juices) bought from food-stalls at Forodhani Gardens in Stone Town, Zanzibar, will cost less than $2 and make a tasty meal.

Egypt, substantial discounts are given for showing one. They even have a black market to supply them.

Getting sponsorship

Unless you are very well connected and virtually assured of getting sponsorship and other such assistance, don't even bother trying. The time spent chasing around after – usually reluctant – 'suits' could be far better spent on organising your trip.

You could be offered equipment or assistance you won't even need and then be expected to do so much in return that you could compromise and even spoil your trip. Lean, mean and independent is the best way to go.

The financial bottom line

In 1997 I travelled by public transport from Cape Town to Cairo in 90 days on about $1 500, an average of $17 a day. And in 2003 bikers I spoke to were still budgeting pretty much the same frugal amount.

But, what will it cost for two people in one vehicle to do the whole trip? For a three-month trip from Cape Town to Cairo inclusive of all normal expenses, fuel, food and sightseeing; but excluding getting you and the vehicle back home, could cost you around $7 000. (For shipping costs see page 12.)

COMPARATIVE PRICES FOR COMMODITIES
(PRICED IN US DOLLARS, AT BEST EXCHANGE RATES)

	DIESEL PER LITRE	PETROL PER LIRE	BEER IN BAR	TEA OR COFFEE	PLATE OF FOOD	BREAD LOAF	CAMP A PERSON	HOTEL A PERSON	BUS KM
South Africa	0,45	0,48	1,00	0,70	3,50	0,50	4,00	12,00	0,03
Namibia	0,43	0,45	0,90	0,60	3,00	0,60	4,00	15,00	0,03
Botswana	0,46	0,48	1,10	0,80	5,00	0,71	5,00	30,00	0,04
Zimbabwe	0,17	0,20	0,40	0,30	1,00	0,10	3,00	10,00	0,02
Malawi	0,58	0,71	0,65	0,42	2,50	0,41	3,50	7,00	0,03
Mozambique	0,70	0,65	0,50	0,20	1,00	0,20	5,00	10,00	0,03
Zambia	0,73	0,61	0,75	0,32	2,20	0,33	5,00	12,00	0,02
Tanzania	0,60	0,69	1,10	0,60	2,65	0,21	5,00	10,00	0,03
Kenya ,	0,55	0,70	1,00	0,60	2,50	0,57	3,00	10,00	0,02
Ethiopia	0,33	0,53	0,70	0,20	1,00	0,30	4,00	7,00	0,02
Sudan	0,31	0,40	n/a	0,18	1,00	0,37	3,00	4,00	0,02
Egypt	0,09	0,20	1,50	0,15	1,00	0,22	2,00	8,00	0,03
Average prices:	0,45	0,50	0,87	0,42	2,15	0,38	3,88	11,25	0,03

	MEAT PER KG	WATER LITRE	RICE PER KG	OIL 750 ML	BEER 375 ML	INSTANT COFFEE	CHEESE PER KG	TEA 250 G	MILK PER LITRE
South Africa	2,59	0,70	0,57	0,70	0,47	3,53	4,12	2,12	0,59
Namibia	5,30	0,59	0,70	0,88	0,47	4,70	4,70	0,70	0,65
Zimbabwe	0,65	0,18	0,39	n/a	0,17	0,30	1,93	0,37	0,12
Malawi	3,00	0,30	0,84	1,00	0,41	1,50	6,60	0,35	0,41
Zambia	3,30	0,33	0,75	1,05	0,45	1,60	7,53	0,66	0,46
Tanzania	2,42	0,34	0,73	1,16	0,66	4,10	9,79	1,00	0,61
Kenya	3,14	0,45	0,75	0,96	0,70	5,38	6,70	0,96	0,64
Ethiopia	1,88	0,47	1,18	1,29	0,35	5,00	4,11	0,59	0,49
Sudan	2,50	0,75	1,13	1,15	n/a	n/a	n/a	0,80	n/a
Egypt	2,66	0,22	0,33	0,83	1,00	1,61	3,78	0,90	0,70
Average prices:	2,77	0,45	0,74	1,00	0,41	3,03	5,47	0,84	0,52

	SUGAR PER KG	CORNED BEEF	COLA 340 ML	POTATOES PER KG	TOMATOES PER KG	FRUIT PER KG	ONIONS PER KG	MAIZE MEAL KG
South Africa	0,66	0,88	0,47	0,59	0,59	0,70	0,22	0,43
Namibia	0,59	1,18	0,41	0,94	1,65	1,40	1,00	0,59
Zimbabwe	n/a	0,86	0,15	0,29	0,40	0,21	0,40	n/a
Malawi	0,56	2,40	0,40	0,50	0,65	0,32	0,70	0,60
Zambia	0,81	1,48	0,35	0,60	0,60	0,59	0,77	0,58
Tanzania	0,84	2,07	0,38	0,29	0,26	0,40	0,21	0,26
Kenya	0,58	1,41	0,36	0,27	0,38	0,63	0,45	0,27
Ethiopia	0,56	1,70	0,18	0,24	0,35	0,35	0,35	1,88
Sudan	0,38	1,10	0,19	1,13	0,38	0,38	0,38	n/a
Egypt	0,39	0,72	0,33	0,29	0,44	0,67	0,20	n/a
Average prices:	0,60	1,37	0,34	0,52	0,58	0,57	0,48	0,67

I gathered these prices at supermarkets, stores and local markets, always trying to find the most favourable or fair price. However, it is very difficult to quote accurately as costs differ so from city to town to village, and can change quickly. They are also often skewed by favourable black-market exchange rates (for example in Zimbabwe). So rather work from the averages and then adjust up or down if the country is cheaper or more expensive.

8 On the road

Driving in Africa can be hazardous, and concentration and care must be taken at all times. Your vehicle is expensive, probably uninsured and is also your ticket home, so look after it! Other than in the south, you will encounter very few road signs, so drive slowly and be alert at all times. If you have a co-driver or passenger, ask them to assist you with the navigation.

Your average daily distance will depend entirely on the road conditions. In South Africa, Namibia, Botswana and even Zimbabwe, you should be able to cover about 800 kilometres a day on tar if you don't dawdle and half that on gravel.

A surprisingly good tarred road cuts through Egypt's Western Desert on the way to the oases of El Kharga, Dakhla and Farafra.

For the rest of the countries described in this book, the averages would have to be decreased to about 600 on tar and 300 on gravel because of poorer road conditions, stray animals, pedestrians and fellow drivers. In northern Kenya, work on about 300 kays a day and in northern Sudan only 200.

Driving on sand

For deep sand or lengthy soft sections, deflate your tyres to around 1,2 kPa. If necessary, down to 0,8 kPa. Although this makes them more vulnerable to wear and tear, it gives the tyre a larger footprint and allows it to 'pancake' instead of digging in when the going gets tough.

Very bad sections are best approached at a slightly higher speed to let your momentum carry you across, instead of trying to power your way through. Keep the steering wheels pointed straight ahead to minimise frontal resistance. Select the correct gear before tackling a bad section, as changing gears causes a drop in momentum and sometimes even a full stop.

Your vehicle should have sufficient ground clearance to negotiate the middelmannetjie (middle ridge) which is common on most sandy roads, so stay in the tracks. Heading off a well-worn track seldom gives you better traction and only degrades the environment by creating more scars on the landscape.

Driving with bad visibility

Driving at night or under dusty conditions is dangerous, so slow down and don't overtake unless 100 per cent sure of a clear road ahead. It's not just other vehicles you have to look out for: animals, pedestrians, rocks and potholes

> In the heat, tiny pockets of air between sand particles expand, making it fluffier and softer, so cover long stretches across sand during the cooler times of the day.

are typical hazards of the African road. Drive with your headlights on even if they don't help you to see better; local drivers may think you are mad but they will make you more visible. Extra spotlights also help, but rather avoid driving at night. Drive with your headlights dimmed in dusty conditions – high-beam lights just reflect off the dust particles. Extra spotlights help for night driving, but avoid driving in the dark.

Driving in game parks

Drive slowly and quietly and stay on the road. Never get too close to animals, especially if they are with their young. Don't get out of your vehicle and never feed the animals. Littering is a cardinal sin; carry all refuse with you until you find an appropriate place to dump it. Remember, it's the animals' natural habitat and you're the intruder.

Negotiating mud and water

If you're not sure of the depth of the mud or water, get out and check, and rather reverse back out to safety than risk yourself and your vehicle. Move slowly through water so as not to form a bow wave. If the fan for the radiator is in danger of spraying the electronics of your petrol-driven vehicle, remove the fan belt. Watch out for black-cotton soil mud which is thick, slippery and can get you very stuck. It's best to avoid the wet season in these regions (see route planning on page 8).

What to do if you get stuck

To avoid getting stuck in the first place, engage your free-wheel hubs and 4x4 drive long before you need them and keep them engaged long after you no longer need them. Use diff-lock sparingly and only if absolutely necessary.

If you do get stuck and you have not broken anything, the first option is to drive out. If you are in mud or sand, try to reverse out of trouble. Stay in the tracks you made going in and, if you have some movement, go forward and back, reversing a little further back each time. A helpful push from passengers and bystanders will help a lot. If in soft sand, deflate tyres to as low as you dare (0,8 kPa) and clear a smooth path in front of the tyres in the direction you intend travelling. If the diff or chassis is resting on the ground, dig it free so that your wheels have weight on them and can grip again.

Don't sink deeper by racing the engine and spinning the wheels, rather go on to option two – getting towed out (sometimes it's the first option). If you're driving in convoy, or someone stops to offer help, have a thick, strong tow rope ready. If it's long enough, your saviour will not get stuck too. A rope with a bit of 'give' in it is better than something such as a steel cable.

Option three is 'jack and pack'. A hi-lift jack with a good base is best to get the wheels up and out of trouble. Pack anything – sand, rocks and branches – under all four wheels and lower them back onto solid traction. Sand tracks and mats are useful, but they're bulky things to carry all the way through Africa just in case you get stuck: rather use what you can find.

Another trick is to jack the whole

back or front of the vehicle free of the ground and simply push it sideways off the hi-lift jack, so that the wheels land on firmer ground.

A winch (manual or mechanical) is another option, but often there is nothing to attach it to. Burying the spare wheel with the winch cable tied to it is hard work, but if you're desperate....

What to do if you break down

If you can't start the vehicle because of a flat battery or faulty starter motor, then you could push it, tow it or run it down a hill to start it in third gear. If another vehicle is on hand, you could also borrow its battery or take jump leads from it.

When the battery is turning a petrol engine over strongly and it still won't start, the problem is probably fuel or spark. Take off the air filter and pour a little petrol into the carburettor. If it splutters and tries to start, there's your problem – the engine isn't getting fuel. Pray that you've run out of petrol or that the fuel pump is faulty, because if it's a faulty carburettor, you should only tackle it with a workshop manual and lots of confidence.

To check the spark plugs, remove them one at a time and, with them still connected and earthed, see if they spark. Some clever people can do this without removing the spark plugs, but I always shock myself. If no spark, then check the wiring around the distributor or the rotor arm or contact breakers inside the distributor. It could also be a faulty coil. And if you're driving a fancy new vehicle with computerised engine control, I am afraid I can't help you. Trouble is, nor can most trained mechanics in Africa, so choose your vehicle carefully.

A diesel engine is less temperamental, but it needs a stronger battery to start it. If the vehicle will not start despite a strong battery, then it could be a faulty injector pump and you will need expert assistance. But beware, new diesel engines can also be a confusing mess of electronics and computers.

Overheating could be caused by a stuck thermostat (remove it), broken or slipping fan belt (replace it) or leak in the cooling system (replace damaged hose or block leak with radiator sealant). It could also be caused by grass and seeds clogging the radiator and building up around the engine and gearbox (a fire hazard).

Watch out for slow-moving transport.

You may break a spring – especially if you're overloaded – and some travellers carry a spare. But, you can usually limp to the next town where the mechanics there should be able to replace it.

Have the vehicle thoroughly serviced and checked before setting out on your journey and maintain it along the way.

How to fix a puncture

Commercial truck tyres with a high ply rating are more suitable than the lighter high-speed variety. Make sure you have strong sidewalls as sharp stones can cut right through others. Maintain the manufacturer's recommended pressures for a loaded vehicle.

If a tubeless tyre has a nail or screw in the treaded area, you can remove the object, seal the hole with a plug and solution and re-inflate the tyre without having to remove it from the rim.

A puncture in a tubed tyre might be repairable with an aerosol sealant kit, but will usually necessitate the removal of the tyre off the rim which, if you don't have split rims, is tricky.

First mark the tyre opposite the valve, so you can replace it properly

---

VEHICLE MAINTENANCE

Check regularly:

- Engine oil
- Coolant
- Transfer case oil.
- Gearbox oil
- Differential oil
- Battery water
- Brake/clutch fluid
- Tyre pressures
- Grass in radiator, under chassis

Replace at recommended intervals:

- Engine oil
- Oil filter
- Air filter
- Fuel filter
- Spark plugs (petrol engines)

---

without altering the balance, then remove the valve from the tube to deflate the tyre fully.

To break the tyre beading off the rim, try placing the jack at the edge of the rim and jacking against something solid – such as the vehicle. If this fails, drive over it repeatedly until it collapses. Then do the other side of the tyre.

Get the bead into the narrowest part of the rim before using your strongest and longest tyre levers to lever the bead over the rim. With the one side of the tyre off the rim, remove the tube, inflate it and identify every little leak by immersing the tube in water.

If it's repairable, roughen up the area around the puncture before applying solution. When the solution is dry to the touch, apply the patch with as much pressure as possible, refit and re-inflate. It might be better to refit a new tube and keep the old one as a spare. If a tubeless tyre needs patching on the inside with a gaiter, then rather refit with a tube.

If you do have an accident...

Basically, the only advice I can offer is – avoid them! No matter what country you have them in, the problems caused by having an accident are enormous.

In Southern Africa, where it's possible to have fully comprehensive insurance and where you can normally trust the police, stop and assess the injuries and damage. Lend assistance, call the police, and, in the case of injuries, call an ambulance. Watch your belongings or get someone you trust to do so – unfortunately there are people who prey on an accident victim's vulnerability. It's a good idea to get the names and addresses of any witnesses too.

> ### You've run out of patches or solution?
> Then pinch the tyre together at the puncture and bind it very tightly with fine, strong twine – I kid you not, this is common practice in Mozambique.

If your vehicle is badly damaged and can't be driven, be sure to negotiate an acceptable deal with a tow truck, otherwise you could be ripped off. If the damage is minor, exchange names, addresses and insurance details.

Killing or injuring domestic livestock is a delicate issue. The owner of the livestock should be liable for your damage, but will rather limp away as fast as possible. They probably won't have the means to compensate you and will demand exorbitant compensation for the animal. If caught in such a situation, it's best to call the police and let them sort it out, although it still might cost you.

As you move north, legalities and rights become blurred and you will have to sweet-talk, brazen and negotiate your way out of most situations. As I said in the beginning, drive carefully and try to avoid accidents.

If you are inexperienced at off-road driving, it would be a very good idea to first enrol in a 4x4 driving course. Then take a few short shake-down trips to test yourself, the vehicle and equipment before setting off to Cairo. The tips and guidelines I have mentioned here can never take the place of lots of practice and experience.

Baobab Valley Camp on the banks of the Ruaha River in Tanzania lives up to its name.

Staying in touch

Internet cafés are springing up all over Africa, but don't forget the fax machine which, although a lower level of technology, still makes a good alternative for keeping in touch. Telephones are dependable in the big cities and some countries have mobile phone networks which you can link up with through roaming agreements with your service provider. Travellers with South African SIM cards (or similar) in their cellphones can have them activated for use in Namibia, Botswana, Zimbabwe, Mocambique, Zambia, Tanzania and Kenya. Satellite phones are an expensive option for those who really must stay in touch all the time. Bushmail, an e-mail system using shortwave radio, works well too.

A laptop, Bushmail and a long-range transceiver may be a little over the top, but if you really *must* stay in touch....

For details, contact Jim Drummond on tel: 011-794-5249 or e-mail: jim@-bushmail.co.za.

It's nice to occasionally update yourself with the latest world news. A good shortwave radio in your vehicle, or a light portable radio, will keep you in touch and also allow you to listen to local music. You'll be able to catch the ubiquitous CNN in almost any bar.

Following the route described in this book, you'll hear dozens of different languages. Fortunately, English is one of them. To communicate, you don't always need to speak the same language; be expressive and use body and sign language. To make it a little easier, here is a list of words in three popular languages: Zulu for the south, Swahili for the east and Arabic for the north.

USEFUL ZULU WORDS		chicken *inkukhu*	meat *inyama*
me/mine *mina*	you *wena*	all *zonke*	fire *umlilo*
hello *sawubona*	goodbye *hamba kahle*	finished *phelile*	medicine *umuthi*
how are you *kunjani*		water *amanzi*	photograph *ifotho*
fine thanks *ngikhona*		man *mnumzane*	woman *unkosikazi*
thank you *ngiyabonga*		old *mdala*	snake *inyoka*
no *hayi*	how much *malini*	train *isitimela*	bus *ibhasi*
yes *yebo*	where *ngaphi*	toilet *ebhoshini*	post office *iposi*
when *manini*	today *namhlanje*	bread *isinkwa*	
tomorrow *kusasa*	yesterday *izolo*	what is your name *ubani igama lakho*	
buy *thenga*	money *imali*	numbers use English	

USEFUL SWAHILI WORDS		chicken *kuku*		food *chakula*		
hello *jambo*	goodbye *kwaheri*	no problem *hakuna matata*				
how are you *habari*		welcome *karibu*				
fine thanks *mzuri*		what's your name *jina lako nani*				
thank you (very much) *asante (sana)*		where *wapi*		tea *chai*		
yes *ndiyo*	no *hapana*	1 *moja*	2 *mbili*	3 *tatu*	4 *nne*	
how much *ngapi*		5 *tano*	6 *sita*	7 *saba*	8 *nane*	
meat *nyama*	bread *mkate*	9 tisa	10 *kumi*			

USEFUL ARABIC WORDS		market *souq*		bread *eesh*	
greetings *salaam al laikoum*		tea *atai*		how much *kem*	
goodbye *ma as salama*		where is the hotel... *fein al fundu*...			
and greetings to you too		what is your name *ismak eh*			
wa al laikoum salaam		1 *wahid*	2 *itneem*	3 *talata*	
thank you *shukran*		4 *arba'a*	5 *hamsa*	6 *setta*	
I want to go to... *ans ayiz aruh*...		7 *seb'a*	8 *thimanya*		
yes *nam*	no *ley*	9 *tesa'a*	10 *ashara*		

10 Using public
transport

It is possible, and some say preferable, to use public transport to get across the continent. Africa and its people are constantly on the move – Somalis travel to South Africa to find work, Malians pass through Sudan and Egypt trying to get to Europe, Nigerians trade between Malawi and Mozambique.

Buses are the most popular way of covering long distances, as trains and the rail network are poorly maintained. Where conditions become too rough or the route too sparsely populated to warrant a bus, then the trucks that you will find on every road or track in Africa will take paying passengers, usually on top of the load or (more expensively) in the cab with the driver.

Public transport takes on many forms in Africa, from overloaded ships of the desert in Sudan (above) to real ships on Lake Malawi (below.)

For shorter distances, the common minibus carries passengers and their loads to every corner of the continent. When the going gets too tough for even these willing workhorses, then the light trucks take over. Boats ply the lakes, rivers and coast and even the lowly bicycle is pressed into service.

Get used to taking your time

The main thing to remember is that, if you want to get somewhere, someone will be willing to take you. It takes a change of attitude to travel this way though. You will have to be patient and prepared for some unscheduled stops, but you will see and experience Africa and its people in a most wonderful way. You will be living on the local person's level – you will not be a threat to them, nor will they be jealous of you. You will be shown courtesy and kindness and learn more about the people, their customs, traditions and language. You will feel a part of the rhythm of Africa.

Public transport in South Africa

If you do decide to take the public transport route, here's more or less what to expect. South Africa's public transport system is fast and efficient. **Luxury coaches** swoop around the country from city to city, keeping to timetables. They are clean, safe and good value for money. The main inter-city buslines are Greyhound, Intercape Mainliner and Translux. Trains are still an option in South Africa, especially for the romance and unique experience of rail travel. The network is wide and timetables are adhered to. There are even a few restored steam trains servicing certain scenic routes. The cities are well serviced by **public buses** and minibus taxis, while Cape Town even has a good suburban rail system. (For bus contacts, see page 14).

Buses leave Cape Town's main railway station en-route to Johannesburg and Pretoria for $47 (Greyhound, Intercape and Translux), to Durban for $55 (Greyhound, Intercape and Translux) and Windhoek for $50 (Intercape). Trains travel from Cape Town to Johannesburg and Pretoria for $35 (6 sleeper) and to Durban for $45 (6 sleeper).

The **Baz Bus** offers a very useful hop-on, hop-off service. It runs comfortable, medium-sized buses up the coast from Cape Town to Durban and on to Johannesburg and back, stopping at all the most popular backpacker lodges. They claim to stop at over 40 towns and 160 hostels en-route and you can break your journey as often as you like. Cape Town to Port Elizabeth costs $85, to Durban $165 and to Johannesburg $195. A great way to see the country.

From Johannesburg, buses leave regularly from the Rotunda at the main railway station and head for Durban ($22 on Greyhound and Translux), Harare ($41 on Greyhound and Translux), Maputo ($25 on Greyhound), Lusaka ($50 on Translux) and Blantyre ($59 on Translux).

Getting around Namibia

Public transport in Namibia is run along similar lines to South Africa. The rail service is a bit run down and less likely to run on time. The exception is the Desert Express, a luxury service that links Windhoek to Swakopmund. With an overnight stop at a quiet siding and visits to rock paintings and a game ranch to watch lions being fed, it's obviously not just travelling from A to B. It's not cheap either at $127 a person double (tel: 061-298-2600, fax: 061-298-2601, e-mail: dx@transnamib.com.na).

Intercape Mainliner runs a bus service to Walvis Bay via Swakopmund and north to Oshikango, as well as its cross-border routes to Cape Town ($50) and Victoria Falls via the Caprivi ($59), tel: 061-22-7847 (Windhoek) or contact them in Cape Town or Johannesburg.

Into Zimbabwe and Malawi

In Zimbabwe, Harare's main intercity bus station is about five kilometres out of town at Mbare Musika. Buses head north to all major towns around the country. The smarter coach companies have depots in the city centre and run services north to Lusaka, east to Malawi and south to South Africa.

Malawi's Shire Bus Company offers an extensive internal service with three levels of comfort: Coachline (with snacks, toilet and aircon), Express (none of the aforementioned and more stops) and the even slower, very basic Speedlink. Other buses and mini buses scamper around all over the country, which makes Malawi an easy country to get around in. From Blantyre, various bus companies run down through Tete to Harare, Beit Bridge and even down to Johannesburg.

A ferry boat, the MV *Ilala*, runs a cheap, weekly service up and down Lake Malawi between Monkey Bay in the south and Nkhata Bay in the north.

Zambia to Zanzibar

Public transport travellers in Zambia are lucky to be able to use one of Africa's few long distance trains, the Tazara service. This express train runs from Kapiri Mposhi, 194 kilometres north of Lusaka, all the way through northeastern Zambia and ends at Dar es Salaam on the Indian Ocean in Tanzania. The twice-weekly service is reasonably fast and efficient and usually runs on schedule.

Their headquarters are in Lusaka (just over the railway bridge from the Kafue roundabout on Independance Avenue), where you can get the latest timetable and buy tickets. In Kapiri Mposhi, follow the railway line east out of the centre for about one kilometre to reach the Tazara terminus. You can buy tickets here too and obtain info, but it is quite chaotic with lots of hustlers and thieves.

The hustle and bustle of the Intercity Bus Terminal is where you want to be for all other transport in and out of Lusaka. International buses leave for Harare once a day and cost $10; to Lilongwe they depart three times a week ($12); daily departures all the way to Dar es Salaam will cost you $16 and take two days. Buses and minibuses leave all the time for all the main towns in Zambia, with minibuses a bit faster and more expensive (to Kapiri Mposhi will cost $4 for a bus and $5 for a minibus).

Other than the Tazara railway line to Zambia, the best overland transport in

Tanzania is on the buses. They crisscross the country between all large towns, the best ones being the 'express' variety. For shorter hops, matatus (minibus taxis) are fine, but travelling in the back of beyond, you will be forced to use a *dala-dala* (light truck).

To reach the islands of Zanzibar and Pemba, you will use one of the large ferries that leave from Dar, unless you want to spice things up with a crossing by dhow (for more info on this, read about Bagamoyo on page 136). For getting around in the game parks of the north, you will have to hook up with a safari in Arusha.

There is one other interesting transport option, the lake ferry from Mwanza, in the south-east corner of Lake Victoria, to Bukoba in the southwest, near the Ugandan border. This service used to go right across to Port Bell (Kampala) in Uganda but was suspended after a tragic sinking of the ferry with great loss of life in 1996. Matatus can now transport you to the Ugandan border from Bukoba, and then on to Kampala.

Kenya to Ethiopia

Kenya's public transport system is similar to Tanzania's, with express buses between large towns and matatus and dala-dalas for the shorter or rougher routes. There is a rail service between Nairobi and Mombassa – very scenic, as it passes through the Tsavo East National Park, but expensive ($55/$38 first/second class).

Heading north to the Ethiopian border can be done in three days. Regular buses can transport you as far as Isiolo, where you must sleep overnight and negotiate a ride on a truck going to Marsabit the next day.

After spending the night in Marsabit, it's negotiation time again and another truck ride to the border at Moyale (sometimes you can get lucky and hitch a ride in a government or NGO Landy, which is a lot quicker, but you will still be expected to pay).

Despite being so mountainous, the road system in Ethiopia is reasonably good with a transport system to match. Although there are no luxury coaches, overcrowding and standing in the aisles are illegal. Buses cover most of the country, yielding to 4x4s and trucks only when conditions become impossible. Buses travel only during daylight hours and, if you intend travelling a long distance, you will be required to be at the bus station at 06h00. The bus will then travel all day, stopping regularly for food, drink and toilets, until the overnight stop (in whatever town takes the driver's fancy).

There are two main bus stations in Addis Ababa. The biggest is the Autobus Terra in the Merkato; the other near the railway station on Ras Makonnen Ave. There is a rail service from Addis down to Djibouti which is really of interest only if you want to get to Dire Dawa. An interesting mode of transport in the towns is the gari (a horse-drawn cart). Another option to consider when travelling in Ethiopia, where the distances are so great, is to use the excellent and reasonably priced domestic flights which fly to every corner of the country, courtesy of the safe and comfortable Ethiopian Airlines.

Getting to Sudan and Egypt

To get to the Sudan border, you will first have to get to Gondar. Then take a minibus for 12 kilometres south to the little town of Azezo, where you will have to find anything going down in the direction of Metema. Where only overloaded 4x4s and trucks dared to go a few years ago, there are now minibuses and the occasional full-sized bus plying the route, as the road has been rebuilt. Although the road across to Gedaref in Sudan has also been rebuilt, transport is infrequent and you might have to jump on a truck.

Sudan's outlying districts are serviced by incredibly basic and strong local buses. Originally based on old Bedford trucks, but now often Isuzus, they are one step up from cattle trucks. The heavy, home-made bodies are constructed of wood and have cramped rows of thinly padded bench-seats. The roofrack and load usually doubles the height of the vehicle and they often break down.

Out in the desert, you will find open trucks with oversized wheels transporting people and goods along the sandy tracks.

But, the most exciting runs of all are in open-backed Toyota Hiluxes, called boksis. Driven at speed across the open desert where there are no roads, the drivers rely on skill and the muscle power of their passengers to get through. But, we've come too far to turn back now, so we'll press on regardless. Fortunately, once you're on tar, you can transfer to quite luxurious coaches with aircon and even toilets. These coaches travel incredibly fast and are not very expensive.

Every town in Sudan has a souq shaabi which serves as the bus station – in Khartoum it's in the south of the city and serves all destinations south and east of the city. In Sharia al-Qasr you will find the bus companies that go north to Karima, Dongola and Wadi Halfa. Omdurman's souq shaabi also sends out buses to the north. The road north to Karima, Abu Dom and Dongola has been hugely improved. What used to be a wild series of tracks through the sand, is now a tarred road as far as Abu Dom. It gets rough further north, but you will still be able to travel in the truck/buses all the way to Wadi Halfa.

The other way to get to Wadi Halfa from Khartoum is by train. This weekly service starts from the central railway station on Sharia al-Geish and heads down the Nile via Atbara. At Abu Hamad, it leaves the river and heads straight through the desert for 370 kilometres to Wadi Halfa. First class costs $22 and second $18.

The only way north from Wadi Halfa is by ferry down the length of Lake Nasser. Tickets are available at any time prior to sailing (northbound weekly on Wednesday afternoons) from the office behind the immigration building. Second class entitles you to a seat down below, or you can lounge on deck for the 20-hour trip. The cost is $28 which includes one meal and a cup of tea (deduct $2,75 if you want to skip the food).

Breakdowns in the Sudan can be lengthy affairs and until it's fixed, you ain't going nowhere.

Travelling around Egypt

Once in Egypt the transport facilities improve vastly. The authorities, however, are so afraid of terrorist attacks on tourists that they try to control your movements and modes of transport. The most comfortable trip that you can do in Egypt (barring flying) has got to be the overnight express train between Aswan and Cairo (13 hours to cover 925 kilometres). First class is air-conditioned, and has reclining seats that allow you to sleep quite comfortably (cost $17,50).

Luxury buses travel up and down from Cairo to Aswan as well as west to the Sinai Peninsular and north to Alexandria. There are bus services linking the oasis towns in the western desert too. Depending on the prevailing security situation, you may or may not be allowed to board certain buses and trains – the rules change all the time, so check before planning your journey.

Travel on the Nile is a must, even if it is only a short ride on a fellucca in Aswan or Luxor. Better still, organise a few days cruising down the river – the captain and his assistant cook for you, and at night you tie up to the bank in some deserted spot and sleep on deck under the stars. You could not have a more fitting finale to an exciting assortment of different modes of public transport through Africa. All that remains now is the chaos of Cairo traffic. Try to avoid its buses and minibuses and rather use the wonderful clean and fast underground railway.

Hope you enjoy it – I know you won't forget it! So, where to now? Well, why not buy a ticket on a bus to Petra in Jordan, or catch a ferry across to Greece or Italy? Or head west through Libya and across north Africa. Or just maybe (no, nobody's that crazy) turn around and head back down again.

Routes in Southern Africa

Southern Africa, the most peaceful region in Africa, offers the most options. Which one you choose depends on your time and what you want to see. A circular route is also an option.

CAPE TOWN TO LUSAKA OPTION 1
via Bloemfontein, Joburg and Harare. Total distance: 3 000 kilometres. Page 58.

For the hasty traveller who wants to head north in the shortest possible time.

CAPE TOWN TO LUSAKA OPTION 2
via Namibia and the Caprivi. Total distance: 3 750 kilometres. Page 74.

A grand tour through Namibia, taking in all the country's main sights.

CAPE TOWN TO LUSAKA OPTION 3
via Botswana and Livingstone. Total distance: 3 000 kilometres. Page 88.

A direct route with optional detours into Botswana's fine wilderness areas.

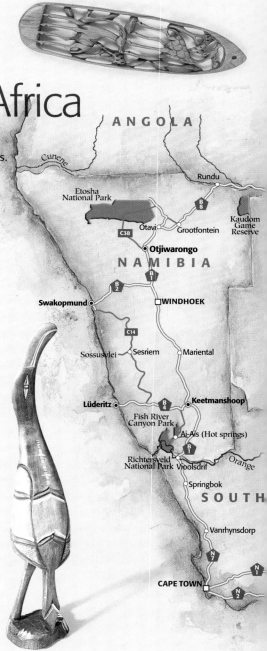

ANGOLA

Cunene

Rundu

Etosha National Park

Otavi   Grootfontein   Kaudom Game Reserve

C38

Otjiwarongo

NAMIBIA

B2

Swakopmund   ☐WINDHOEK

C14

Sossusvlei   Sesriem   Mariental

Lüderitz   Keetmanshoop

Fish River Canyon Park

Ai-Ais (Hot springs)

Richtersveld National Park   Vioolsdrif   Orange

Springbok

SOUTH

Vanrhynsdorp

CAPE TOWN ☐

ZAMBIA

Kafue National Park

Mongu

Sitoti

Katima Mulilo

Kazungula

Livingstone

Victoria Falls

Chobe National Park

Moremi Wildlife Reserve

Nata

Sowa Pan

Francistown

BOTSWANA

Mahalapye

GABORONE

Mafikeng

Vryburg

LUSAKA

Chirundu

Zambezi

Mana Pools National Park

HARARE

ZIMBABWE

Hwange National Park

BULAWAYO

Masvingo

Musina

Polokwane

Kruger National Park

Liwonde National Park

Gorongosa National Park

Quelimane

Beira

Vilankulo

MOZAMBIQUE

Inhambane

N

Pretoria

JOHANNESBURG

SWAZILAND

MAPUTO

Kroonstad

Kimberley

BLOEMFONTEIN

LESOTHO

Umfolozi Game Reserve

Richards Bay

AFRICA

DURBAN

Umtata

Three Sisters
Beaufort West

Mossel Bay

Port Elizabeth

East London

Indian Ocean

Don't miss
◆ Cape Point ◆ Gold Reef City
◆ Great Zimbabwe ◆ Kariba
◆ Sossusvlei ◆ Etosha
◆ Okavango Delta ◆ Kafue
◆ Moremi, Chobe ◆ Victoria Falls

Cape Town to Lusaka

via Bloemfontein, Johannesburg and Harare 3 000 km

11

If you're in a hurry to get up north and want to take the most direct route, then this is for you. Good, fast highways whisk you up through Beitbridge into Zimbabwe. There you have the option of visiting the Great Zimbabwe Ruins, Victoria Falls, Mana Pools National Park and Kariba before striking into the heart of Zambia.

To start your journey in style, I suggest heading down the Cape Peninsula to Cape Point, the most appropriate place to start any African journey. Take De Waal Drive out of the city centre and stay with the M3 as it sweeps along the majestic chain of peninsula mountains.

Whether you leave from Cape Agulhas (above) or Cape Town (right), the bridge over the Zambezi below Victoria Falls (left) is a good 2 700 km away.

Views of the city, Table Bay and the winelands of Paarl and Stellenbosch in the distance make this a very scenic drive, so take your time. Head for Muizenberg on the False Bay coast and follow the road past the popular seaside suburbs of St James, Kalk Bay, Fish Hoek and the historic old naval base of Simon's Town.

Lots of good accommodation and restaurants might entice you to stay or at least, if the weather's warm, stop for a swim along the way. I'm particularly fond of quaint little **Kalk Bay** with its fishing harbour, Brass Bell Pub built on the rocks and a number of well-stocked antique shops.

Cape Point is in the **Cape of Good Hope Nature Reserve**, so pay the entrance fee of $3 and drive down to the parking area at the point. From there it's a short climb up to the lighthouse that marks the beginning of your journey. Look north, make a wish for a safe and exciting trip and then, climb down to your vehicle, start up, and be off on the journey of a lifetime!

On your way back up the peninsula, consider turning west (left) as you exit the reserve to follow the Atlantic seaboard via scenic **Chapman's Peak Drive** (scheduled to re-open at the end of 2003 after extensive repairs). **Hout Bay's** harbour offers boat trips

and seafood while beyond lies beautiful **Llandudno, Camps Bay, Clifton** and **Sea Point** for upmarket accommodation, dining and swimming (bring your bikini). You will end up at the **Waterfront**, Cape Town's tourist mecca. With trendy shops, restaurants, bars and cinemas, it is popular with locals and tourists alike. Boat trips leave from here to **Robben Island** and helicopter flips can give you a bird's eye view of the peninsula.

Where to stay in Cape Town

Most of Cape Town's centrally situated backpackers and affordable accommodation establishments are to be found around the upper end of **Long Street** – you will be surrounded by all the coolest restaurants, pubs and clubs too. Places such as **Carnival Court**, 255 Long Street, tel: 021-423-9003, fax: 021-423-9166, e-mail: info@carnivalcourt.co.za, website: www.carnivalcourt.co.za and **Long Street Backpackers**, 209 Long Street, tel: 021-423-0615, fax: 021-423-1842, e-mail: info@longstreetbackpackers.co.za, website: www.longstreetbackpackers.co.za are but two of the many, which all charge in the region of $7 for dorm beds, $11,50 for singles and $17,50 for doubles. The surrounding areas of Kloof Street and the suburb of the

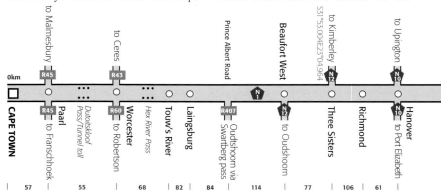

Gardens are also good places to look, but remember parking is a problem.

Moving out of the centre, you will find a huge selection of accommodation in the suburbs of **Sea Point** and **Green Point**, many of them within walking distance of the Waterfront. Try **Big Blue**, 7 Vesperdene Road, Green Point. tel: 021-439-0807, fax: 021-439-8068, e-mail: big.blue@mweb.co.za, website: www.bigblue.za.net or **Brown Sugar**, 1 Main Road, Green Point, tel 021-433-0413, fax: 0860-10-2291, e-mail: brownsugar2000@hotmail.com, website: www.brownsugar.get.to or **Carnaby's**, 219 Main Road, Three Anchor Bay, tel: 021-439-7410, Fax 021-439-1222, e-mail: carnaby@netactive.co.za, website: www.carnabybackpacker.co.za.

Another good option is the modern **Road Lodge**, situated alongside the highway at N1 City. They charge $24 a room that can sleep up to three people (reservations tel: 0800-11-3790, website: www.citylodge.co.za).

Cape Town's most central caravan and camp site is **Hardekraaltjie**, Duminee Street, just off Voortrekker Road in Bellville (tel: 021-946-2006, fax: 021-948-7225). They charge $8,85 double for camping and also have little four-bedded cabins with fridge and stove, but no bathroom, for $17. Just

past Simon's Town, on the way down to Cape Point, is the attractively situated **Oatlands Village** (tel: 021-786-1410, fax: 021-786-1162) which offers camping for $11 double and self-catering cottages for $43 double. Another beautifully positioned camp site is the **Berg River Resort** (tel: 021-863-1650, fax: 021-863-2583), on the banks of the Berg River on the R45 road between Paarl and Franschhoek (ideal for exploring the wine routes). Camping is $11 double and cottages $28.

Where to eat, drink and enjoy

Simple – stroll around the Long and Kloof Street area or head for the Waterfront. Cape Town is famous for its spicy **Cape Malay** cooking and fresh seafood dishes. It is also the undisputed jazz capital of South Africa (and some would say of Africa). Music venues change all the time, so check out the local press, or ask around.

Where to shop

Cape Town is very First World and has malls, malls and more malls. The best are very good and have a huge selection of specialist shops, supermarkets and discount outlets where you will be able to find all you need.

The biggest and best are: The **V & A Waterfront** in the city centre, **Canal**

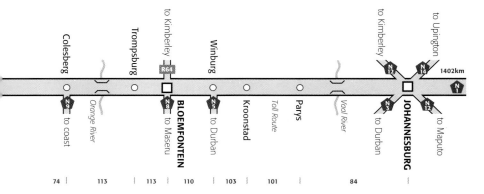

Walk on the N1 heading out of town and **Tyger Valley Centre,** up Durban Road off the N1 in Bellville.

Information

Cape Town is blessed with an excellent tourist **information centre** on the corner of Burg and Castle Streets, tel: 021-426-4260, e-mail: captour@iafrica.com. They stock hundreds of free pamphlets and maps (also for the surrounding regions). Relax at the onsite internet café. There is also an excellent Namibian tourist office in the Standard Bank Centre, Heerengracht, Cape Town.

What to do in Cape Town

A visit to **Robben Island** is a must. The boat trip across Table Bay is a worthwhile excursion on its own and the guided tour of the island, which is now a World Heritage Site, is expertly conducted by former inmates and warders of the prison. The terminal for tickets and tours is at the old Clock Tower at the Waterfront, tel: 021-419 1300, website: www.robbenisland.org.za. Tickets cost $18.

The **Two Oceans Aquarium** at the V&A Waterfront is well worth a visit too. Although a bit on the pricey side at $6, it has a mind-boggling variety of marine life in excellently constructed tanks, including a huge glass fronted one, containing sharks and other large species (tel: 021-418-3823, website: www.aquarium.co.za)

Climb Table Mountain – very cautiously. Every year people are rescued off the mountain, so go with someone knowledgeable, or walk along the contour paths on the lower reaches. Even the tame-looking **Lions Head** can be dangerous when the weather turns foul. Or you can cheat by taking the **cable car** (tel: 021-424 8181, cost: $6/$11 single/return)

You cannot leave Cape Town without visiting one of the many **wine routes** that crisscross the surrounding countryside. There are 10 within easy day trip distance of the city – Paarl, Stellenbosch, Wellington, Franschhoek, Constantia, Worcester, Hermanus, Helderberg, Durbanville and Swartland – and many estates offer gourmet meals as well. The Cape is justifiably famous for its wines, go out, taste them and stock up for the lean weeks ahead. Get hold of a current copy of *John Platter's SA Wines* for all and everything about the regions and their wines.

Heading up the N1 to Joburg

Breaking away from the fleshpots of cosmopolitan Cape Town ain't easy, but one day you'll find yourself cruising out of the city along Table Bay

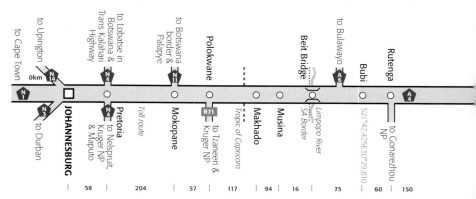

Boulevard and barreling down the N1 highway. The suburbs drop behind you and the winelands of **Paarl** beckon one last time as you are given the choice of driving over the spectacular **Du Toitskloof Pass** or taking the quicker and easier option of the tunnel (toll $2) At some point the magnitude of driving to Cairo will hit you – just concentrate on tackling the small daily details and you'll find that they will build into "the big trip" by themselves.

On the other side of the mountains, you will pass **Worcester** – beware of speed traps when passing through. Further on, the table grape vineyards of the **Hex River Valley** are a beautiful sight, especially when the leaves turn to red and orange in autumn, but the countryside becomes dry and scrubby beyond that as you enter the wide open spaces of the **Great Karoo**.

The ribbon of tar that is the N1 becomes straighter and longer and higher speeds are tempting, but be careful, as this is a busy route. The railway junction of Touws River, with its graveyard of rusting old steam locomotives, is passed at 180 kilometres. Forty-five kilometres on, a real graveyard for casualties of the Boer War is just off the road on the right at S33°14.380 E20°28.517. Ten kilometres further, also off to the right, is the won-

derfully restored and furnished **Lord Milner Hotel** which has a fascinating Boer War history. Accommodation costs $35/$55 single/double in the main building, a little less in the garden cottages and $20/$33 single/double in the charming old annexe. A private museum, vintage train and cars and a great little pub/restaurant make this a popular stop on the long dry road north.

Laingsburg, at 260 kilometres, is a good place to pitstop as fuel, clean toilets and fast food is available from a couple of large petrol stations. The town's dependence on sheep farming is the reason for the "Dra Wol" (wear wool) sign laid out in white stone on the hillside as you leave town and, as you head north, sheep is about all you'll see for the next 200 kilometres. Well-signposted laybyes with shaded tables and benches break the monotony until the **Prince Albert Road** is reached. Turn off here if you've planned a route via the ostrich town of **Oudtshoorn**. It will take you through the quaint little village of **Prince Albert**, and then over the rugged, steep **Swartberg Pass** and eventually to the **Garden Route** on the Indian Ocean coast (see page 102).

At 460 kilometres from Cape Town, **Beaufort West** makes a good overnight stop. The main street is lined with

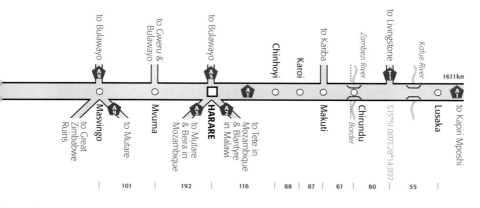

fuel stations, fast food outlets and accommodation. The **municipal camp site** on the right as you enter the main part of town costs $7,50 to pitch a tent and $14 for a caravan (be careful though, during winter the Karoo nights are icy cold). There is a large choice of B&Bs which charge from $12 single and $20 double (in summer, look for one with a pool). The **Formula 1 hotel** has rooms which sleep up to three for $23 and on the way out of town there is the **Wagon Wheels Motel** with rooms ranging from $12 to $23 single and $21 to $35 double. Camping is $6 a site and $1,75 a person. Beaufort West also has good breakdown and vehicle repair facilities as well as a selection of supermarkets and shops.

Seventy five kilometres north of Beaufort West lies the bustling truckstop of **Three Sisters**, named after three nearby hills. B&B is available at the **Three Sisters Guestfarm** for $11 a person sharing. Just north of the truckstop, at S31°53.004 E23°04.964, is the important **turnoff to Kimberley** via the N12 (see page 90). Towns are far apart in the Karoo, so make sure you always have enough fuel. In 2003 this section of the N1 was being upgraded, so take care through the single-lane stop-start deviations.

Richmond and **Hanover** are long drives apart and have the usual, basic amenities, while **Colesberg** is well endowed with truckstops and accommodation. From the upmarket **Merino Inn** on the south side, through the cheaper guesthouses ($7 a person) and camp site in town, to the comfortable **Viltra Inn** ($12/$17 single/double) at the northern exit, Colesberg caters for all budgets. The smooth, straight N1 highway crosses the **Orange River** and rolls on, bypassing little towns such as **Trompsburg** and **Edenburg**, both of which have fuel and accommodation.

Bloemfontein, at 1 000 kilometres from Cape Town, is a large city with all amenities. There are supermarkets, agents for all major vehicle manufacturers and good medical facilities. Accommodation at **Taffy's Backpackers**, 18 Louis Botha Street, tel: 051-31-4533 is inexpensive at $4,75 in a dorm, $6 a person double and $3,50 camping. There are also quite a few well signposted B&Bs. Discover more about **Lord of the Rings** author JRR Tolkien's birthplace by phoning Bloem info at 051-405-8489.

The N1 bypasses Bloemfontein, so unless you particularly need to enter the centre, refuel at one of the large garages on the ringroad. Out of town accommodation, however, is more difficult to find. Your best option is **Tom's**

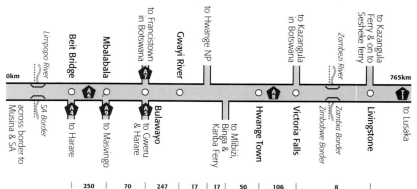

SOUTH AFRICA

Capitals: Pretoria (administrative), Cape Town (legislative), Bloemfontein (judicial)

Official languages: English and 10 other indigenous local languages

Area: 1 221 000 square kilometres

Population: 45 million

Visa requirements: Not required for most holiday visitors

Time: UT +1

International dialling code: +27

Currency and rate: rand (R) and cents; R8,50 =$1

Climate: Generally warm and sunny. Summers hot, winters cold

Highlights: Cape Town and the winelands of the Western Cape, gameviewing in Kruger and other national parks, Drakensberg, The Garden Route

Driving: On the left. A good system of tarred roads

Accommodation: Plentiful and a wide variety; camping, backpackers, B&Bs, hotels and luxury lodges

Food, shops and fuel: Cosmopolitan selection of restaurants, delis and supermarkets. Fuel available all over

Tourism info: Satour, tel: 011-778-8000, fax: 011-778-8001, e-mail: info@southafricantourism.com, website: www.southafricantourism.com

---

Place, 35 kilometres south of Bloemfontein. Look for exit 153 signposted to Koppieskraal at S29°24.568 E26°07.906. It offers fuel, food, camping ($2,50 a site plus $1,25 a person) and cottages for $15/$19 single/double.

Winburg, 110 kilometres beyond Bloemfontein, has basic amenities, but Kroonstad, at the same distance again, is better. Accommodation in chalets at the Kroon Park Resort is from $11,75 a person sharing and camping $5 a person (tel: 056-213-1942, fax: 056-213-1941). You will now be travelling on one of the best roads in Africa – the N1 becomes a toll road from here all the way through to Makhado (Louis Trichardt). It's not cheap, but well worth it for the speed and ease with which you can zoom through the heavily built-up areas of Gauteng.

Traffic will pick up, and you will have to keep a sharp eye out for road signs on the freeways and fly-overs. Fuel and food is available at large truckstops along this route, but if you want other amenities or services you will have to venture into the city. In fact, the Johannesburg/Pretoria area is probably the best place in Africa (if not the world) to equip and stock an overland safari.

Where to stay in Gauteng

There are various backpackers that offer camping and secure parking. Airport Backpackers, 3 Mohawk Street, Rhodesfield, Kempton Park, Johannesburg. Tel/fax: 011-394-0485, e-mail: airportbackpack@hotmail.com. Dorms and rooms between $8,50 and $14 a person, and camping $4,75. With similar prices are Eastgate Backpackers, 41 Hans Pirow Road, Bruma, Johannesburg. tel: 011-616-2741, fax:

011-615-1092, e-mail: egatebp@netactive.co.za, and **Ranch Hostel**, Inchanga Road, Witkoppen, Johannesburg. tel: 011-708-1304.

North South Backpackers, 355 Glyn Street, Hatfield, Pretoria. tel: 012-362-0989, fax: 012-362-0960, e-mail: northsouth@mweb.co.za, website: www.northsouthbackpackers.com. Dorms are $7,50, rooms $11,75 and camping $5 a person.

Pretoria Backpackers, 425 Farenden Street, Clydesdale, Pretoria. tel: 012-343-9754, fax: 012-343-2524, e-mail: ptaback@netactive.co.za, website: www.ptabackpackers.co.za. Dorms cost $7,50 a person and rooms between $15 and $29.

Word of Mouth, 430 Reitz Street, Pretoria. tel: 0800-108-102, fax: 012-343-9351, e-mail: info@wordofmouthbackpackers.com, website: www.wordofmouthbackpackers.com. Dorms and camping are $7,50 and rooms $20 double a night.

Where to eat and what not to miss in Gauteng

One of the trendier suburbs to hang out, eat and drink in is **Melville**. For African Jazz head for **The Baseline** (tel: 011-482-6915), the **Xai Xai Lounge** a Mozambiquan-style bar and **Nuno's Restaurant** (011-482-6984) serves Mediterranean food. Across the road, **Unplugged** is a great late night spot. Melville has its own website at www.virtualmelville.co.za.

If you stay over in Joey's, go and see **Gold Reef City,** a working museum based around an old mine just south of the city. From the restored mine village

---

GAUTENG SHOPS THAT STOCK EVERYTHING FOR:

The outdoors

Campworld (10 branches),
tel: 012-329-2259,
website: www.campworld.co.za

Outdoorsman (eight branches),
tel: 012-328-7167,
website: www.the-outdoorsman.com

Outdoor Warehouse (five branches),
tel: 0800-03-3051,
website: www.outdoorwarehouse.co.za

Safari Centre,
Joburg tel: 011-465-3817
e-mail: bryanston@safaricentre.co.za,
Pretoria tel: 012-348-3253,
e-mail: menlyn@safaricentre.co.za,
website: www.safaricentre.co.za

4x4 rentals

Rainbow Camper Hire,
tel: 011-396-1860, fax: 011-396-1937,
e-mail: info@rainbowcamperhire.co.za,
website: www.rainbowcamperhire.co.za

Bundu Rent,
tel: 011-425-3758, fax: 011-425-3619.
e-mail: gw@bundurent.com,
website: www.bundurent.com

Vehicle sales and servicing:

Halfway Toyota, Fourways,
tel: 011-465-7774, fax: 011-465-7899
e-mail: dp@halfway4ways.co.za,
website: www.halfwaytoyota.co.za

Other vehicle makes are well represented. Check phone directory

with working shops and saloons, head underground in a miners cage for a tour of the old workings. They also have a new **Apartheid Museum** (011-496-1822).

For a guided tour of **Soweto**, call Jimi's Face to Face Tours on 011-331–6109 or e-mail face2face@-pixie.co.za. **Gauteng Tourism** is on tel: 011-327-2000, fax: 011-327-7000, e-mail: tourism@gauteng.net, website: www.gauteng.net.

Pretoria to the border

The N1 continues north past Pretoria, along the **Kranskop toll road**, bypassing all towns on the way except **Polokwane** (Pietersburg), where it annoyingly cuts right through town. You will have to dodge thronging pedestrians and double-parked taxis as you slowly fight your way through the main street. The road north, although still a toll road, has some rigorously-enforced 60 kilometres an hour speed restrictions through built-up areas – also watch out for stray animals.

Makhado (Louis Trichardt) is a pleasant town at the foot of the **Soutpansberg** and a comfortable place to overnight. The municipal camp site is great value with good security and well-shaded sites, and costs only $4 a site a day. Three kilometres north of town is the beautifully situated **Clouds End Hotel**. Set in a forest with a variety of birds and small game, they charge from $20 a person B&B, or they also have camp sites.

The climb out of Makhado and through the mountain passes of the Soutpansberg is a wonderful scenic drive with farm stalls and mountain lodges along the way. After 95 kilo-

---

USEFUL CONTACTS IN GAUTENG

Vehicles and accessories

Halfway Toyota, Fourways,
tel: 011-465-7774

Big Country 4x4 & Outdoor, Menlyn,
tel: 012-348-0826,
e-mail: bruce@bigcountry4x4.com,
website: www.bigcountry4x4.com

4x4 Warehouse, Cnr William Nichol and Bruton roads, Bryanston, Johannesburg, tel: 011-706-9295,
e-mail: 4x4@4x4warehouse.co.za,
website: www.4x4warehouse.co.za

RV Centre, Johan le Roux Road, Meyerton, tel: 016-362-0431,
e-mail: rvcentre@webmail.co.za

Wayne's 4x4, Jakaranda Street, Hennopspark, Centurion, Joburg,
tel: 012-653-0309, fax: 012-653-0309

Bush Miles, Fourways Value Mart, Witkoppen Road, tel: 011-467-4476,
fax: 011-467-4484,
e-mail: info@bushmiles.co.za,

Camping and Safari Gear

Army Co, 60 Mitchell Street, Pretoria West, tel: 012-327-3282,
fax: 012-327-1194,
e-mail: army@armystores.co.za,
website: www.armystores.co.za

---

metres **Musina** (Messina) is reached – the last South African town before crossing into Zimbabwe. Although the exchange rate across the border makes most things cheaper there, there are often shortages in Zimbabwe, so try and check with south-bound travellers about what to stock up with before leaving South Africa. Musina has super-markets, fuel and most other services including accommodation. The Impala Motel charges $20/$22 single/double for self-contained rooms, and the **Baobab Caravan Park** has chalets for $20/$24 single/double and camp sites at $4,75 a stand plus $1,75 a person.

The short 16-kilometre drive to the border is often lined with queues of heavy trucks waiting to clear customs. Drive right past them and enter the South African border post. If you have avoided the busy school holiday or long-weekend periods, your formali-ties should be dealt with quickly and efficiently. Cross the Limpopo River via the new bridge (no charge, but a toll fee of $8,25 if coming from the other direction). The Zimbabwean side is less efficient but also fairly quick if your documents are in order. Corrupt offi-cials like asking for a South African police clearance certificate to prove that your car is not stolen – you might want to get one. Remember to buy third-party insurance for the vehicle outside at the agency kiosk if you don't already have Comesa Insurance.

Zimbabwe has been suffering from severe shortages of fuel and some food-stuffs as well as runaway inflation and devaluation of the local currency. There has also been some civil unrest, so make enquiries before you enter the country.

Discovering Zimbabwe

The Zim side of the border has fuel, basic accommodation and a money changing forex bureau (don't change on the street, it's too dangerous). Heading north, the road forks – left via the A6 to Bulawayo and on to Victoria Falls, and right to Harare on the A4.

For Victoria Falls, take the A6

The **A6 to Bulawayo** is 340 kilometres of good, tarred road with little traffic. Bulawayo is a large city with all the amenities you could wish for, including major motor dealerships and super-markets. If you are camping, the cen-trally situated Municipal Caravan Park is reliable and good value at $2 and has chalets for $6 a person.

Another value option is **Hitch Haven**, 7 Hillside Road, Hillside, tel: 019-46274, e-mail: hitchhaven_2000@-yahoo.com. Camping is $2, dorms $4, rooms $10 a person. Although **Burke's Paradise**, 11 Inverleith Drive, Burn-side, tel: 019-46481 does not offer camping, it's a popular backpackers with dorms for $4 and rooms for $8 a person. Another option is the beauti-fully situated chalets and camp site in the **Matobo National Park**. After pay-ing the once-only entrance fee of $10, camping is $3 a person and chalets $7 double. The park is also well worth a visit for the fabulous views, granite hills, balancing rocks, rock art and grave of **Cecil John Rhodes**.

The road remains good and reaches the turnoff to the **Hwange National Park** at 280 kilometres. Hwange is Zim's largest and most popular game park and has excellent viewing of the Big Five. The main camp is about 30 kilometres off the A8 and offers inex-pensive accommodation in chalets ($7 double), cottages ($11 double) and camping ($4 a person).

The town of **Victoria Falls** (at 440 kilometres) has been crossed off the itineraries of many travellers, as the Zimbabwean government becomes more and more unpopular. This has benefited **Livingstone** (see page 96) on the Zambian side of the Falls. It's probably worth spending time on both sides as there is so much to see and do here.

The old established **Council Rest Camp** (tel: 0113-4210) is well situated in the centre of town and good value at camping $2, rooms $5 a person. There is much other accommodation, from backpacker's lodges to five-star resorts in and around the town, but if you like to get away from the hustle and bustle, head upstream past the golf course and swanky Elephant Hills Hotel to the **Zambezi Caravan Park**. Camping costs $5 a person and includes spotting the game that passes through to drink at the river.

For Harare take the A4

The **A4 north of Beit Bridge** is a fine road with regular laybyes – keep an eye out for a huge walk-in baobab tree at one. Also watch out for livestock on the roads. At 75 kilometres you will reach the legendary **Lion and Elephant Motel** on the banks of the Bubi River. Halfway between Johannesburg and Harare, this beautiful spot boasts clean, comfortable accommodation in family rooms at a very reasonable $4/$6 single/double plus $1 an extra bed, and camping for $1 a person. There's a great bar – the Bubi Trap with darts and a fireplace – a restaurant (where breakfast costs $1), small game park and swimming pool. If it's snacks you're looking for, try their famous biltong and pies.

Dropping into places like the Lion and Elephant is one of the things that makes travelling through Africa such a pleasure – you'll probably even manage to change money safely and at a good rate with one of the locals in the bar.

Dragging yourself away from the pleasures of the Lion and Elephant, it is 215 kilometres to the town of

---

ZIMBABWE

Capital: Harare

Official languages: English, Shona and Sindebele

Area: 390 500 square kilometres

Population: 11,5 million

Visa requirements: Not required for most holiday visiters

Time: UT +2

International dialling code: +263

Currency and rate: Zimbabwe dollar Z$900=$1

Highlights: Victoria Falls, Great Zimbabwe Ruins, gameviewing in national parks and Kariba Dam

Climate: Pleasant, temperate climate with summer rainstorms

Driving: On the left. A good system of tarred roads

Accommodation: Good selection of camping, hotels and lodges to suit all budgets

Food, shops and fuel: Good restaurants and supermarkets, but experiencing severe shortages of fuel and some foodstuffs in 2003

Tourism info: Zimbabwe Tourism, tel/fax: 014-70-5085, website: www.tourismzimbabwe.co.zw, or the South African office on tel: 011-616-8532, as it has the best information

Masvingo, where most services can be found. If you intend visiting the fascinating Great Zimbabwe Ruins, look for the turnoff 23 kilometres south of Masvingo (S20°06.725 E30°49.330) The stone ruins, lying less than 30 kilometres away, are well worth a visit for their mysterious magnificence. Entrance costs $5; there is camping at $2 and rooms for $9.

Masvingo has a Toyota dealership, truckstop, supermarkets, bank, fast food and a variety of accommodation. The Masvingo Caravan Park is on the Mutare road in an attractive setting and charges $1 a person, while non-campers can head for the Backpackers Rest, Dauth Building, corner Robertson and Josiah Tongogara avenues (tel: 0139-65503) where dorms cost $1 a person, double rooms $2 with secure parking.

The road continues for 293 kilometres through good ranching country punctuated by granite kopjes until the capital city of Harare is reached. No matter what problems beset Zimbabwe, Harare seems to be impervious. The nation can be starving, petrol might be unobtainable and the government falling, but this beautiful tree-lined city and its people happily get on with business.

Most amenities are available and while there might be shortages, or certain imports unobtainable, Zimbabweans have always "made a plan" and are good at fixing things that other countries would simply throw away and replace.

Where to stay in Harare

Harare does not have must-see sights, but with its central situation in Zim, it is the hub of the country with lots of

USEFUL CONTACTS IN HARARE

Landrover Sales and Repairs, 32 Telford Road, Harare, tel: 014-75-2342, e-mail: irman@mail.co.zw

Toyota Zimbabwe, 153 Robert Mugabe Road, Harare, tel: 014-73-8503

Puzey and Payne (for Mitsubishi, Peugeot, VW and Mazda), Second Avenue, Harare, tel: 014-70-4441, e-mail: puzeys@puzeys.co.zw

Haddon Motors (for Nissan and Isuzu), tel: 014-74-6656, 3 Samora Machel Avenue East, Harare, e-mail: haddons@samara.co.zw

Bike-a-rama, Corner Lytton and Canberra roads, Workington, Harare, tel: 014-66-8017

Motor Cycle City, 3 Lisburn Road, Workington, Harare, tel: 014-75-5629

Tyre Treads, Seke Road, Harare, tel: 014-77-1822

Mr X-haust, Mr Tyre, 26 Nelson Mandela Road, Harare, tel: 014-77-2984

Fasfit (five branches) for silencers, shock absorbers, tel: 04-74-9861

National Tyre Services (various branches), tel: 014-77-1224

Eezee Kamping (for camping supplies), 95 G Silundika Street, tel: 014-62105

BOC Gases (for gas refills), Hull Road, Industrial Sites, tel: 014-75-7171

The Great Zimbabwe Ruins near Masvingo in Zimbabwe will intrigue and impress you.

good accommodation and where you can chill out at restaurants and clubs. Because of Zimbabwe's current unpopularity you won't find the hoards of overland travellers of years gone by and some establishments might even have closed down.

These were still battling on: **The Econet Camp** (ex Coronation Park) is a municipal site with dodgy security, but great value for money (S17°50.139 E31°06.222). A four-bedded chalet costs only $4 and a camp site for two is a ridiculous $0,40! (It's the wacky black-market exchange rate that does it). The nicest backpackers is **It's a**

Small World, 25 Ridge Road, Avondale, tel/fax 014-33-5341, e-mail: mail@backpackerslodge.com, website: www.backpackerslodge.com. In a quiet neighbourhood near to the city, this neat and well-run lodge offers travel info, internet access, laundry facilities and secure parking as well as a pool, bar and restaurant. They charge $6 for a dorm bed, $10/$15 for a single/double and $20 for an en-suite double.

The best city centre lodge is **Palm Rock Villa**, corner Selous Avenue and Fifth Street, tel: 014-70-0691. As their charges are not dollar related, it costs only $2/$3 for single/double and $4 for a large self-contained room. There are two out-of-town camps. The greener and more attractive one is quite far out and difficult to find: **Backpackers and Overlanders Lodge**, tel:014-57-5715, e-mail: conxshon@samara.co.zw is out on the Twentydales Road Extension, opposite the expensive Mbizi Game Park and Lodge. Set in beautiful gardens, they charge $3 for camping, $6 for a dorm bed, $13 for a double room and $16 for a two-bedded cottage. The other camp, **The New Rocks**, is in Caledon Avenue, Hatfield, tel: 014-57-6371, e-mail: jakeharp@samara.co.zw and is a bit cheaper than the above.

Harare to Lusaka

(For route to Malawi, see page 114.)
The 490-kilometre **A1** road from Harare to Lusaka via **Chirundu** passes through **Chinhoyi** at 116 kilometres. The caves of the same name are eight kilometres north of town and hardly worth the rather high national park entrance fee. There is, however, a nice inexpensive camp site there (no need to pay park fees).

At 290 kilometres from Harare, the untidy little town of **Makuti** marks the turnoff to **Kariba**. This 74-kilometre road winds through the hills, offering views of the lake. Kariba's attractions are limited to houseboat stays and cruises and it is also the eastern terminus for the ferry service along the lake to **Mlibizi**. (In South Africa, Frontline handles ferry reservations: tel/fax 021-556-6133, e-mail: rfline@iafrica.com). There's a good selection of lakeside camp sites, but watch out for hippos, crocs and elephants.

Continuing north from **Makuti**, it is about 12 kilometres to the headquarters of the wonderfully wild **Mana Pools National Park**. Although the turnoff to the park is another 12 kilometres north, all administration is handled here. Prior booking is essential (although you might be lucky and get in on a cancellation) and the road into the park is very rough, but what makes it all worthwhile is the wild, unfenced and untamed camp on the banks of the great **Zambezi**. All the big game are found here and most wander through the camp site. With almost unrestricted walking allowed in the park too, Mana Pools is a rare and exciting place.

The border post of **Chirundu** is reached at 40 kilometres past the Mana Pools turnoff and it gets hotter and very humid as the road winds down the escarpment to the **Zambezi**. Chirundu also offers adventurous canoe trips down the river through the national park.

The border crossing should be painless and if you had bought Comesa insurance on entering Zimbabwe, it should still be valid for Zambia. The Zambian government is trying hard to

curb corruption and has a phone number posted up to report such unlawful incidents. It seems to be working, as the days of virtual banditry by the traffic police seems to have thankfully ended.

Discovering Lusaka

The road becomes the **T2** and winds up the escarpment again, where at 80 kilometres it is joined by the **T1 from Livingstone** and continues for another 60 kilometres to Lusaka. You'll have travelled more than 3 000 kilometres and be well on your way to Cairo – at least the end of the beginning.

About 10 kilometres south of Lusaka at S15°30.261 E28°15.583 is the turnoff to one of the nicest places to stay around Lusaka, **Eureka Camping**

Park. Well run on the family farm by Doreen van Blerk, it adjoins a small private game park. Shady sites, comfortable chalets, swimming pool and a bar with pool table, cold beers and hot steaks makes it a must for any overlander. Camping costs $5 a person, basic A-frames $20 double and self-contained chalets $30 double. Tel/fax: 01-27-2351, e-mail: eureka@zamnet.zm.

Driving on into **Lusaka**, you pass the industrial area on your left and then cruise through the city on the aptly named **Cairo Road** (at least you know you're on the right road). If you turn right at the circle at the northern end, you will find the huge new Manda Hill Shopping Centre. Everything is available there, from a large well-stocked supermarket to all types of specialist shops and a smart, efficient fuel station.

Lusaka also has a good backpacker's called **Chachacha**, 161 Mulombwa Close, tel/fax: 01-22-2257, e-mail: cha@-zamtel.zm, website: www.zambiatour-ism.com/chachacha. Between the Great East Road and Church Road, it is quite difficult to find and a bit cramped, but is a good base with phone, internet, communal kitchen and good security. Rates: camping is $3 a person, dorms $6 and rooms $12/$14 single/double. About 50 kilometres north of Lusaka, on the **Great North Road**, is the very pleasant **Fringilla Farm Lodge**, tel: 01-61-1199, fax: 23-3885, e-mail: fringill@zamnet.zm, website: www.fringillalodge.com. Set in fertile farmlands, it is like a village with a butcher, baker and dairy, all selling lovely farm-fresh produce. A bar, restaurant and pleasant gardens make this a great stopover (single cabin $28, flat that sleeps four $40 and camping $5 a person).

ZAMBIA

Capital: Lusaka

Official language: English

Area: 252 600 square kilometres

Population: 9,1 million

Visa requirements: Required by most, but not South Africa and other neighbouring states.

Time: UT +2

International dialling code: +260

Currency and rate: Zambian Kwacha ZK4 500=$1

Climate: Pleasant and warm all year. Hotter and thunderstorms from November to April

Highlights: Victoria Falls, gameviewing in Kafue and South Luangwa parks

Driving: on the left. Road network good, but poorly maintained.

Accommodation: Backpackers and campers well catered for, luxury lodges in game parks.

Food, shops and fuel: Not many restaurants, supermarkets in main towns, fuel widely available

Tourism info: The best Zambia National Tourist Board office is in South Africa, tel: 012-326-1847, fax: 012-326-2140, e-mail: zahpta@-mweb.co.za, website: www.africa-in-sights.com/zambia

Cape Town to Lusaka

via Namibia and the Caprivi 3 750 km

Heading north through Namibia, this route is a gentle introduction into African travel. Good roads and infra-structure and comfortable camp sites encourage you to explore the Namib Desert and the well-stocked game reserves of the north. Once through Caprivi, you have the option of taking the direct road to Lusaka via Livingstone and the Victoria Falls, or the more adventurous western route through Barotseland.

From Cape Point (see page 59), head to the centre of Cape Town and the N1, which starts at the Waterfront.

Left: Bushmen still follow their old traditions in isolated parts of Namibia. Right: Skeletons of old trees dot the landscape at Dead Vlei near Sesriem.

At about 12 kilometres from the city centre, just past the large Canal Walk shopping mall, turn left (north) onto the N7. Very soon you'll be in the rolling wheatlands of the Swartland, bypassing farming towns such as Malmesbury and Piketberg. This fine tarred road passes over the Piekenierskloof (160 kilometres), a good spot to pull over and enjoy the view and a snack while checking your vehicle.

The irrigation farms along the Olifants River produce wonderful citrus and plenty of wine, so stock up for the long road ahead. A few days hiking through the magnificent wilderness area of the nearby **Cedarberg** would be great, but with a long way to go, we head for **Vanrhynsdorp** at 300 kilometres. With two large petrol stations and fast food outlets just off the road, it makes the ideal pitstop. Heading north once again, the surrounding countryside becomes drier as we are now in **Namaqualand**. The spring flowers that carpet the hills and plains in September and October are world famous, but even out of season the large variety of succulents is worth looking out for.

Little towns and villages flash by. At 560 kilometres you reach **Springbok** – a convenient place to pull into, with supermarkets, garages and good affordable accommodation. The **Namaqua Tourist Information Office** is next to the post office and can be contacted at tel: 027-718-2985, fax: 027-712-1421, e-mail: tourismbk@namakwa-dm.co.za, website: www.namakwa-dm.co.za. Approaching from the south, you'd have noticed the **Kokerboom Motel and Caravan Park** (tel: 027-712-2685, fax: 027-712-2017). They offer motel-type accommodation for $18/$30/$45 single/double/triple and camping for two for $6. There is another camp site, the **Springbok Caravan Park**, two kilometres out on the road to the nature reserve which has overnight rooms for $12 double and **Cat Nap** (027-718-1905), back in town, charges $7 a person for backpackers' accommodation. The **Springbok Lodge and Restaurant** (tel: 027-712-1321, fax: 027-712-2718, e-mail: sblodge@intekom.co.za), centrally situated in Voortrekker Street, is something of an institution in the town as they offer a variety of tourist services and accommodation at $12 a person sharing.

If you overnighted in Springbok, you'll cover the 125 kilometres of good tarred road to the border at **Vioolsdrif** by midmorning. The wide **Orange**

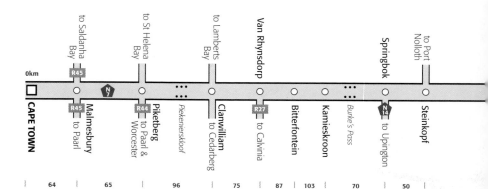

River beckons for a quick swim in the heat, but the painless and swift border formalities must be dealt with. You will be required to pay $7,50 for a Cross Border Charge Permit which must be kept and handed in at a border post when exiting Namibia again.

Entering Namibia

As the fuel in Namibia is slightly cheaper than in South Africa it's become traditional to stop at the motel at **Noordoewer** to refuel and down your first celebratory Namibian beer. The road north (B1) is hot, barren and straight, but uncrowded and in excellent condition. **Grünau**, 140 kilometres from Noordoewer, has fuel and basic accommodation at the **Grünau Motor Chalets and Caravan Park**, tel: 026-2026, fax: 026-2017. But, if you can make it, rather continue for another 160 kilometres to **Keetmanshoop**, where the pleasant Wendy Biwa dispenses tourist information from her office in the town's old restored post office, tel: 063-22-1266, e-mail: cwb@webmail.co.za.

The shops in Keetmanshoop are well stocked (especially with biltong), the garages can handle any breakdowns and accommodation is varied and plentiful. The **municipal camp** site costs $3 a person plus $2 a car; the **Central Lodge**, Fifth Avenue, tel: 063-22-5850 and Bird Mansions, Sixth Avenue, tel: 063-22-1711 both charge $20/$35 single/double, and the **Canyon Hotel**, Fifth Avenue, tel: 063-22-3316 is $30 a person. There is also a camp site and bungalows at the BP garage just south of town, which means you don't have to turn into Keetmanshoop.

The direct route to Windhoek

The road north is simple and straightforward, but can get very hot, so carry spare water. Many Namibians drive with their lights on during the day, a safe habit that more drivers in Africa should copy, especially on dirt roads. At 225 kilometres from Keetmanshoop, you will reach **Mariental** – a good pitstop, with all the usual amenities of a small town including the **Mariental Hotel**, tel: 063-24-2466, fax: 063-24-2493, e-mail: mrlhotel@-iafrica.com.na. Accommodation ranges between $15 and $45 a person. The nearby **Hardap Dam** is popular with travellers and offers camping at $10 a site and double chalets at $15. Booking is through Namibia Wildlife Resorts in Windhoek (see page 82).

The remaining 260 kilometres to Namibia's capital city, **Windhoek**, is

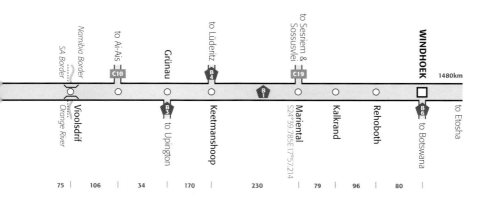

75 | 106 | 34 | 170 | 230 | 79 | 96 | 80 |

broken only by the town of **Rehoboth**, so it is important to plan your refueling stops. The roads around Windhoek are all new and well signposted and the city is compact and laid back. But, before you explore this pleasant spot and down too many draft beers, let's consider a more adventurous, interesting and scenic drive up from the south.

The scenic road to Windhoek

A word of warning before we leave the smooth, tarred surface of the B1 highway. Some of the C and D roads have been re-prioritised – a euphemism for "they've changed the numbers". Old maps will show incorrect numbers and, to make matters worse, some roads are still signposted with old numbers, so use a good up-to-date map (Namibia Map 2002, published by Projects and Promotions, Windhoek, tel: 061-25-3981, e-mail: proprom@iafrica.com.na is good).

The scenic route through Namibia starts 142 kilometres north of **Noordoewer** where you turn left (west) off the **B1** and head towards **Ai-Ais** on the **C10**. A well-graded gravel road (all gravel roads in Namibia are regularly maintained and graded) of 73 kilometres brings you to the hot springs of Ai-Ais. Set in the magnificent **Fish River Canyon**, the resort offers a large

warm-water swimming pool, private indoor baths, shop, restaurant and comfortable accommodation in four-bedded flats for $26, four-bedded huts for $18 and camping at $10 a site.

Many visitors come for the spectacular four- or five-day hike through the canyon. Suitable only for the very fit and well equipped, this 90-kilometre hike starts from **Hiker's Point**, ends at Ai-Ais and needs meticulous preparation. There is no accommodation, day and night temperatures are extreme and once you're in, there's no way to bail out of the hike – it's not for the faint-hearted. Information and bookings through **Namibian Wildlife Resorts** in Windhoek (see page 82).

The road north takes the **C37** past the spectacular canyon view point and on via the **C12** to the junction with the **B4**. Turn left (west) here and you'll be on your way through the harsh, dry **Namib Desert** and down to **Lüderitz**. Along the way, turn right (north) off the road about 20 kilometres west of the little town of **Aus** to try and spot the elusive desert horses. Thought to have descended from the animals abandoned by the German Schutztruppe at the start of the First World War, these feral hoses are thriving under very difficult circumstances.

Little visited, but interesting for its

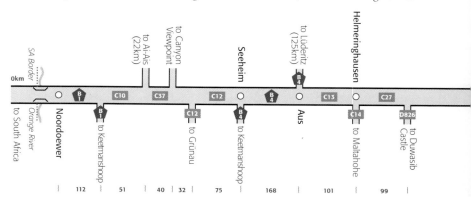

old German colonial architecture, Lüderitz is a good place to chill out in. There's lots of accommodation: **Zum Sperrgebied Hotel**, Bismarck Street, tel: 063-20-2856, fax: 063-20-2976 costs $28/$35 single/double, including breakfast and has a lively bar with colourful locals and a pool table; **The Backpackers' Lodge**, 7 Schinz Street, tel/fax 063-20-2000 charges $4 in a dorm and $5 a person sharing a twin room and is a typical friendly, helpful backpackers' haven; camping is available at **Shark Island Camp Site**, tel: 063-20-2752, fax: 063-20-3213. In an attractive location, but sometimes very windy, the sites cost $10, bungalows $20 and even the lighthouse is to rent at $50 a night!

On the way into Lüderitz, you will have passed the old ghost town of **Kolmanskop**. Abandoned 50 years ago after the area's great diamond boom, the desert is slowly encroaching and burying the fascinating old buildings there. Permits must be bought at the **Kolmanskop Tour Co** in Lüderitz for the twice-daily tours and cost $1,50, or pay $2,50 for an all day pass which is great if you want to take photographs at sunrise or sunset.

Head east back to Aus, and then north on the C13 towards **Helmering-hausen**. After 100 kilometres and just four kilometres before Helmering-hausen, turn left onto the **C27** and drive for 100 kilometres. Here the **D826** turns off to the right and after about 25 kilometres you will be greeted with the unusual sight of the old sandstone fortress, **Duwisib Castle**. History tells of a captain in the Schutz-truppe who married an American heiress, built the castle on a huge 50 000 hectare farm and was then killed in the Battle of the Somme during the First World War. Duwisib lives up to its evocative past with opulently furnished rooms and a sparkling fountain in the courtyard. Camping is $8 a site, bungalows are for hire on the neighbouring farm for $10.

Head back to the C27 and swing north for 150 kilometres to **Sesriem** (S24°29.208 E15°47.934). Namibia Wildlife resorts has an office and camp ($13 a site) here as well as selling fuel, cold drinks and basic foodstuffs. If you have not been able to book ahead in the main camp site, which is comfortable and attractive under great thorn trees, then you will be banished to the noisy and smelly emergency camp. Buy your permits for **Sesriem Canyon** and **Sossusvlei** from the office and turn left first to explore the canyon. Park your vehicle and clamber down into the narrow little gully – the stagnant pool

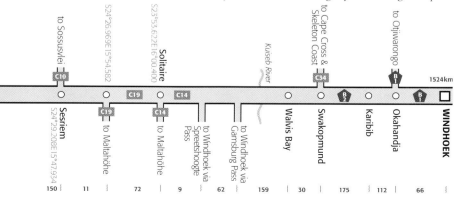

at the end of the canyon is used by the birds, which nest in the walls, and small game which visit at night.

The road down to the vlei is 60 kilometres of new tar and follows the course of the **Tsauchab River**. It's open from just before dawn to just after sunset, so avoid the inevitable heat of midday and visit at the more photogenic early or late times of the day. Assuming you have a 4x4, continue through the 2x4 parking area (S24°43.786 E15°19.313) onto the very-churned-up sandy track which takes you another five kilometres right to Sossusvlei and **Dead Vlei**.

Dead Vlei is to the left and requires a hike over the dunes, but it is worth the effort to see the starkly beautiful landscape of the skeletons of trees left to die when the vlei dried up some 500 years ago.

Sossusvlei is larger and sometimes visited by lonely gemsbok. Like all the other dry pans, it is a dry bed of fine powdery mud, unless of course you are lucky enough to coincide your visit with the once-in-a-decade phenomenon of torrential rain and a water-filled vlei. Water birds fly in and the area comes alive with animals of all varieties. Quite a unique sight.

Continue north on the C27 for 11 kilometres to a junction (S24°26.969

E15°54.582), turn left and take the **C19** for 72 kilometres to the crossroads settlement of **Solitaire** (S23°53.622 E16°00.400). Everyone stops at Solitaire – for fuel, emergency repairs, accommodation and, best of all, to browse and eat at the small trading store. Meet **Moose**, the colourful character who bakes **world-famous apple crumble** and organises water to be dropped off for thirsty round-the-world cyclists, travelling through the desert. It costs $17 a person B&B at the lodge, $6 a person in a bungalow and $3,50 to camp. Breakfast costs $3; other meals are $5. There is a cool inviting reservoir to swim in when the heat becomes unbearable – a veritable paradise in this hot, dry part of the world (tel: 061-24-0375, fax: 061-25-6598, e-mail: afrideca@mweb.com.na, website: www.namibialodges.com).

Leaving Solitaire, turn left into the **C14** which takes you all the way to **Walvis Bay** and then **Swakopmund** via the **Kuiseb Canyon** in the **Namib-Naukluft Park**. Alternatively, nine kilometres out of Solitare, you can cut straight up to Windhoek via the spectacular **Spreetshoogte Pass** on the **D1275** or the almost-as-impressive **Remhoogte Pass** on the **C24**.

Swakopmund is Namibia's playground – beaches, trendy restaurants

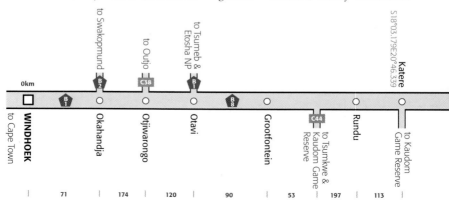

and lots of accommodation in this resort town of lovingly restored old German colonial buildings. Brave the icy **Atlantic** waters for a swim or relax in the heated olympic-size pool just up from the beach. Visit the **Hansa Brewery** for a guided tour and then stroll the streets to absorb the atmosphere and architecture of this old colonial town. Enjoy delicious German confectionery, breads, cured meats and sausages as well as good seafood at any one of the town's many restaurants.

Camping is not really an option here as the few sites where it is permitted are out of town, along the exposed coast. The best place for affordable, self-catering accommodation is the **Swakopmund Municipal Restcamp** on the Walvis Bay side of town (tel: 064-410-4333, fax: 064-410-4212, e-mail: swkmun@swk.namib.com, website: www.swakopmund-restcamp.com). Rates are: $16 for two in a basic fisherman's hut, $30 for four in a holiday flat, $44 for six in a spacious A-frame and $50 for six in a luxurious rest house. **Karin's Attic** at 37 Post Street offers backpackers' accommodation at $5 for a dorm bed and $10 for a single room (tel: 064-40-2707, fax: 064-40-3057, e-mail: kattic@iafrica.com.na).

To get to Windhoek from Swakopmund, you have the choice of the grav-el surface of the C28 through the mountains of the **Khomas Hochland** (320 kilometres), or the slightly longer tarred B2 to **Okahandja** and then on to Windhoek (350 kilometres).

If you've opted to skip Windhoek and head directly north, drive out of Swakop on the C34 along the coast to **Henties Bay**, or even further north to **Torra Bay** before heading inland. Southern **Kaokoveld** and **Damaraland** have some exciting trails and camping possibilities, but are unfortunately beyond the scope of this book – we might never get to Cairo if we get lured into the wonderful wild northwest of Namibia. Make your way to **Outjo** on the **C38** and then head north to **Okaukuejo Camp** in **Etosha National Park**.

Exploring Windhoek

The Namibian capital is a clean, safe and well organised city with plentiful accommodation to match, from the relatively expensive ($73/$86 single/double) **Windhoek Country Club**, to the numerous B&Bs, guesthouses and backpackers' lodges.

Coming in on the B1 from the south, **Arebusch Travel Lodge** is safe, clean and spacious, and situated on the left about 10 kilometres short of Windhoek, tel: 061-25-2255, fax: 061-25-

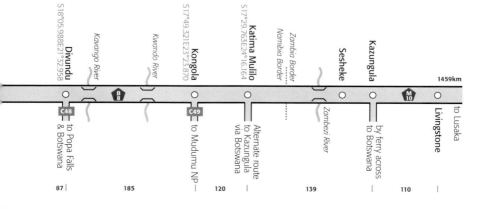

1670. A well-equipped chalet with kitchen, television and air-con costs $30 for two, a double room (sharing facilities) is $20 and camping $4 a person. A very popular backpackers' lodge is the **Cardboard Box**, corner of Johann Albrecht and John Meinert streets, tel: 061-22-8994. fax: 061-24-5587, e-mail: cardboardbox@bigfoot.com, website: www.ahj.addr.com. Camping costs $3, a dorm $5 and a double room $20. A swimming pool, pool table, lively bar and restaurant and good internet connection make this a great place to rest and recharge. The in-house **Crazy Kudu Safaris** can organise anything for you, tel: 061-25-6580, fax: 061-25-6581, e-mail: namib.safari@crazykudu.com, website: www.crazykudu.com. **Rivendell Guest House** at 40 Beethoven Street (tel: 061-25-0006, fax: 061-25-0010, e-mail: rivendell@toothfairy.com, website: www.rivendell-namibia.com) is more upmarket but still very affordable at $16 double or $22 if self-contained.

About 20 kilometres west of the city along the **C28** is the small **Daan Viljoen Game Park**. With no dangerous game, you can walk or cycle around and accommodation is available in the form of self-contained bungalows with kitchens for $25 double and camping at $9 a site. Book through

Namibia Wildlife Resorts. All resorts and camp sites in Namibia's national parks and other protected areas are now owned and run by **Namibia Wildlife Resorts Ltd**, a company fully owned by the government. They handle all bookings for accommodation and are situated at the corner of John Meinert and Moltke streets, tel: 061-23-6975, fax: 061-22-4900, e-mail: reservations@mweb.com.na, website: www.namibiawildliferesorts.com.

A helpful and central private tourist information centre is the **Tourist Junction** at 40 Peter Muller Street, tel: 061-23-1246, fax: 061-23-1703, e-mail: marketing@touristjunction.com, website: www.touristjunction.com. They offer information and bookings for all accommodation and transport, as well as public phones and internet.

You should visit the **Alte Feste Museum**, on a rise overlooking the city on Robert Mugabe Drive (open every day, but closed for lunch on Saturdays and Sundays, admission is free). There are two well-stocked supermarkets in the city; Pick'n Pay in the **Wernhil Park Shopping Centre** in Mandume Ndemufayo Avenue and Shoprite on Stubel Street, but other specialist shops also offer an amazing selection of international delicacies and imports.

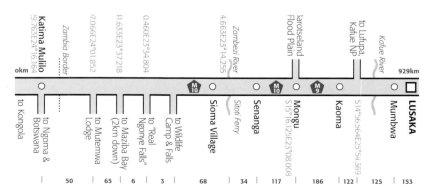

NAMIBIA

Capital: Windhoek

Official languages:
English and Afrikaans

Area: 824 300 square kilometres

Population: 2 million

Visa requirements: Not required
for most holiday visitors

Time: UT +2

International dialling code: +264

Currency and rate:
Namibian dollar N$8,50=$1

Climate: Hot and dry with summer
rainfall, mostly in the north

Highlights: Fish River Canyon,
Sossusvlei and Etosha National Park

Driving: On the left. Good system of
tarred and well-maintained gravel roads

Accommodation: A wide variety of
B&Bs, backpackers, hotels and lodges

Food, shops and fuel:
German influence in restaurants and
delis, supermarkets are well stocked
and fuel is always available, but long
distances between stops

Tourism info: Namibian Tourist Office,
tel: 061-290-6000, fax: 061-25-4848,
e-mail: info@namibiatourism.com
website: www.namibiatourism.com

The best place for motor spares and accessories, as well as all outdoor equipment (including fishing and hunting gear and a good selection of maps and local guide books) is **Cymot/Greensport**, 60 Mandume Ndemufayo Avenue, tel: 061-23-4131, fax: 061-22-1011, website: www.greensport.com.na, e-mail: greensport@cymot.com.na.

Trappers Trading in Wernhil Park, tel: 061-22-3136 stocks a good selection of practical outdoor clothing. For changing money, use **American Express** at **Woker Travel Services**, 6 Peter Muller Street, tel: 061-23-7946, fax: 061-22-5932, or **Thomas Cook**, corner Independence Aveue and Post Street.

From Windhoek to Etosha

The **B1** continues north out of Windhoek – and don't worry if you didn't refuel before leaving, as you reach the junction town of **Okahandja** after only 70 kilometres. A big curio village, sell-ing mostly wood carvings, is situated at the southern entrance to the town, opposite a Shell petrol station.

The wide, tarred **B2** turns off to Swakopmund here, but stay on the equally good B1 for 130 kilometres to **Otjiwarongo**. You can't miss the **Otjiwarongo Backpackers** behind their brightly painted wall. The quickest way north is to stay on the B1 to **Otavi**, but you'd miss one of the best game parks in the world, **Etosha National Park**.

Take the tarred **C38** out of **Otjiwarongo** for 180 kilometres, straight into **Okaukuejo Camp** via **Outjo**. Booking for any accommodation other than camping is essential for Etosha (contact Namibia Wildlife Resorts in Windhoek). Accommodation in the three camps varies from rooms to luxury bungalows and will cost between $35 and $45 double, camping throughout costs $13 a site for up to eight people and two vehicles. You will sometimes be told that the camp site is full, but be patient and persistent, there's usually room for one more camper. No-one checks the camp sites, as long as you have paid for each night that you have stayed in the park, you will have no problems when leaving.

The best part about Etosha is its waterholes on the edge of each camp. Floodlit at night, they offer fantastic game viewing 24 hours a day. There's nothing better than sitting comfortably, sundowner in hand, watching the parade of game come down to drink in the last rays of the setting sun. The camps are clean; shady and well run, and each has a swimming pool, restaurant, petrol station and a shop selling almost everything (they obviously have their priorities right as ice cold beer is always plentiful, but they sometimes run out of fresh fruit and vegetables).

Drive the 70 kilometres east to the next camp, **Halali**. The roads in the park are well-maintained gravel, but can be quite dusty. Stick to the speed limit of 60 kilometres an hour. and enjoy the park – sit with binoculars at waterholes, watch birds, wait for the animals to come to you. Halali is also smart and neat with a waterhole in a lovely position below a hill which forms a natural grandstand. With all the amenities and comforts, this smart camp, like the others in Etosha, is ideal for an overnight stay or a relaxing longer stay.

The most easterly camp, 75 kilometres from Halali, is also the most picturesque. **Namutoni Camp** started life as a German colonial outpost and still boasts the original fort – a really impressive Beau-Geste-type structure, complete with look-out tower and waving palm trees. The most comfortable accommodation is in the luxury

4X4 HIRE IN NAMIBIA

Into Namibia, 76 Sam Nujoma Drive, Windhoek, tel: 061-25-3591, fax: 061-25-3593, e-mail: admin@intonam.com.na, website: www.intonam.com.na

Mpengu Car Hire, 9 Tunschel Street, Pionierspark, Windhoek, tel: 061-25-6946, fax: 061-25-6945 e-mail: mpengu@iafrica.com.na

Avis, Eros Airport, Windhoek, tel: 061-23-3166, fax: 061-22-3072, e-mail: avis@mweb.com.na, Website: www.avissainbound.co.za

Sani, Eros Airport, Windhoek, tel: 086-100-2111, e-mail: mail@sanirentals.co.za, Website www.sanirentals.co.za

Triple Three Rentals (vehicle hire in Swakopmund and Walvis Bay), tel: 064-20-0333, fax: 064-40-3191, e-mail: 333rentals@namibnet.com, website: www.333.com.na

bungalows overlooking the waterhole, but the historic rooms in the old fort are my favourite.

North of Etosha, into Caprivi

Drag yourself away from the wonders of Etosha and head, via the 'bottomless' **Lake Otjikoto**, to **Tsumeb** and on to **Grootfontein** (stay at **Die Kraal**, just out of town on the road to Rundu). Refuel and restock at this regional centre before tackling the long (250 kilometres) **B8** to **Rundu**.

The road is tarred all the way and the turnoff into town is at a big Shell garage (S17°55.950 E19°46.270). This town has a frontier feel to it as it lies on the banks of the **Kavango River** which forms the boundary with Angola. It has well-stocked supermarkets, shops and garages to supply the Caprivi and a large part of southern Angola.

Head for the **Sarasunga River Lodge** which is beautifully situated under trees on the banks of the river (S17°53.458 E19°46.922). This quiet and peaceful spot has a bar, restaurant and swimming pool.

For one of the roughest and wildest game-viewing opportunities in Africa, look for the signposted turn off (S18°03.179 E20°46.339) to **Kaudom Game Park** 115 kilometres east of Rundu. This isolated reserve in the sandy wastes of northeastern Namibia requires you to be totally self-sufficient with fuel, water and food for the entire duration of your stay. The very sandy and rough track requires a 4x4, good driving skills and deflated tyres to reach the Kaudom boundary (S18°23.366 E20°42.965) at 55 kilometres. Another 13 kays along the eastern side of the fence will bring you to the dry river bed of the **Cwiba** (S18°26.424 E20°44.018).

Only 12 kilometres more brings you into **Kaudom Camp**. Fees are payable at the office (S18°30.322 E20°45.216), which is protected from marauding elephants by a deep moat. (Fees: $2,50 a vehicle entrance, $2,50 a person a day, $10 a camp site or $12,50 for a bungalow that sleeps four). The camp is very basic with no electricity and questionable water. The area teems so with elephants, that the staff (and campers) spend sleepless nights chasing them away from the camp site. A few roads follow the dry riverbeds in the vicinity of the camp where most game can be seen congregating around waterholes.

It is also possible to drive for approximately 77 kilometres right through the park to **Sikereti Camp** in the south and then another 63 kays to **Tsumkwe**. From there it is 205 kilometres of reasonable gravel back to the tarred road to **Grootfontein**. Quite an adventure and best done in the company of at least one other well equipped vehicle. The best map and guide book to this area is produced by Jan Joubert and available at Cymot/Greensport in Windhoek.

Back on the B8, continue for 94 kilometres along the wide tarred surface to the petrol station at **Divundu** (S18°05.988 E 21°32.958), which has a bakery, supermarket, motor scrapyard and mechanic. This is also the turnoff south to **Popa Falls**, **Mahango Game Park** and on into **Botswana**. Popa Falls is more of a cascade than a waterfall, but still a pretty sight on this the **Kavango River**, which feeds the immense swamps of Botswana. The government rest camp at the falls was being renovated late in 2002 but for $1,50, you could still catch a leaking dugout across to the view site. Beautiful, green, grassy camp sites are available just a bit further on at **Ngepi Camp** for $1 a person.

A big, strong bridge carries you across the **Kavango River**, and after 185 kilometres along the **B8** you will be stopped at a roadblock as you cross the **Mashi River** at **Kongola**. To visit the **Mudumu** and **Mamili** national parks, turn south here onto the **C49**, a good gravel road that loops around and eventually ends up at **Katimo Mulilo**.

Twenty kilometres down this road, I suggest you turn off (S17°49.321 E23°23.870) to the luxurious **Namushasha Lodge**. Situated on the high banks of the Kwando River, it overlooks a floodplain with good game viewing and fantastic birdlife. You can take a boat to a colony of carmine bee-eaters – I counted about 500 nests in the river bank – and see kingfishers, wattled cranes and fish eagles along the way. It will cost you $50/$60 single/double for bed and breakfast per day in the very comfortable chalets and $5,50 a person to camp.

Katimo Mulilo is the capital of eastern **Caprivi** and has all you need. Around the main square you will find the supermarket, bank, bakery and Katima Toyota next to the Caltex garage (fill up for your excursion into western Zambia). For accommodation, try the **Hippo Lodge** (tel: 067-35-2685), on the eastern outskirts of town. Solid self-contained rooms, set in lush gardens cost $15/$20 single/double and camping at $2,50 a person.

This area forms quite a crossroads. You can head south to **Ngoma Bridge** and into **Botswana**. Continue south and you will reach **Maun** and the **Okavango Swamps**. Drive east to **Kasane** and you have the choice of heading south on a fine tarred road to **Francistown**, east across the border to **Victoria Falls** in Zimbabwe or north across the **Kazungula Ferry** ($12 a vehicle) to **Livingstone** in Zambia. It's no wonder that smugglers and bandits loved this little corner of Africa – they could always jump across any convenient border and stay one step ahead of the law.

Across the border into Zambia

Aiming ever northwards, turn left at S17°29.763 E 24°16.164, just out of Katima Mulilo, for Zambia's **Wanela** border post. This is a quiet, laid-back,

easy border crossing. Namibia will ask for the Cross Border Charge Permit you bought on entering the country and the Zambian side are impressed with a carnet, but need $12 insurance for a month (if you don't already have Comesa).

To get to **Livingstone** and on to **Lusaka**, take the ferry across the **Zambezi** at **Sesheke**, just across the border (a new bridge is under construction).

For a more interesting and rugged route, head for 60 kilometres up the western bank of the Zambezi to the comfortable **Mutemwa Lodge** (turn off at S17°07.066 E24°01.852). This road, and all the way north to **Senanga** is sandy and rough and suitable only for 4x4s. The lodge is run by Gavin Johnson and situated on the banks of the mighty Zambezi with a beautiful view of the river and plains beyond. There are six luxury double en-suite tents, bar/restaurant and wooden deck over the river. They are justifiably expensive at $220 a person, but that does include all meals and activities (there is a cheaper rate for South Africans). Camping is $5 a person at their shady riverside site. Contact 2mutemwa@bushmail.net or check out their website at www.mutemwa.com.

Seventy kilometres past Mutemwa at S16°41.633 E23°37.218 is a burnt-out sign to the burnt-out resort of **Maziba Bay**. Drive two kilometres down to the river to a large sandy beach which invites fishing (a 3,5 kilogram tigerfish was pulled out when I was there) and swimming (don't, there are crocodiles). Pitch your tent or free-camp in the abandoned bungalows overlooking the mighty Zambezi. Filiciano is the watchman – tip him if you're feeling generous.

At S16°40.460 E23°34.804, 5,5 kilometres past the Maziba turnoff, is a sign to 'The Real Ngonye Falls'. Two kilometres down the turnoff, you will come to a parking area where local boys will look after your car ($2) and escort you down to a dugout canoe on the river. Negotiate a fee for the boatman ($2 return) and guide ($2) and you will be paddled across and head off on a 45-minute hike to the main cataract of the Ngonye Falls. The falls are hugely impressive as the thunderous, green mass of Zambezi water turns white and foams and tumbles over the rocks to regain its green hue in the maelstrom below. If Victoria Falls had not existed, the world would be beating a path to Ngonye.

The remaining 55 kilometres of rough 4x4 track to the ferry across the Zambezi at Sitoti (S16°14.663 E23°14.255) takes about two hours. (The turnoff to the Angolan border at Shangombo is near here.) On a wide, still bend in the river, the ferry takes you across ($10 a vehicle, passengers free) to the eastern bank, where it is another rough 20 kilometres to Sinanga.

A tarred, but potholed, road leads to Mongu, 105 kilometres away. Mongu is a regional centre and has all services, fuel (the first since Katima Mulilo) and a big Shoprite supermarket. A great place to buy local leather and basket crafts is the Women's Co-operative next to the petrol station on the right as you leave town. Mongu is not the sort of place you will want to stay in, but if you have to, try the Ngulu (tel: 07-22-1028) Lyambayi (tel: 07-22-1271) or Sir Mwanawima Hotels (tel: 07-22-1485).

The wonderful, tarred M9 highway leads east out of Mongu, through some of the most abused forests in Africa, and

Two recommended books on the region: The Africa House by Christina Lamb, a fascinating biography of Stewart Gore-Brown who build himself a feudal paradise in Northern Rhodesia. The No 1 Ladies Detective Agency by Alexander McCall Smith, a quaint sort of Miss Marple in the bush story. Precious Ramotswe's agency in Gaborone finds wayward husbands, exposes conmen and tackles witchcraft.

reaches the turnoff to the Kafue National Park at 308 kilometres (S14°56.564 E25°54.369). The good news is that the game is returning to the Kafue as poaching has been curtailed. It is also uncrowded and costs only $10 a person a day, $5 a vehicle a day and $5 a person a night to camp at Lufupa Camp (S14°37.007 E26°11.486).

There is also a Lufupa Lodge ($80 a person a day, full board, including game drives and boat trips on the river).

Beware of the swarms of tsetse flies on game drives – a necessary evil as they make it impossible for domestic animals to survive here. Also keep an eye out for a magnificent pack of wild dog in the area around Lufupa.

The remaining 280 kilometres of M9 highway steadily deteriorates through Mumbwa (where you can get fuel) until, by the time you're approaching Lusaka, the surface is more potholes than tar. Entering through the industrial area, you will run straight into Cairo Road and the centre of town.

After the rough conditions of western Zambia even Lusaka looks inviting, so head for Eureka Camp (see page 72) and chill.

13

Cape Town to Lusaka

via Botswana taking in the Okavango Swamps, Moremi, Chobe Game Reserves and Livingstone 3 000 km

A fairly direct route which takes you on good roads through the Northern Cape and the unspoilt wilderness of the Kalahari. Botswana offers the chance to detour into two of the great game reserves of Southern Africa, as well as taking a trip into the swamps. With good road connections in all directions, you also have the option of linking up with most other routes through Southern Africa.

Follow the N1 highway out of Cape Town and up through Beaufort West to Three Sisters (see page 64).

Left and right: Nothing could be more relaxing than being poled serenely through the Okavango Swamps. Above: A colourful bee-eater.

Just past the Shell truckstop, S31º53.004 E23º04.964, turn north onto the N12 and after 63 kilometres you will reach the quaint little town of **Victoria West**. At 600 kilometres from Cape Town, you might be looking for a place to stay. The town has many smart B&Bs at around $12 a person sharing, budget accommodation in the main street at $7 a person sharing and a rather forlorn looking public camp site. An annual festival for independent indigenous films is held in the **Apollo Theatre**, the town's restored Art-Deco cinema (e-mail: apollotheatre@intekom.co.za, website: www.apollotheatre.co.za)

The **N12**, quieter than the N1 and in excellent condition, continues for 111 kilometres to **Britstown** which has food, fuel, B&Bs and a municipal camp site. You leave the Karoo behind you as you travel the 132 kilometres to **Hopetown** (keep an eye out for donkey carts on the road).

Hopetown is where the first diamond was discovered in South Africa. Stop in at the **Noordkaap Landboudienste** premises in town and see the window pane that old Rosen, the general dealer, scratched with that very diamond. Comfortable, homely accommodation is available next to the police station at **Die Stalle Guesthouse** (tel/fax: 053-203-0007) at $22 for a self-contained double, including a large breakfast. There is also a municipal camp site nearby.

To see the first old wagon bridge to have been built across the Orange River, cross the new bridge, pass the truckstop (which also has accommodation) and take the first turn left at S29º35.193 E24º07.036. It's a couple of kilometres down this road.

For Anglo Boer War buffs, this is the start of the **Battlefields Route**, and cemeteries, blockhouses and memorials dot the veld on either side of the road all the way to **Kimberley**. For assistance and information on Kimberley and the whole region, visit the new **Visitors Centre** in Bultfontein Road in the city – the N12 takes you right past it (tel: 053-832-7298, fax: 053-832-7211, e-mail: dvcadmin@kimnet.co.za, website: www.kimberley-africa.com).

Don't pass through this historic diamond mining city without at least visiting **The Big Hole** and **Open Mine Museum Village**. This largest excavation in the world is open everyday from 08h00 to 18h00 and costs $2. The fascinating old mining village has been restored and you can even try your luck

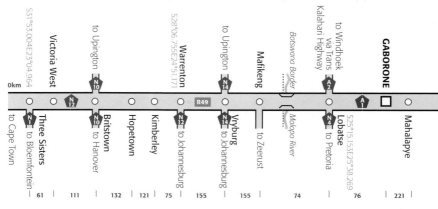

on a diamond dig – \$0,60 a bucket. Other attractions in Kimberley include guided underground mine tours and a **Ghost Trail**.

As to be expected, there is a large selection of accommodation in Kimberley. Camping is centrally available at the **Big Hole Caravan Park** (tel: 053-830-6322) and costs only \$2,50 a site plus \$1,25 a person. Inexpensive rooms are available close to the information centre at **Stay a Day**, 72 Lawson Street, tel: 053-832-7239 for \$10 single. The busy Carrington Road, Belgravia, also not too far from the info centre, is where you'll find the **Carrington B&B** (tel: 053-832-1983), **Carrington House** (tel: 053-831-6191) and **Carrington Lodge** (tel: 053-831-6448) ranging in price from \$20 to \$30 single.

At **Warrenton**, 74 kilometres from Kimberley, turn off left (S28°06.755 E24°51.171). The **R49** crosses the **Vaal River** and runs parallel with the railway line through the fertile **Vaal-Harts Irrigation Scheme** for 155 kilometres to **Vryburg**. There is no fuel on this stretch of road. Although Vryburg has all the amenities of a regional town there is no need to stop for more than fuel and food before continuing for another 156 inhospitable kilometres to **Mafikeng**.

Mafikeng is a bit of a nightmare to navigate through as there are so few road signs and so many crowded taxi ranks and shopping centres.

For accommodation try the **Garden View Guest Lodge**, corner North and Havenga streets, tel: 018-381-3110, or the nearby **Getaway Guest Lodge**, corner Tillard and Baden Powell Streets, tel: 018-381-1150. They are both run by the same group and prices range from \$14/\$21 single/double (sharing facilities) to \$21/\$30 single/double (self-contained).

Look for signs pointing north to **Ramatlabama** (the Botswana border) to get out of Mafikeng.

Into Botswana

It is only 26 kilometres to the border post where the service is quick and courteous, as long as you are not carrying any meat products (banned because of the danger of spreading foot-and-mouth disease). The post is open daily from 06h00 to 20h00 and money can be changed (at a poor rate) for paying the \$2 road tax. The **A1**, a wide, well-maintained tarred road, runs for 49 kilometres to the meat processing town of **Lobatse**. Just before the town, at S25°15.153 E25°38.269, is

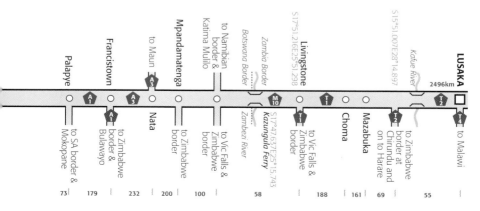

the turnoff left onto the **Trans-Kalahari Highway**, which whisks you quickly over 800 kilometres of good tarred road through the desert to the Namibian border at **Buitepos** and on to Windhoek.

Staying on the A1, it becomes very busy for another 76 kilometres into the capital city of **Gaborone**. Gaborone is a soulless city of fancy new buildings built with the vast income that the government makes from diamonds. It is growing so fast that the roadsign planters can't seem to cope, which makes it a bit difficult to find your way.

There is quite a good museum depicting the ancient history of Botswana and an adjoining art gallery with interesting, metal sculptures in Queens Road, just off The Mall. Although there are many hotels and lodges in and around Gabs, the two that are of particular interest to over-landers are the St Claire Lion Park and Citi Camp.

Driving north from Lobatse, you turn off left to the **Lion Park** (S24°49.326 E25°49.318) about 20 kilometres short of Gabs. The rustic camp site lies three kilometres down a dirt road and costs $2 a person entrance plus $4 a person to camp (tel: 37-2711). The attraction here is being disturbed by the sound of lions roaring at night, and although the place has a bit of a zoo feel to it, you can really get up close to the big cats. The other place, **Citi Camp** (tel: 31-1912, e-mail: citicamp@info.bw), is conveniently situated at the junction of Nelson Mandela and Nyere Drives, close to the city centre (S24°38.323 E25°54.576). With neat and clean ablutions and nice shady sites, it is good value at $6 a person. Bungalows are also available at $20/$30 single/double.

BOTSWANA

Capital: Gaborone

Official languages: English and Setswana

Area: 582 000 square kilometres

Population: 1,5 milliion

Visa requirements: Not required for most holiday visitors

Time: UT +2

International dialling code: +267

Currency and rate: Pula P5,50=$1

Climate: Hot and dry with summer rains

Highlights: Okavango Delta and surrounding game reserves, bushmen paintings in Tsodilo Hills

Driving: On the left. Roads vary from tarred highways to sandy tracks

Accommodation: From basic camping in game reserves to lodges and luxury tented camps

Food, shops and fuel: Restaurants, supermarkets and fuel only available in big towns, keep well stocked if out in the bush

Tourism info: Botswana Tourism, 035-3024, fax: 030-8675, e-mail: botswanatourism@gov.bw, website: www.botswanatourism.org

The **Department of Wildlife and National Parks** is situated in the government enclave off Khama Crescent opposite the end of Queens Road, tel: 58-0774, fax: 58-0775, e-mail: dwnp@-gov.bw. And if you need transport, cars and 4x4s can be hired from **Avis**, Sir Seretse Khama Airport, tel: 31-3093, fax: 31-2205, e-mail: avisbots@botsnet.bw.

Heading north on the wide, tarred A1 you will pass through small towns where the speed limit must be adhered to. Thorn trees and mopani dot the red sands of the Kalahari as the **Tropic of Capricorn** is crossed – watch out for the jagged tar edges along this stretch of road.

At 221 kilometres past Gabs, the town of **Mahalapye** is reached and you have the chance to refuel and restock with food. There are also banks and accommodation. There is road construction ahead and at 10 kilometres short of **Palapye** you will find the turnoff to northern South Africa, which links up with the **N11** and joins the **N1** at **Mokopane** (Potgietersrus). Palapye has a camp site, food, fuel and B&Bs – watch out for signs as the main road bypasses the town.

Beyond Palapye the road is potholed and there is construction around **Serule**. Make sure you stop at railway crossings – traffic cops lie in wait. North of Serule you will pass through a foot and mouth control post. Don't have meat products with you, they will be confiscated. The road north to **Francistown** is lined with piles of firewood for sale. It is so stupid that in this relatively rich country, where the authorities could be supplying alterna-

Giraffes browsing in the woodlands of Moremi Wildlife Reserve in Botswana.

tive fuel, scarce and much-needed trees are fast being wiped out and desertification is spreading.

Francistown is a pleasant overnight stop at 450 kilometres from Gaborone. The best place to head for here is the beautiful **Marang Hotel** situated about five kilometres out of town on the banks of the **Tate River** (follow the signs from the circle in town). Although very smart and upmarket ($76/$88 single/double in rooms and chalets), they also offer camping ($10,50 a site plus $5,50 a person) tel: 21-3991, fax: 21-2130, e-mail: marang@info.bw.

A cheaper option between town and the Marang is the **Satellite Guest House**, tel: 21-4665, fax 20-2115. A new and modern motel-type place, they have secure parking and charge $28/$36 single/double for air-conditioned, en-suite accommodation. The **Budget Bed** (no phone) next door is cheaper but not as nice.

If you were to carry on straight along the A1, you would cross the border into Zimbabwe at **Plumtree** and then get to Bulawayo. Although, at the time of writing this, it was politically incorrect (and some said dangerous) to be visiting Zim, its popularity will grow again – visit it while it's still cheap and uncrowded.

Take the **A3** northwest out of Francistown towards **Nata** and **Kazangula**. After about 20 kilometres you will reach a new little camp called **Africamp**. Camping costs $4 a person and a self-contained double rondavel $32.

The tarred A3 is in good condition and not very busy. Soon you will start seeing baobabs; watch out for stray livestock. At **Dukwe** there is another foot-and-mouth control post where you will have to disinfect your footwear and drive through a dip. About 17 kilometres south of Nata is the turnoff (S20°17.372 E26°18.114) to **Nata Bird Sanctuary**, a great place to view the aquatic birds that congregate on the edges of **Sowa Pan**. Camping is also available at $5 a person plus $2 a vehicle.

A far better option is to carry on for another seven kays to the turnoff (S20°13.535 E26°15.913) to **Nata Lodge** (tel: 61-1210, fax: 61-1265, e-mail: natalodge@info.bw, website: www.natalodge.com). This beautiful oasis of green offers the comfort of a huge thatched bar/restaurant/lounge with stone fireplace for chilly winter evenings and a cool, inviting pool for the hot, sunny days. Their menu offers an extensive selection including fish and chips for $5 and steak and chips for $8,50. Dining is by candlelight on the patio under spreading trees. Self-contained chalets and luxury tents cost $65 and $54 respectively, while camping is $5 a person (smart afro-chic in the stylishly decorated ablution block).

Nata is at an important crossroads - west to Maun and the swamps, and north to Chobe and Zambia. It is a long way in any direction, so stock up with food and fuel.

There is accommodation at the **Sua Pan Lodge** behind the Shell station (rondavels $29/$38 single/double and camping $5 a person, tel 61-1220.)

I will not describe the route west through Maun and then north via Moremi and Chobe Game Parks to link up with Kazungula in great detail, as it is quite a long detour. But, if you have time, it can offer some of the best wilderness experiences in Africa. The 310 kilometres of tarred road from Nata to Maun passes turnoffs to some amazing places such as Kubu Island on Sowa Pan, Makgadikgadi Pans National Park and Nxai Pan National Parks with Baine's Baobabs.

For all these places, and indeed the whole of Botswana, I fully recommend you get hold of the excellent *Shell Tourist Guide to Botswana*. Written and illustrated by Veronica Roodt and published by Shell Oil Botswana, it consists of a concise, but detailed tourist guide book and a separate series of maps with over 270 GPS co-ordinates. Sold together in a folder, it's available

The splayed hooves of the lechwe allow it to negotiate the swamps in Botswana.

from Shell Oil Botswana, PO Box 334, Gaborone (tel: 35-3025, fax: 37-3155) at selected Shell service stations in Botswana or most good outdoor supply shops in southern Africa. Cost about $12.

Gateway to 'the swamps'

Maun is the gateway to the **Okavango Delta** (also called the **Swamps**) and has grown phenomenally over the last decade or so. A good selection of shops allows you to stock up with virtually anything you need while accommodation is available in hotels and camps attractively situated along the banks of the **Thamalakane River**.

Getting into the Swamps needs organising, and can be quite expensive, as your only options are to fly or be poled in by *mokoro* (dug-out canoe). The wonderfully untamed **Moremi Wildlife Reserve** is just north of Maun and should not be missed. All camps are wild and unfenced - try and stay at **Third Bridge**.

You will need 4x4 traction for the sandy tracks in this part of Botswana, especially as you head north into **Chobe National Park**. **Savuti** in the centre and **Serondela** up on the Chobe River in the north are the camps to head for. You can then drive to Katima Mulilo in Namibia and on into western Zambia or to Kazungula and across to Lusaka, via Livingstone.

To continue our main route north from Nata, the tarred road is in good condition with little traffic. The countryside is wild and you will probably see game along the way. After 200 kilometres the little town of **Mpandamatenga** is reached. A dirt road turns east here to cross the border into Zimbabwe. Keep on the tar, and you will reach the turnoff to **Panda Rest Camp** a kilometre north of town. This shady, locally-run camp offers self-contained chalets for $34/$45 single/double and camping at $4 a person (tel: 7163-5328)

There is another 100 kilometres to the border at **Kazungula**. This spot is unique in Africa, as four countries meet here. From Kazungula you can head west into Namibia, cross the ferry north into Zambia or drive east into Zimbabwe to Victoria Falls. Although there is no town at the border, petrol and take-away food is available.

The pretty little town of **Kasane** lies on the banks of the Chobe, about 12 kilometres west of Kazungula and has a bank, supermarket and a variety of accommodation. Your best bet is the **Chobe Safari Lodge**, tel: 65-0340, fax: 65-0437. They are conveniently close to the entrance gate to the **Chobe National Park** and offer sunset cruises on the river. Rooms start at around $30 a person and camping costs $6.

Across the Zambezi

The **ferry at Kazungula** (S17°47.637 E25°15.743) is one those very special Spirit of Africa places. Not only do four countries meet here, but it is also the confluence of two mighty rivers, the Chobe and Zambezi. The inevitable queue of heavily laden trucks and trailers lines the road, while down at the river's edge women stand with piles of goods, plentiful in Botswana but in short supply in Zambia. African trade, big and small at an African crossroads.

The Botswana border is fast and efficient, and then you head down to the river. Fortunately smaller vehicles go to the head of the queue, so soon you're gingerly manoeuvring your vehicle up the ramp of the ferry. You snap off photographs as the engines churn and kingfishers dive, while in the background, the two rivers mingle as they have done since the beginning of time.

All too soon you're jolted back to the chaotic reality of getting your vehicle off the ferry and up to the crowded Zambian borderpost. You pay ferry fees of $10 a vehicle at a small shed on the Zambian side.

If the vehicle you are driving does not belong to you and is not registered in your name, then you must have a letter full of passport numbers and preferably on an official letterhead from the owner, to whom it may concern, giving you, the driver, permission to be using the vehicle and to take it across borders.

If you do not have valid third party insurance for Zambia, then try to buy **Comesa Yellow Card Insurance**. Ask for it to be validated for all the countries that you still intend visiting – it will save you having to buy again at every borderpost.

The first section of Zambian road away from the river is so badly potholed that you will be restricted to a maximum of 30 kilometres an hour. After five kilometres you reach a T-junction, turn right and find an even worse tarred road which, fortunately, improves over the 60 kilometres to **Livingstone**. You will arrive at **Mosi-Oa-Tunya Road** in the town centre – turn right to drive down to the Falls. Livingstone has benefited a lot from the troubles in Zimbabwe as more and more tourists want to now view the **Victoria Falls** from the Zambian side.

There is a carpark at S17°55.622 E25°51.864 where you must buy your ticket ($10 a person) to view the falls; there is also an information centre and a huge variety of curios on sale. Take a raincoat and something to protect your camera from the spray.

A network of paths takes you to all the best viewpoints for this most magnificent of sights. To get away from the crowds and hustlers, pull off the road just above the falls, sit at the edge of the mighty Zambezi and watch the river disappearing in a cloud of spray.

There are a few expensive luxury hotels right at the falls; the cheaper options are in town. One of the nicest places to stay is the **Maramba River Lodge**, halfway between the falls and town. With a pool and bar/restaurant on the banks of a river within the Mosi-Oa-Tunya National Park, it has grassed, shady camp sites for $5 a person, safari tents at $20/$25 single/double and self-contained chalets for $30/$40 single/double. Tel/fax: 03-33-4189, e-mail: maramba@zamnet.zm, website: www.maramba-zambia.com.

A perennial favourite in town is **Fawlty Towers**. Situated at the Kazungula Road intersection, the walled private garden contains a sparkling pool and a lush garden of trees and grass. Rates are: $5 a person camping, $8 for a dorm bed, $20 in a double room and $30 for a self-contained double room, Tel/fax: 03-32-3432, e-mail: ahorizon@zamnet.zm).

Both the above places can assist with bookings on booze cruises, whitewater rafting, microlight flights and bus travel in any direction.

Botswana's deserts give refuge to some of the world's few remaining Bushmen.

The final stretch to Lusaka

Take the **T1** out of Livingstone to get to **Lusaka**. This road was in a shocking condition, but has been rebuilt, which makes the 350 kilometres to **Mazabuka** a pleasure to drive now. Maz calls itself "the sweetest place on earth" because of its large sugar estates and has supermarkets, garages and banks. It makes a nice quiet place to change money and shop before getting into big, brash Lusaka.

Another 69 kilometres brings you to the main Chirundu to Lusaka road (**T2**) at **Kafue**, and from there it is only 55 kays to the capital (see page 72).

Routes in Central and East Africa

This region has it all: tropical off-shore islands, historical ruins, the highest peak in Africa and some of the best game parks on the continent.

CAPE TOWN TO DAR ES SALAAM
via Mozambique. Total distance: 5 750 kilometres. Page 100.

This mighty coastal route starts out easily, but deteriorates further north.

Don't miss
- ◆ Kilimanjaro ◆ Ilha de Mozambique
-   ◆ Lake Malawi ◆ Kilwa
-   ◆ Shiwa Ngandu ◆ Masai Mara
-   ◆ Zanzibar ◆ Ngorongoro
- ◆ Serengeti ◆ Malunge Mountains

LUSAKA TO MBEYA
via eastern Zambia and Malawi. Total distance: 1 600 kilometres. Page 122.

Avoiding Mozambique, this is a continuation of the route through Malawi.

HARARE TO LILONGWE
via Tete and Blantyre. Total distance: 1 000 kilometres. Page 114.

This Malawi detour is an attractive alternative to the road through Zambia.

LUSAKA TO NAIROBI
via the Great North Road. Total distance: 2 900 kilometres. Page 130.

This reasonably quick and painless route cuts through East Africa's heart.

THE SAFARI ROUTE
via the Serengeti and Masai Mara. Total distance: 550 kilometres. Page 140.

This route is for game-park junkies and includes East Africa's finest.

N

Serengeti Plain

C12 B3 □ NAIROBI

KENYA

B144

A 104

Kilimanjaro

Arusha

TANZANIA

B1

Segera

A 14

Kisigo Game Reserve

Morogoro

A 7 □ DAR ES SALAAM

Rungwa Game Reserve

Rungwa National Park

Iringa

Rufiji

A 104

Mbeya

R104 B345

Selous Game Reserve

Kilwa

B2

ZAMBIA

Isoka Karonga

Mtwara

Nyika National Park

247

T 2

Mocimboa da Praia

Vwaza Game Reserve Mzuzu

Ruvuma

246

Mpika

243

Luangwa National Park

Lake Malawi

106

MOZAMBIQUE

Pemba

M 1

Chipata

LILONGWE

Kapiri Mposhi

Petauke

M 12

T 4

Liwonde

T 4

M 10

M 1

106

LUSAKA

M 3

Alto Molócué

232

EN 8 Ilha da Mozambique

T 2

Chirundu

103 □ BLANTYRE

Tete M 2 Milange

104

Nyamapanda

EN 7

A 1

Zambezi

Chinhoyi

A 2

Quelimane

□ HARARE

ZIMBABWE

14 Cape Town to Dar es Salaam

via South Africa's East Coast and Mozambique 5 750 km

This epic drive up the coast of Africa starts from the icy waters of the Cape and ends on the warm, palm-fringed beaches of East Africa. The road is easy enough in the south, but becomes rough and adventurous as the road deteriorates through Mozambique and southern Tanzania. It also offers the chance to visit the historical islands of Ilha de Mozambique, Ibo and Kilwa.

Pick up the N2 out of Cape Town and head past the airport towards Somerset West (about 55 kilometres), then up Sir Lowry's Pass. At the top there's a viewpoint where you can stop to bid the Fairest Cape *tot siens*. Passing through the Hottentots Holland Mountains, you enter the apple-growing region of Elgin.

Opposite: The Church of Our Lady of the Bulwarks on Ilha de Mozambique is reputed to be the oldest European building in the southern hemisphere. Below: Macua women paint their faces with a white paste made from crushed bark to keep their skin soft and protect it from the sun.

This is a busy and dangerous stretch of the N2, so take care. At Botriver, there is a turnoff to the seaside resort of Hermanus – popular in summer for its swimming and in winter for whales.

As you travel through undulating wheatfields to reach Caledon, look out for flocks of the endangered national bird of South Africa, the blue crane. This is where you should turn south if you want to visit **Cape Agulhas**, the southernmost tip of Africa.

You could drive the 75 kilometres to **Bredasdorp** and then another 30 to the lighthouse at Aghulhas. You just might be disappointed – there are no cliffs or rocky points, just a museum (entrance $1). Heading back, take the R319 out of Bredasdorp to return you to the N2 at **Swellendam**.

Well-spaced towns with all amenities line this comfortable highway and there are numerous laybyes where you can stop to rest and picnic. But don't let the wide open road tempt you into breaking the speed limit as the traffic cops are notorious around here.

Turnoffs to the right lead to many seaside resorts, while turning to the left would take you to the foot of the Langeberg and through quaint, steep little passes into the Little Karoo beyond.

Along the Garden Route

At **Mossel Bay** (400 kilometres from Cape Town) you reach the sea again and start the **Garden Route**, an all-year-round holiday destination. The next 300 kilometres or so is a paradise of beaches, forests, mountains, rivers and attractive towns. The N2 bypasses Mossel Bay and, as fuel and food is available at two large truckstops on the Cape Town side of the town, it is only necessary to enter the town if you need accommodation. Try the **Park House Backpackers**, 121 High Street, tel: 044-691-1937, fax: 044-691-3435, e-mail: meyer@mweb.co.za. It is an attractive old stone house with wide verandas. Camping is $3,50, dorms $5,50 and double rooms $15.

The **Dias Museum** (corner of Church and Market streets) has a full-sized replica of the caravel that Portuguese explorer Bartholomeu Dias sailed around the tip of Africa in.

The road continues as a wide dual-carriageway past beaches, lagoons and little resorts such as **Groot Brak River**. It swings inland to pass the town of **George** – not the most attractive place along this coast, but very well serviced with shops and garages. If you are a golfer, this is heaven, with the great

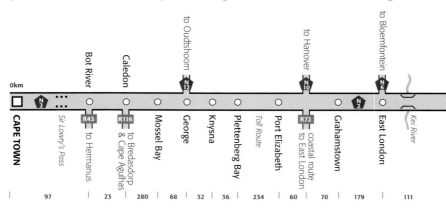

Fancourt and George courses.

Stick strictly to speed limits as you drive through the beautiful **Kaaimans River Pass** and down to the picturesque village of **Wilderness**. The beach looks perfect with its white-capped waves in an azure sea crashing onto a beach that stretches into the distance, but be careful of strong currents.

This is South Africa's Lake District and the road becomes a scenic drive with lakes on your left, sea on your right and hotels, camps and B&Bs all around.

At 500 kilometres from Cape Town you will reach the lagoonside town of **Knysna**. It would be difficult to imagine a more beautiful setting – a lagoon that opens to the sea through two high headlands and a backdrop of lush indigenous forests. It also has its own brewery and extensive oyster beds. What more could you ask for?

There is a wide variety of accommodation available. The comfortable **Highfields Backpackers**, 2 Graham Street, tel: 044-382-6266, e-mail: highfields@hotmail.com offers dorm beds at $8 and double rooms for $20 in a characterful old house with views high on the hill behind town.

The **Caboose** is an attractive wooden log hotel offering rooms fitted out like train compartments for $15/$20 single/double (corner Grey and Potter streets, tel: 044-382-5850, fax: 044-382-5224, e-mail: knysna@caboose.co.za, website: www.caboose.co.za)

Other, more upmarket, guesthouses and B&Bs are plentiful in and around town. Camping is available on the far side of the lagoon at **Lake Brenton**, tel: 044-381-0060. On the way down to the Heads are Woodburn Caravan Park, tel: 044-384-0316 and Monks Caravan Park tel: 044-382-2609. All charge around $8,50 a person a night.

Prices fluctuate between seasons so check at the excellent Tourism Office in the main street, which offers a free booking service and can advise on the many hiking trails in the area. Tel: 044-382-5510, fax 044-382-1646, e-mail: knysna.tourism@pixie.co.za, website: www.knysna-info.co.za.

Places to eat at are plentiful too. For oysters, head out to Thesen's Island where the Knysna Oyster Company offers tours, tastings and good food at their **Oyster Tavern,** tel: 044-382-6941. Down on the waterfront, below the railway station, is **The Oystercatcher**, tel: 044-382-9995. Built out over the water, they charge only $4,50 for six oysters and offer a selection of

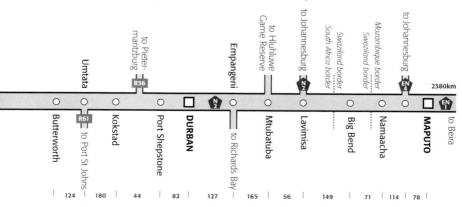

tapas too. Next door, at the **Knysna Quays**, is the fine deli/restaurant, **34° South**, tel: 044-382-7331. Wine sales, sushi bar, oyster bar, fresh fish and the largest selection of chilli sauces in the world make this a must.

If, like me, you can't miss a good brewery tour, then drop in at the **Mitchells Brewery** (tel: 044-382-4685) at Arend Street in the industrial area. They hand-make real ale and offer tours at 10h30 every week day.

Entering the Eastern Cape

Drag yourself away from Knysna and 37 kilometres further, through lush forest hiding small farms and hippy communes, brings you to **Plettenberg Bay** with its great beaches – and more golf courses. Beyond here you will encounter a toll road which is cheap at only $1 as the wide road whisks you over **Bloukrans Bridge**, where they offer the "world's highest bungi jump" and on through pristine forest towards the surfing mecca of **Jeffreys Bay**.

A good place to stop for fuel and food along here is at the Petroport at **Storms River Bridge** – they also have clean toilets, public phones and a picnic area.

A dual-carriage road takes you the last 45 kilometres into **Port Elizabeth**.

Keep an eye out for the N2 signs once you're in PE – the road system is a bit confusing. It is also not easy to find fuel close to the main road through town, so wait until you're out the other side and stop at the Caltex Truckstop at intersection 761.

At 60 kilometres beyond PE there is a confusing three-way intersection (intersection 797). If you drive straight through, you will head inland to Cradock and Middelburg, eventually ending up on the N1 to Johannesburg. To stay on the N2, keep left. If you want to take the R72 which follows the coast all the way to East London, then make sure you turn off at intersection 798. I told you it was confusing!

Staying on the N2, you will soon reach the university city of Grahamstown, home to the highly popular and entertaining Arts Festival every July. The buzziest place to stay is the **Old Gaol Backpackers** in Somerset Street, tel: 046-636-1001, e-mail: oldgaol@-hotmail.com. There are many B&Bs in the city and a municipal camp site is in Gray Street (tel 046-622-3241).

The 121 kilometres to **King William's Town** is a bit dodgy as stray animals and road works always seem to make things interesting. This is **Settler**

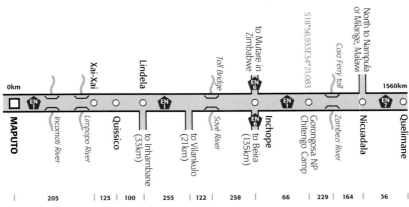

Country, so named because of the English settlers who came out in 1820 and the Germans who followed a few years later. The names of towns and villages reflect this history in places such as Bathurst, Port Alfred, Fort Beaufort, Hamburg, Berlin and Potsdam.

If you had come up along the coast on the R72, you would have passed through the picturesque seaside town of **Port Alfred**. Originally founded as a port on the banks of the Kowie River for the settlers in the area, Port Alfred and other little lagoonside villages along this stretch of coast now serve as holiday resorts and offer pleasant beaches and boating.

There are two camp sites in town, the **Riverside Caravan Park**, 26 Mentone Road tel: 046-624-2230 and **Medolino Holiday Resort**, 23 Stewart Street, tel: 046-624-1651, both charging about $7 a site. A very pleasant B&B at $17 a person is **Turning Tides** at 8 Van der Riet Street, tel/fax: 046-624-4700, e-mail: johncase@telkomsa.net. **Station Backpackers** is in the old railway station building (backpack@-thestation.co.za). Although there are no longer any scheduled services, an excursion train runs day trips up to the old settler town of Bathurst.

Into East London

East London, 59 kilometres from Grahamstown, is a city with all the services you might need for restocking, replacing or repairing. There is a very pleasant, grassed **camp site** under shady trees out by the beach at **Nahoon**. Run by the municipality, it charges $7 a site out of season and $10 during school holidays (tel: 043-722-6015).

The funkiest backpackers in town is the **Sugarshack**, which is a beach-bum's paradise on the Esplanade right above Eastern Beach, tel: 043-722-8240, e-mail sugarsk@iafrica.com. They give free surfing lessons, allow free use of surfboards, boogie boards and wetsuits, and charge $6,50 for dorm beds, $16,50 doubles and $4 for camping in the small garden. The **Kat Leisure Group** seems to run most of the hotels and lodges around East London. Their **Express Lodge** on the corner of Fleet and Fitzpatrick Streets is close to the city centre and Eastern Beach and charges $18/$25 single/double, while their **Reef Lodge** is attractively situated down at Nahoon Beach and charges $23/$29 single/double. Reservations tel: 0800-42-2433.

The Wild Coast

North of East London is **Transkei**. It will be your first taste of 'real' Africa – the Africa of round mud huts, thatched with grass, clustered on hilltops. It is also the less picturesque Africa of stray animals and dangerous roads, so stay alert while travelling the 365 kilometres of tarred road from EL to **Umtata**.

Along the way you will pass turnoffs down to the coast. These rough dirt roads lead to quiet, but comfortable little resorts at places such as **Morgan's Bay**, **Mazeppa Bay** and **The Haven**. Coffee Bay is a chilled-out place that offers alternative, holistic, space-cake-type living on the beach. Hiking, surfing, cultural tours – the whole 'thang'. Camp at **Campers Cove** ($4 a person) or stay in the dorms ($5) and double rooms ($15) at Bomvu Paradise (both contactable on tel/fax: 047-575-2073, e-mail: bomvu@intekom.co.za, website: www.bomvubackpackers.com). The **Coffee Shack** is a bit of a legend. Right on the beach and into surfing and other adventure sports, they have camping for $4 a person, dorms for $6,50 and double rondavels for $17 (tel: 047-575-2048, e-mail: coffeeshack@-wildcoast.com).

Rather than stay in Umtata, plan your day so that you drive the remaining 315 kilometres through to the **Kwazulu-Natal South Coast** or turn down onto the R61 and drive 95 kilometres to **Port St Johns**. Enjoying a bit of a revival, this old colonial port is now popular with dudes and dudettes wanting to follow an alternative lifestyle. Is it because it is such an 'African' place in South Africa, or could it be the annual marijuana growers competition which is supposed to be held nearby?

You could do some lazy river rafting on the **Umzimvubu River** or visit a sangoma (traditional healer), but be careful, the lifestyle is infectious, and you might stay longer than you had planned. Stay at **Second Beach**, about

five kilometres down the coast. **Amapondo Backpackers** offers dorms at $6 a person, double rooms at $14 and camping costs $3,50, tel/fax: 047-564-1344, e-mail: amapondo@wildcoast.co.za. The more upmarket **Ikaya le Intlabati** charges $16 for double rooms and $24 for their colourful garden cottages (tel/fax: 047-564-1266)

The N2 turns east at **Kokstad** and joins the Kwazulu-Natal South Coast at **Port Shepstone**. Sixteen kilometres before Port Sheppy is the turnoff left to the **Oribi Gorge National Reserve**. This 1 800-hectare forest reserve has great hikes and some wildlife. Stay at the charming and economical **Oribi Gorge Hotel** (tel/fax: 039-687-0253, e-mail: oribigorge@worldonline.co.za). You can cover the 127 kilometres to Durban via the big, fast freeway or take the scenic R102 route which hugs the coast and meanders from beach to beach through dozens of little resort towns, all of which have reasonably priced hotels and camp sites.

Durban and beyond

Durban is the third largest city in South Africa and the busiest port, but it is also a holiday destination for thousands of upcountry visitors who flock to its

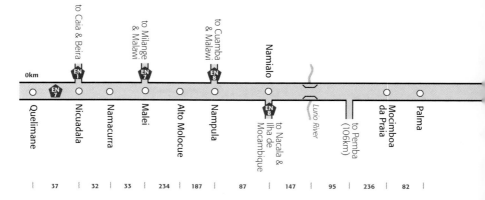

beachfront over long weekends and school holidays.

There is a lot of accommodation in and around Durbs. A popular place with overlanders is **Tekweni Hostel**, 169 Ninth Avenue, Morningside, tel: 031-303-1433, fax: 031-303-4369, e-mail: tekwenihostel@global.co.za, website: www.tekweniecotours.co.za. Dorms cost $7 a person, doubles from $19 and camping $6.

After you've had your photo taken in a rickshaw and eaten a good hot Indian curry (Durbs has a large Indian community, descendants of labourers brought out in the 19th century to work on the sugar plantations), stock up with supplies and head north.

The N2 continues north out of Durban as a toll road and passes a string of North Coast resorts. But you'll probably have had your fill of beaches by now and want to see the Big Five.

At 220 kilometres from Durban, you will pass **Mtubatuba** where you can turn off to the **Hluhluwe/Umfolozi Park** which at 96 000 hectares is one of South Africa's largest game parks and has a good stock of all the main animal species. Unfortunately, they do not offer camping facilities, but do offer affordable self-catering rondavel accommodation. Entrance costs $5 a vehicle plus $1,50 a person. Book through **Kwazulu-Natal Wildlife**, tel: 033-845-1000, fax: 033-845-1001, website: www.rhino.org.za.

A convenient alternative is the **Isinkwe Bush Camp**. At 30 kilometres north of Mtubatuba, take the Bushlands turnoff right for one kilometre. Set in pristine indigenous bush, they offer dorms ($7 a person), doubles ($18) and camping ($5), as well as safaris and day tours into the nearby parks and reserves. Tel: 035-562-2258, fax: 035-562-2273, e-mail: galago@-futurenet.co.za, website: www.africasafari.co.za/isinkwe.

The coast along here is all protected as the **Greater St Lucia Wetland Park** and includes such places as **Lake St Lucia** and **Sodwana Bay** – great for bird-watching, fishing and diving.

The N2 now swings inland and will take you all the way to Johannesburg if you don't turn off and cross into **Swaziland** at **Golela**. The border is hassle free, as is the drive via **Nsoko** and **Big Bend** to **Siteki**. There is a choice of two border posts to pass through into Mozambique, **Namaacha** or the more direct **Goba** route which is 30 kilometres shorter, but untarred. You

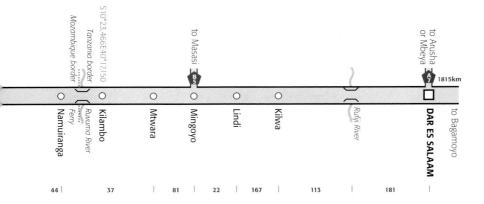

will only be traversing Swaziland for 164 kilometres, so don't bother dallying and head straight down to exciting, vibrant **Maputo**.

Another way to cross from northern Kwazulu-Natal into Mozambique is to take the coastal route through the border at **Ponta do Ouro**. Not recommended for sedan cars, the road turns off just north of **Mkuze** and passes through **Jozini** on its way down to the coast at **Kosi Bay**. The track north of the border is subject to flooding in the rainy season. It passes the **Maputo Elephant Reserve** (no phone) where there is a good camp site which costs about $17,50 for two people and a vehicle a night. You might see elephants and hippos; the lagoons and beaches are a breeding ground for turtles.

Into Mozambique

Mozambique's long civil war devastated its tourist industry, along with just about everything else. But, who could resist its seafood, beer and beaches for too long? Now there's a revival and tourists are flocking back, especially from South Africa. Maputo has a Mediterranean feel to it and has good music and nightlife.

The old camping area **Campismo Maputo** along the beachfront near the new Holiday Inn has good ablutions and security and charges $15 for two people and a vehicle. The **Carlton** and **Central** hotels are centrally situated and close to each other in Rua da Bagamoyo. Charges range from $10 for a plain single to $30 for a good double. **Fatima's** is a popular backpacker's hostel up in Avenue Mao Tse-tung that has camping for $3,50, dorms for $6,50 and double rooms for $15.

If you have the time, take the ferry across to **Inhaca Island**. It leaves from the long jetty near to the docks and costs less than $2 each. It takes about three and a half hours to cross the 35 kilometres to the island. You can stay in the swanky **Inhaca Hotel** or in reed huts (book at Fatima's in Maputo). The coral reefs are full of colourful fish and there are a couple of small restaurants around the market.

Highway **EN1** north out of Maputo is a good tarred road. **Xai-Xai**, 205 kilometres from Maputo, was badly damaged in the 2000 floods and it is currently not worth stopping there for more than fuel and food. There is a caravan park 10 kilometres away at the beach ($8,50 a person).

Quissico lies 120 kilometres further up the EN1. The camp site there was washed away, but no-one minds if you free-camp under the palm trees. **Inhambane**, another 133 kays away (watch out for potholes on the road down to the coast), is the oldest settlement along this coast and has attractive tree-lined avenues along the waterfront.

If it's beaches you're looking for, then drive 22 kilometres to **Praia do Tofo** on the seaward side of the peninsula. **Hotel Marinhos** is a pleasant enough place that charges around $22 for a double room, while at **Casa Azul Backpackers**, just south of the hotel, they charge $6,50 single. Diving is the popular sport here and it's well catered for at **Diversity Dive** behind the hotel. There is also a camp site up at the lighthouse.

Vilankulo is 275 kilometres from

MOZAMBIQUE

Capital: Maputo

Official language: Portuguese

Area: 801 600 square kilometres

Population: 19 million

Visa requirements: Required by all (not issued at border)

Time: UT +2

International dialling code: +258

Currency and rate: Meticais Mt 30 000=$1

Climate: Tropical with summer rains

Highlights: Beaches, fishing and diving. Also offshore islands, including Ilha de Mozambique, a World Heritage Site

Driving: On the left. There are a few new tarred roads around Maputo and Beira, but the rest are potholed and not maintained

Accommodation: Quite plentiful between Maputo and Vilankulo, but rather scarce further north, though it is improving

Food, shops and fuel: Good seafood and Portuguese cuisine in restaurants. Very few supermarkets, so shop in markets. Fuel availability adequate and improving

Tourism info: For the best information, contact the Mozambique National Tourist Co in Johannesburg, tel: 011-339-7275, fax: 011-339-7295, website: www.mozambique.mz

Inhambane and serves as the little port to the **Bazaruto Archipelago**. The town also has fuel at the traffic circle as well as a bakery and shops. The **Dona Ana Hotel** has occupied the best position overlooking the jetty for more than 50 years and its roof-top patio is a great place for sundowners – double rooms start at $17,50. The camp site on the beachfront charges $3,50 a person. Just south of the camp are rooms to rent for about the same price – they're unmarked and unnamed, so you'll have to ask.

Up the road, 94 kilometres from Vilankulo, is the seaside town of **Inhassoro**. Here you will find many South African ski-boat fishermen – the beer and banana brigade – as well as the **Hotel Sita** and a camp site with good ablutions just above the beach.

Turn left for Zim, right for Beira

The EN1 runs for 64 kilometres from the Inhassoro turnoff up to the bridge across the **Rio Save**. There is a $6 toll which, surprisingly, you pay only if heading north. Another 258 kilometres brings you to the intersection with the main **Mutare to Beira highway (EN6)**.

Turning left here would take you up into Zimbabwe, through Mutare and on to Harare – from where you could branch out north to Lusaka via Chirundu, east to Blantyre via Tete or back to South Africa via Beit Bridge.

Turn right and drive for 135 kilometres if you want to visit **Beira**, if only to stock up at the big new Shoprite supermarket there. Beira is Mozambique's second largest city and attractive enough with some interesting old colonial buildings. The **Biques Camp**

Site is about five kilometres east of town along Praca de Independencia and costs $3,50 a person. Backpackers head for **Pensao Messe** on Rua Daniel Napatina ($10 double), and for a good meal try the **Restaurante Arcadia**.

Before turning north towards **Gorongosa National Park** at the intersection of the EN1 and EN6, make sure that you have filled up with fuel at Gondola, Chimoio or Dondo, as there are no garages along this next stretch. Although there is a new filling station under construction at Inchope, and black market fuel can usually be bought at Gorongosa and Caia, it is nearly 500 kilometres to a secure supply at Nicuadala.

The Gorongosa National Park was once the pride and joy of colonial Mozambique, but existed only in name during the long civil war. The animal numbers are now increasing and the park is being revitalised by dedicated personnel. Entrance costs $20 and camping at **Chitengo** (S18°58.933 E34°21.083) is another $10 a person. There are still old landmines around, so stick to the roads and tracks.

A good new road has been built past Gorongosa to **Caia** which passes through pristine forests and villages. There are no major roadblocks along this stretch, but the police will check your documents on the outskirts of each large village.

Although there is no accommodation at Caia, there is a new camp site at **Catapu**, on the left 12 kilometres beyond the Inhaminga/Inhamitanga turnoff and 30 kilometres before Caia. An impressive ferry carries you across the Zambezi at Caia ($5 a vehicle) and a tarred road runs to **Nicuadala**, where you have the choice of driving the 37 kilometres down to **Quelimane** or keeping left towards **Nampula**. Quelimane is Mozambique's fourth largest town and has most amenities if you need assistance.

The road to Malawi

If you have decided to follow a route north through Malawi, you have two options. The first would be to not cross the Zambezi by ferry at Caia, but to drive upstream to **Sena**, cross the old railway bridge there (check first if it has been repaired) and enter Malawi through **Nsanje**. Your second option is to drive 33 kilometres north from **Nicuadala** to the little town of **Malei**. Here a road turns off to **Milange** on the Malawian border, from where it is a short comfortable ride on to Blantyre.

Ilha, a World Heritage site

From the intersection at **Nicuadala** the road is still good tar for 300 kilometres as far as **Molocue**. Thereafter it deteriorates and is badly potholed for the remaining 187 kilometres to **Nampula**. There are no camp sites in Nampula so, if you want to stay here, try **Pensao Marques** or **Centrale** (rooms $5), or the more upmarket **Pensao Parques** (double rooms $15). There is a pleasant camp site and restaurant situated between the insulbergs, about 20 kilometres out on the Rapale road, but a better bet is to head straight for the coast.

From Nampula, drive 85 kilometres to **Namialo**. Don't turn north yet – that

The main north road through south and east Africa is good, but venture off it and ... be warned.

road takes you to Pemba – carry on straight in the direction of **Nacala**. At eight kilometres past **Monapo**, turn right and head for one of the African coast's most attractive destinations, **Ilha de Mozambique**. This historical and architectural gem well deserves its status as a Unesco World Heritage Site. Its early history is lost in the mists of time, but probably was visited by Chinese and other eastern and middle-eastern seafarers before becoming a Shirazi shipbuilding and trading port.

Ilha was captured by Portugal in 1507 and became the naval and economic hub as well as the capital of Portuguese East Africa. Grand forts, cathedrals, hospitals and residences were built and the island prospered.

As the importance of other ports like Lourenço Marques grew, Ilha became a sleeping beauty – even the civil war

bypassed the island. So it lies today, five centuries later, a mouldering maze of vine-covered buildings crying out for restoration – go and see it while you can!

The narrow 2,5-kilometre long island is connected to the mainland by a causeway. Turn left as you arrive on Ilha and then down the second right lane. Look out for a sign **Casa de Luice** to get to the little guesthouse run by Mira and Luis. They will assist you with information, rooms, camping and food.

Drive on past the reed hut town to the area around the central square and governor's palace, now an interesting museum. The palace also houses the official tourist information centre and can help with accommodation. Next door is the old church, now the Sacred Art Museum and across the road is the **Restaurante Ancora D'oura**.

On the furthest tip of the island lies the massively formidable **Fort of Sao Sebastao** and its tiny neighbour, the **Church of Nossa Senhora Baluarte**. Spend a few days here exploring the island and you might not want to leave. There is a very good camp site, **Camping Casuarinas**, on the mainland side of the causeway. It costs $4 a person and has a cool bar and hot restaurant.

The road to Tanzania

It is 424 kilometres from Ilha to Pemba, and best done in one run. Retrace your route to **Namialo**, where you must turn north to cross the **Lurio River** (242 kilometres). The road is reasonable old tar and passes through **Metoro** before reaching the huge deep bay of **Pemba**.

The best part of Pemba is the old part, down near the harbour where you will find the inexpensive **Hotel Maritimo** ($5 a person). The newer part of town has upmarket hotels, bars and restaurants and other services including garages, internet cafes and an international airport, but the real action is six kilometres away down at **Wimbe Beach**, which has a tourist complex, bars and restaurants and a dive centre.

A couple of kays beyond Wimbe Beach and away from the crowds is the shady **Caju Camping** (S12°57.950 E40°34.016). With no electricity or piped water, it's very rustic – you heat water in a bucket to shower. They charge $4,50 a person to camp and serve evening meals for $3,50.

Russell runs the **Blackfoot Bar** where you will meet all the unscrupulous expats who are ruining the forests and marine life around here, but they do know everyone and everything and will phone Mtwara in Tanzania to organise the ferry across the Ruvuma River for you.

Drive back for 87 kilometres towards Metoro and then turn north to get to **Mocimboa da Praia** and beyond to Rovuma River, the border of Tanzania.

An interesting side trip along the way is a visit to **Ibo Island**, one of the many small islands in the **Quirimba Archipelago**. Not easy to get to, you must first make your way to the beach at **Quissanga** and then find a dhow going across to the island (the last house on the left will store your vehicle).

A bit like a miniature Ilha de Mozambique, Ibo has crumbling buildings along the waterfront and an old fort where traditional silversmiths make delicate jewellery with the most rudimentary tools. For years the only accommodation was **Casa Janine**, where camping costs $2,50 and a double room $11, but recently other houses have opened their doors to travellers.

Another good detour on your way up to Mocimboa is to turn off the main road at Macomia and drive on a good gravel road down to the coast at **Mucojo** (you could also get here by travelling up the coast from Quissanga).

At the beach, turn left and drive north through the palms for seven kilometres to **Pangane** village. Carry on through Pangane to the spit of land where Ashim Abibacar and his family run a rustic little camp (S11°59.966 E40°32.633). Nothing is too much trouble – they will cook mouth-watering fish dishes for you and organise dhow trips and snorkelling. A camp site will cost only $6 for two.

Mocimboa da Praia has accommodation, a bank and other basic amenities, but it is also the end of the tarred road. **Palma** is 82 kilometres north along a narrow sandy track – watch out for speeding locals – and after another 44 kays you will reach the **Ruvuma River**, the Tanzanian border.

Pedestrians cross by dugout canoe, but for a vehicle you will need the ferry operated by Philip Mtupa (PO Box 378, Mtwara, Tanzania, tel: 0741-50-3007 cellphone: 0748-50-5007). If you have booked ahead, he should be waiting for you. Otherwise, you might have to wait for about 48 hours. The ferry can operate only at high tides and costs $30, whether you are one vehicle or the maximum of four. Pay for the ferry in Mozambican or Tanzanian currency.

The Mozambican customs and immigration office is very basic and simple, as is the **Kilambo** border post across the river in Tanzania. Although Kilambo is only a village and has no amenities, you can at least change metacais into shillings here.

Head straight to **Mtwara** (37 kilometres) where you will have to start getting used to a new country, currency and food. There's not a lot to Mtwara, but if you want to stay over, try the **Tingatinga Guesthouse** two kilometres out of town towards the beach where self-contained doubles cost $7,50.

The road north is reasonable tar for the first 80 kilometres until the intersection at **Mingoyo**. Turn right here. The road deteriorates for the next 22

kays to **Lindi**. Although Lindi was part of the Sultinate of Zanzibar and an important slave port, there is little left to see now. The only reasonable place to stay is the **Nankolowa Guesthouse** which charges $6 for a double room and $9 for self-contained with fan.

You have 167 kilometres of reasonable gravel road to the turnoff to the most impressive ruins on the East African coast, **Kilwa**.

There are actually three Kilwas. The first one you come to is **Kilwa Kivinje**, the old Omani slave-trading centre. Now very much boarded up, its buildings and Zanzibar-styled doors hint at its past glory. The second is **Kilwa Masoko**, the modern market town with hotel, restaurants and bus station. Try the pretentiously named **Masoko Hilton Hote**l which charges $8 for a double with fan.

The third is **Kilwa Kisiwani**, an island two kilometres offshore. To visit this island with its impressive ruins, you must first obtain permission from the **Kilwa Cultural Centre** opposite the post office in Kilwa Masoko. Although you will need to show your passport and fill in forms, there is no charge. You can also organise a dhow to take you across from here.

The ruins include a fort, the 14th-century Great Mosque and the Sultan of Kilwa's palace. You will probably have the ruins to yourself as, sadly, very few tourists get down this way.

The dirt road continues for another 160 kilometres, crossing the **Rufiji River** on a newish bridge, before reaching tar at Kibiti for the final 135 kays into **Dar es Salaam**.

15 Harare to Lilongwe
Via Tete and Blantyre 1 000 km

Travellers taking this route would avoid Zambia, pass through the Tete province of Mozambique and enter southern Malawi at Blantyre. This enables you to explore the Mulanje mountains and other parts of the south before travelling virtually the whole length of Malawi, passing directly into Tanzania at the northern end of the lake.

Head east out of Harare along Samora Machel Avenue to where Enterprise Road forks off to the left. This will take you out onto the A2 and into the countryside.

Right: Game viewing by boat on the Shire River in Liwonde National Park, Malawi.
Below: Tons of terns on the Shire River.

It is 238 kilometres on a good tarred road to the border at **Nyamapanda** where the Zimbabweans and Mozambicans vie with each other to see who can hassle you the most.

Leaving Zim is fairly straightforward, but the Mozambican officials will check your visas and then want $15 for vehicle insurance (if you don't already have), $6 for a temporary import permit (if you don't have a carnet) and $1,50 each to stamp your passport.

It is 49 kays of good tar from the border to the intersection at **Luenha** (S16°50.183 E33°16.425). Turn left here and travel another 95 kilometres to the regional centre of **Tete**.

This town has a long history of trade, as it lies on the banks of the mighty Zambezi. Long before the Portuguese built a fort here, Omani Arabs were sweating up this route to trade for gold and slaves – the history of even earlier incursions has been lost in the annals of time.

The **Motel Tete**, on the banks of the Zambezi as you enter the town is a pleasant enough place with good vehicle security, but rather expensive at $50 for a double room. A much cheaper option (usually open to negotiation) is the **Pensao Alves Melo**, up from the

governor's palace in town. There is a new camp site on the opposite bank of the river, **Jesus de Bom**. Turn right coming off the bridge and it is slightly downstream. Built by a South African missionary, Riaan Terblanche, under the auspices of the church, it charges $3 a vehicle and $1,50 a person. (e-mail: roym@mweb.co.za).

A Pescina, on the townside riverbank just downstream of the bridge, offers reasonable accommodation, camping and a restaurant, but is usually full. A single/double is $16/$19 a person. A pleasant place to enjoy a sundowner and tasty meal is the **Complexo Turistico Jemba**, on the riverbank upstream from the bridge.

A word of warning, the traffic police around Tete are evil and corrupt. Always wear your safety belt, keep your speed way down and never cross the solid white line down the middle of the road. No U-turns or anything remotely dodgy – they will get you and fine you heavily. The cops on duty on the bridge are particularly bad. There is a small toll fee to pay when crossing the bridge, but it must be paid in local currency. Taking into account all the problems you may encounter in Tete, it is probably better to travel the 612

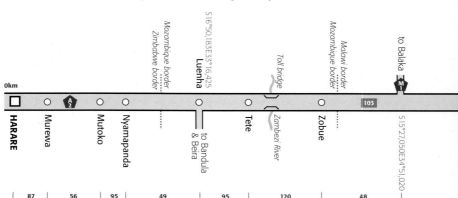

kilometres straight through from Harare to Blantyre in one day, but hey, think of the excitement you'd miss!

The M1 to Blantyre

The border post at **Zobue** is chaotic on the Mozambican side - you will be mobbed by money-changers, hawkers and hustlers. The Malawians will charge you $20 for road tax and another $26 for insurance if you do not already have cover.

The road is 110 kilometres of good tar all the way to Blantyre. You will encounter a couple of tame roadblocks along the way and at about halfway, pass the turnoff north to Lilongwe.

Although most of the tarred roads in Malawi are in good condition – some are being reconstructed – the gravel roads in rural areas are not regularly maintained and can be in very poor condition, depending on when they were last graded.

Keep a sharp eye out for the Malawian drivers, who like to stop their trucks and buses in the middle of the highway and never pull off the road in the event of a breakdown.

The M1 brings you into the centre of **Blantyre** at the circle on Glen Jones Road. Turn left and drive down to the

A fisherman repairing his fishing nets on the shore of Lake Malawi.

clocktower circle. Keep left, under the railway bridge and first left again, and you will drive straight into **Doogles Lodge** (S15°47.031 E35°00.898), the

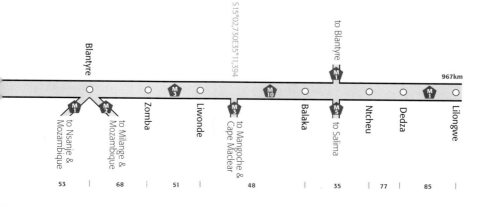

most popular place to stay for travellers (tel: 01-621-128, e-mail: doogles@africa-online.net). Charges are camping $2,50 a person, dorm beds $5, double chalets $10 and self-contained garden suites $18 double. They have one of Blantyre's most popular bars, a pool, TV lounge, good internet connection and serve good food. Mark and Billy are helpful and knowledgeable, and there is good security.

Another highly recommended place which is quieter and popular with volunteer workers on extended stays is **Kabula Lodge** (tel: 01-62-1216). Go up Glyn Jones Road, past the expensive and classy Mount Soche Hotel, and follow the signs. Accommodation ranges from $7 basic singles to $20 self-contained doubles and includes the use of well equipped kitchens. If

Crossing the Shire River on the road between Blantyre and Monkey Bay in Malawi.

you want to spoil yourself a bit, head for the **Alendo Hotel** at 15 Chilembwe Road. This new, clean hotel is centrally situated in attractive gardens and is run by the Malawi Institute of Tourism for training purposes. Charges are $60 for a single and $80 for a double, inclusive of breakfast.

Right across the road from the Alendo is **Chez Maky** (tel: 01-62-2124) a popular daytime restaurant serving continental food and great coffee while jazz schmoozes in the background. **The Cactus Bar**, down Schlater Road, has a Wild West theme and is the spot where most expats hang out.

Blantyre is the commercial capital of Malawi and has an extensive industrial area where you can have your gas refilled (BOC Gas) or your car repaired.

The **Chichiri Mall**, on Kamuzu Highway, is a large new shopping centre housing a big, well-stocked Shoprite supermarket. There are also banks, a pharmacy, DHL and various fast-food joints. Just above the turnoff to Doogles is the new **Mwaiwathu Private Hospital** where you can go for any medical emergency.

Blantyre is the hub of an extensive transport network. Cross border coaches head through Tete to Harare and on to Johannesburg, intercity busses fan out to all of Malawi's major cities, and local slowcoaches and minibusses serve the towns and villages closer by. Most leave from the bus depot near Doogles. Oh yes, nearly forgot, **Carlsberg Breweries** up on Malimidwe Road in the industrial area (tel: 01-67-0222) runs a great tour and tasting on Wednesday afternoons.

Firewood is precariously transported by bicycle down from the Zomba Plateau in Malawi.

From Blantyre you might want to run down to the **Mulanje Mountains** (about 100 kilometres) for a spot of hiking (**Tiyende Pamodzi Scouts**, tel: 01-52-7307, can guide you).

On the way down, you will pass through the beautiful tea-growing area around **Thyolo**. Take a tour of the **Satemwa Tea Estate** (S16°03.213 E35°06.749) and stay in the luxurious but affordable historic tea-planters bungalow (tel: 01-47-3430; fax: 01-47-3368; e-mail: 113213.233@compuserve.com).

The **M2** which continues through **Mulanje** will take you across the border into Mozambique. The road then runs down to **Mocuba**, where it joins the main **Highway 7**. North will take you to Nampula, Pemba and on into Tanzania, while south goes down the coast to Beira and Maputo (see page 110).

To Lake Malawi

To head north via the lake, take the **Kamuzu Highway** through the suburb of **Limbe** and follow the signs to **Zomba**. It is only 70 kilometres to this ex-capital of Malawi which nestles at the foot of the **Zomba Plateau**. This is another good hiking area with good birdlife. Recommended accommodation up on the plateau is the bungalow and camp sites at the **Kuchawe Trout Farm**.

Liwonde town is another 51 kilometres up the M3 and notable only for its proximity to Malawi's best game reserve, **Liwonde National Park**. It is quite difficult getting into the park by road, especially after heavy rains and often visitors are ferried in by boat up the **Shire River**. There are two camps in the park, **Chinguni Lodge** in the southern hills and **Mvuu Lodge and**

MALAWI

Capital: Lilongwe

Official languages: English and Chichewa

Area: 18 500 square kilometres

Population: 11 million

Visa requirements: Not required by most holiday visitors

Time: UT +2

International dialling code: +265

Currency and rate: Malawian Kwacha MK=$1

Climate: Pleasant and temperate, rains from November to March

Driving: Good main tarred roads, others poor

Highlights: Beaches and diving at the lake, hiking on the Mulanje Massif and game viewing in Liwonde and Nyika national parks

Accommodation: Various comfortable and picturesque resorts along the shores of Lake Malawi, backpackers in main towns, and camping and lodges in national parks

Food, shops and fuel: Good restaurants and supermarkets in main towns, otherwise markets. Fuel freely available, but petrol a low octane blend

Tourism info: Malawi Department of Tourism, tel: 01-62-0902, e-mail: tourism@malawi.net, web: www.malawi.net

---

Camp on the Shire River in the centre. Game stocks are building up and an ambitious attempt is underway to re-introduce rhino and other endangered game. The best viewing, particularly of the excellent birdlife, is from a boat on the river (organised from the lodges).

Chinguni is the best option for tight budgets as it is easy to get to and charges $40 a person for full board in en-suite double rooms, $10 for dorm beds and $5 a person to camp. Tel 08-83-8159, fax: 08-84-6517, e-mail: chinguni@africa-online.net.

Getting to Mvuu is more difficult as the roads in the park are often washed away. It then entails driving up to Ulongwe (S14°50.957 E35°10.374) on the Mangochi road and heading down to the west bank of the river (S14°50.621 E35°17.375), opposite the camp. A boat then ferries you and your luggage across.

Mvuu Lodge is very exclusive and costs $240 a person a night inclusive of three meals and three game activities a day. Mvuu Camp is next door and charges $140 a person in en-suite chalets, also inclusive of meals and game drives. Self-catered camping is a much more affordable $8 a person. Park fees are an extra $5 a person and $2 a vehicle. Contact Central African Wilderness Safaris on tel: 07-71393, fax: 07-71397, e-mail: info@wilderness.malawi.net.

During the early 1990s **Cape Maclear** was the spot that every over-lander had to visit while travelling through east and central Africa. Not so popular now, it has a bit of a rundown air about it. Its laid-back atmosphere and proximity to the **Lake Malawi**

National Park, however, still make it a good place to visit.

Turn right just north of Liwonde, (S15°02.730 E35°11.394) to **Mangochi**. Pass through Mangochi after 77 kilometres and continue up the lake for another 60 kays to just before **Monkey Bay**. The turnoff to Cape Maclear is at a Total garage (S14°07.610 E34°55.081), then it's about another 16 kays.

Steven's Resthouse (S14°01.804 E34°49.969) started it all and for a long time was the only place to stay - there are now too many places all vying for too few tourists. The current best is **Fat Monkeys** on the eastern end of the beach and away from the village. Basic rooms are $5,50 double and camping costs $1 a person. There is a lively bar and a restaurant where meals are served for about $3,50. The security is good too. The **Scuba Shack** at Steven's offers four-day open water dive courses for $195 as well as casual dives for $20.

On to Lilongwe

There is what appears to be a short-cut across to the **M5** and up to **Salima** that saves you driving all the way back down to Liwonde. It looks impressive on the maps and even has a number, the **M10**.

However, it is a rough track and is often impassable after rain, so check before using it. The junction (S14°10.202 E34°56.619) where you turn west is six kilometres south of the Total garage.

After about 60 kilometres you will reach the main **M5** road at either **Golomoti** or **Mua**, depending on the condition of bridges.

Mua Mission (turnoff S14°17.151 E34°31.150) is worth a visit for its ethnographic museum and wood-carving workshops, but otherwise, it is just a straight run up to **Salima** from where you can head west to **Lilongwe** or continue north along the lake (see page 126).

Passengers, livestock and supplies being transferred onto Malawi's lake ferry, the MV *Ilala*.

16

Lusaka to Mbeya
via eastern Zambia and Malawi 1 600 km

If you have the time, then this is a good alternative route to the rather tedious Great North Road through northwestern Zambia. You can visit the wonderfully isolated South Luangwa National Park before crossing into Malawi, where you can spend a lazy interlude at a lakeside resort, freshening up for the dusty safari circuits of East Africa which lie ahead.

From the circle at the northern end of Cairo Road in Lusaka, turn right and take the Great East Road out past the Manda Hill shopping centre. You'll pass the agricultural showgrounds and the trade fair grounds.

Left: Kayaking on Lake Malawi. Right: Popular all over East Africa, bao is like backgammon played with stones on a carved board.

Then the university and eventually the turnoff to the international airport. The road has a good tarred surface, but beware of corrupt transport officials trying to rip you off with false accusations of speeding. There are also dangerous bends and steep descents through the hills as you drop down the escarpment. At **Nyimba**, 340 kilometres from Lusaka, you will cross a spectacular suspension bridge. Here you can buy beautiful baskets, hats and mats at stalls along the road. Watch out for potholes from **Minga**.

The quiet, secure roadside camp of **Zulu's Kraal** (S14°17.773 E31°19.797) is reached at 408 kilometres, just the right distance to stop for the night (tel: 71217). It is situated right at the turnoff to **Petauke** and consists of small A-framed chalets ($8 double) and a grassy camp site ($3 a person). An adjoining workshop is able to do repairs to your vehicle if needed. There is also a smart BP service station close by.

The road worsens beyond here, as you pass through the pretty little town of **Sinda** (**Sinda Motel** offers rooms and camping). Cyclists, pedestrians, stray animals and crater-sized potholes keep your speed down as you pass through **Katete**.

At 126 kilometres from Zulu's Kraal you will reach the regional centre of **Chipata** (466 kilometres from Lusaka). A large town with all amenities such as banks, Shoprite supermarket and garages, this is also where you turn north to get to the South Luangwa National Park.

If you are looking for accommodation, drive through town and, nine-and-a-half kays further, turn in (S13°41.695 E32°43.029) to the **Yellow Chicken Camp**. Run by eco-friendly Steve and Cathy, they charge $4 for camping and $10 a person in attractive ethnic huts. Fresh poultry and dairy products are complemented by home-grown veggies to produce tasty, filling meals for $5.

The wilds of South Luangwa

To get to **South Luangwa National Par**k, head to the Lusaka side of Chipata and turn north at S13°37.838 E32°37.544, just west of the arch (why do so many African towns build these tatty monstrosities that only debase what they are meant to glorify?).

Although it is only about 130 kilometres to the park entrance, the road is so bad that it will take you almost three hours. It is also poorly signpost-

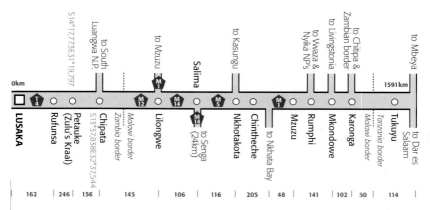

ed and easy to lose your way.

At 44 kilometres you will enjoy a short section of tar through some steep hills. At 69 kays turn sharply left (S13°18.112 E32°13.227). You'll pass a Catholic Church at 109 kilometres and get onto a tar road and T-junction at S13°12.369 E31°55.113. Left goes to **Mfuwe Airport** and right takes you straight to the bridge across the Luangwa River and into the park.

Accommodation in the park is exclusive and expensive, so most visitors stay just outside along the banks of the Luangwa River. **Flatdogs Camp** (turnoff S13°06.182 E31°47.175) has moved from the old crocodile camp and is now to the left of the bridge, just before you cross over into the park. Comfortable self-catering chalets cost $30 a person, camping under shady trees is $5 a person and kennels (small, rustic huts) or tree platforms $10 a person. There is a good bar and restaurant and gamedrives into the park are offered at $25 a person. Elephants, hippos and other game wander through the camp all the time as the river is in the front garden (e-mail: flatdogs@-campafrica.com, website: www.camp-africa.com).

To get to **The Wildlife Camp**, turn down at the sign-posted intersection (S13°06.583 E31°47.684) and drive for six kilometres. Also attractively situated on the banks of the river, they offer self-catering chalets at $20 a person and camping at $5 (tel/fax: 062-45026, e-mail: wildlife@super-hub.com or maplanga@netactive.co.za).

The old crocodile camp (turnoff right at bridge), which has re-opened

as **Crocodile Valley**, charges $12 a person in basic chalets and $3 for camping. Both of the above also offer game drives with excellent guides.

Entry into the park costs $20 a person for 24 hours plus $15 for your vehicle. There is a small network of roads that never strays too far from the river and the wildlife is quite plentiful, especially the birds.

The little town of **Mfuwe** sometimes has fuel at the BP garage, but don't bank on it. A place you should visit is **Tribal Textiles** where they design and produce unique hand-painted textiles. Watch them working and then buy a bed cover, wall hanging or table linen (e-mail: gillie@zamnet.zm, website: www.africantribalcrafts.com). Outside is the **Mango Tree Craftmarket**, selling beautifully created curios made from sustainable natural bush resources.

Crossing into Malawi

The border is about 30 kilometres east of **Chipata**, past the **Yellow Chicken Camp**. The Zambian side is rough and simple to pass through, but you then have to drive for another 13 kilometres to reach the Malawian post at **Mchinji**.

Although the formalities are handled swiftly and honestly, it costs a fair bit to bring a vehicle into Malawi. First you pay $20 road toll/tax at the weighbridge, then $1 for a temporary import permit (nothing if you have a carnet) and finally $11 for a car and $26 for a light truck for insurance (if you do not already have the Comesa cover).

The tarred road is in excellent condition and little used, so you will cover the 100-odd kilometres quickly and soon be entering the capital city of Malawi, **Lilongwe**. The city is a bit weird in that there is a perfectly good old town where everything interesting happens and then there is the 'Capital City', built specially for bureaucrats, where nothing interesting happens.

Coming in on the **M12**, you will hit the circle on **Kamuzu Procession Road** – turn right and cruise on down into the quaint little colonial centre of Lilongwe. Pass the Total garage on your left, the Nico Shopping Centre at the next traffic light and then down the hill to another circle (S13°59.363 E33°46.206). Turn right here and you'll already be leaving the city – Malawi is a small-scaled country.

To get to the best place to stay in town **Kiboko Camp**, pass the golf club (camping in the pleasant grounds costs $5 a person), at the next circle, turn left and you will see Kiboko on the corner. It's run by a well-travelled Dutch couple. Dorms cost $5 a person, chalets $12 a person and camping $3. It's safe, secure and your hosts have plenty of free advice and info on the country. Tel: 01-82-8384, fax: 01-75-4978, e-mail: kiboko@malawi.net, website: www.kiboko-safaris.com.

Just above the post office in Mandala Road is the recently refurbished **Imperial Hotel**. This old 1940s establishment offers smart, central accommodation ranging between $25/$40 single/double to $50/$80 for self-contained rooms. The vibey Harry's Bar beckons below for drinks and food (e-mail: imperial@malawi.net).

Lee's Forex Bureau in the Nico Mall will change money for you; you will also find a couple of pharmacies in the mall. Tyres, exhausts and motor spares are available in the industrial area behind the mall and agents for Toyota, Nissan and Land Rover are all nearby. The best shop to restock is Shoprite supermarket, next to the mall. You can buy all your curios in front of the post office.

Off to laze at the lake

Head out on the **M1** and turn off (S13°54.065 E33°47.481) onto the M14 to **Salima**, 106 kilometres away. Drive through Salima (watch out for the many bicycle taxis pedalling to and fro with passengers on their carriers) and another 22 kays to the end of the road in **Senga Bay**. You drive straight through the gates of the classy **Livingstonia Beach Hotel** – rather expensive at about $150 a person, tel: 01-26-3222, fax: 01-26-3452, e-mail: livingstonia@lemeridienmalawi.co.mw – but next door is the beautifully situated **Steps Camp Site**. Good facilities, grass, trees and an inviting beach make this one of the nicest camp sites in Malawi and it costs only $4 a person (contact the Livingstonia Beach hotel). The nearby **Red Zebra Café** is a good place to eat, with main meals costing about $3,50.

To follow the lake north, drive back to Salima and turn up (S13°45.556 E34°23.346) onto the tarred **M5** – it's 116 kilometres to **Nkhotakota**. Fifteen kilometres south of the town is the well-signposted turnoff (S13°02.972 E34°17.783) to **Nkhotakota Potteries**. They produce some very attractive pottery which is sold at their gift shop. You

Be very careful where you decide to take a swim – crocodiles are ubiquitous.

can enjoy a full breakfast or three-course dinner in the spotless little restaurant for around $4,50 and even stay in one of their self-contained rooms for $10 a person. If you are interested in attending an all-inclusive weekend pottery course, they offer two nights accommodation, all meals, tuition and use of the workshop, as well as a session with local village potters making traditional pots for only $60. Tel: 01-29-2444, fax: 01-22-3131.

The coast between Nkhotakota and **Nkhata Bay** has some of the most attractive beaches and comfortable accommodation on Lake Malawi, but make sure that the road is open – sometimes the bridge across the **Dwambazi River** washes away, making this route impassable.

The first resort you reach is the upmarket **Ngala Beach**. This beautiful lodge is popular with honeymooners and charges $35 a person in luxury chalets, inclusive of breakfast (e-mail: ngala@malawi.net, website: www.nga-labeachlodge.co.za). The next place north is the backpacker's and overlander's haven of **Kande Beach** (S11°56.197 E34°06.649), 42 kilometres beyond the Dwambazi River bridge. There is lots to do, with boats, sailboards and snorkelling equipment for hire as well as a Padi diving school on the premises and horse riding stables nearby. With a busy bar and restaurant, twin-bedded beach huts for $11, dorm beds for $4 and camping at $2 a person, it is no wonder most travellers stop in here (tel: 01-35-7376, e-mail: kandebeach@hotmail.com, website: www.kandebeach.com).

There are two wonderful little lodges between Kande and Chintheche, each with their own private beaches. The first is Tony and Denise Jackson's **Makuzi Beach** which charges $18/$28 single/double in rooms, $42/$68 in en-suite chalets (all inclusive of breakfast) and $3,60 a person for camping (tel/fax: 01-35-7296, e-mail: makuzibeach@-sdnp.org.mw). The next piece of paradise is **Nkhwazi Beach**, just two kays up the road and another two down to the water's edge. Run by the hospitable Jim and Elsje Davidson, the attractively decorated chalets sleep four and cost $27, while grassed and shady camp sites are only $2,50 a person (satellite tel: 0871-76265-8745).

The last accommodation before the road swings inland is the upmarket **Chintheche Inn**. It has a swimming pool and tennis court and charges $55/$80 for comfortable self-contained rooms inclusive of a hearty breakfast, and only $5 a person for the best camp site in Malawi. Bookings and enquiries through Central African Wilderness Safaris in Lilongwe, tel: 77-1153, fax: 77-1397, e-mail: info@wilderness.-malawi.net, website: www.wilderness-safaris.com.

After swinging inland, you will reach an intersection (S11°36.607 E34°16.118) where you have the choice of turning right down to **Nkhata Bay** or left up to **Mzuzu**. Nkhata Bay was once on every traveller's itinerary, but is now a bit of a backwater. There is a pretty little harbour where the lake ferry puts in, a good diving school too, and I'm told the space cake is still cooking, but the buzz has gone. **Big Blue**, run by Bryn Evans, is an old favourite on the corner as you arrive in town. They charge $4 a person in quaint wooden huts built over the water on stilts, $3 in dorms and $1,50 a person camping. Security is good (important in Nkata Bay), tel: 35-2370, e-mail: bigblue@sdnp.org.mw.

The new hotspot is **Mayoka Village**, situated on a steep slope on the other side of **Ilala Bay**. The attractive bar and restaurant is right on the water's edge and serves some great steak, fish, baguette and even real humus and freshly squeezed fruit juice.

Accommodation is cheap at $2,50 in a chalet and $1 a person for camping (contact them through caredotcom@-sdnp.org.mw for attention Mayoka Village). There are a couple of small supermarkets in town, but nowhere to change money.

Heading out from Nkhata Bay

There is no good road further up the coast from Nkhata Bay, so head back inland. **Mzuzu**, 48 kilometres up the road, is the regional centre and has a forex bureau in the main street as well as most other amenities. Rejoin the tarred **M1** (S11°27.619 E34°00.867) and hurry on through the highland forests, passing the turnoff to **Rumphi**.

With so many other great game parks to come, I really can't recommend turning off here to visit **Vwaza** and **Nyika** national parks (also note that it is not feasible to drive through these parks and out the other side, only there and back).

The road drops down to the lake again at **Chiweta**. Be careful around here, they are rebuilding the road and you will encounter deviations which can cause you to miss turnoffs. The turn-off for **Chitimba Beach Camp Site** (S10°35.034 E34°10.174) is just past Chiweta and leads to an attractive lakeside camp with double reed huts for $10, dorm beds for $3 and camping at $2 a person. They serve meals and drinks at the beach bar and offer 4x4 trips up to the mission station of Livingstonia.

I would fully recommend the excursion up to Livingstonia Mission if you have a 4x4. The narrow, steep track up the escarpment is a series of switchback bends that gains over 700 metres in height in 16 kilometres.

As you slog up this Rift Valley pass, you are rewarded with fabulous views of the lake and eventually the spectacle of a Victorian village in the middle of the African bush. The stone buildings, all more than a hundred years old, house a school, hospital, college, clock tower and impressive church. The atmospheric old Stone House was built as the residence of Dr Robert Laws and is now accommodation for visitors ($3 a person and a plate of food, $2, (S10°36.708 E34°06.790). Visit the museum in the same building.

Karonga is the most northerly town along the M1 and has been in the limelight after an important find of the virtually intact 12-metre skeleton of a dinosaur said to be 100 million years old. Subsequent digging unearthed the 2,5-million-year-old jaw of an early hominid. A new museum, situated opposite the town assembly, will house these important finds. There is also the interesting history of First World War battles between the English and Germans around the town.

The nicest place to stay is at **Club Marina** on the lakeshore ($8/$12 single/double, tel: 36-2391). Next door is the more basic **Mufwa Lake Centre** which charges $6 for a self-contained double and offers camping at $3 a person. Between the two, under a tree at the edge of the lake, you should find someone selling fine pottery that has

A dugout canoe is sometimes the only way available to cross a river in Africa.

been transported across the lake from the renowned pottery community of Matema Beach in Tanzania.

Unless you want to head back into Zambia, don't take the M26 road up to the border at Chitipa – they are improving it, but it is still very bad. Stay on the M1 and head north out of Karonga for 50 kilometres to the Tanzanian border where the formalities will be similar to those at the Tunduma border post (see page 132). There remains 132 kilometres of mostly tar to the Tanzanian town of **Mbeya** where you join the main road (**A104**) which takes you all the way up to **Dar es Salaam** (see page 134).

Lusaka to Nairobi

17

via the Great North Road, Dar es Salaam and Arusha 2 900 km

The easy, uncrowded and fast Great North Road allows you to really eat up the kilometres on the first part of this section. Kundalila Falls and the interesting Shiwa Ngandu Estate, with its therapeutic hot springs, keep you entertained in Zambia, before you pass into Tanzania where Zanzibar, Mount Kilimanjaro and great game resources make the rest of this route a must.

Driving out of Lusaka along Cairo Road, one can't help but feel a sense of purpose – this is the Great North Road (T2). It's sad to see the devastation of the forests and the truckloads of charcoal heading for the city.

Above: The bush telephone – a woodland kingfisher. Left: You can shop right at Shop Left in Isoka, northern Zambia. Opposite: Ornately carved and studded doors are a feature of the narrow alleys of Stone Town, Zanzibar.

So rather focus on the productive farmlands around Fringilla's and the Ploughman's Arms. The road is good tar with only a few bumps and road-works between Kabwe and Kapiri Mposhi. You might be stopped at road-blocks on the Great North Road, but will glide through with a few pleas-antries if you are wearing your seat-belt, can show your insurance and have emergency triangles. Fuel is avail-able all the way to Tanzania – but cheaper across the border.

At **Kapiri Mposhi**, 180 kilometres from Lusaka, the T2 turns east at S13°55.528 E28°40.004 and improves.

Beyond **Mkushi**, at S13°33.102 E29°39.559 is **Sweet Waters Guest House** (turn off left), run by Vernon Cantlay. It costs $18/$23 single/double and $2 a person camping.

Fuel is available at **Serenje** and about 60 kilometres beyond, at S13°04.207 E30°38.050, there is the signposted turn-off to **Kundalila Falls**. Drive 14 kilometres down a good dirt road to the car park where Samuel will rush to meet you on his bicycle. He charges you an official $3 to view the falls and $10 a person to camp – exor-bitant he agrees, but he's trying to get it reduced by the department in Lusaka.

Take the rickety bridge across the river to view the falls from above – very impressive as they tumble 65 metres down the escarpment – but be careful, as the path is dangerous and slippery. A path to the left leads down to the beau-tiful pool below, ideal for swimming in.

Carry on for 89 kilometres past Mpika to the turnoff left to **Shiwa Ngandu Estate** at S11°13.329 E31°49.575. From the quaint old red-bricked office, an impressive avenue of trees leads up to the imposing old English manor house surrounded by beautiful gardens. Named after the Lake of the Royal Crocodile, it still has its original furni-ture. The guided tour is well worth it.

Away from the main house is the rustic but comfortable **Kapishya Lodge**, pricey at $100 a person sharing with full board. The real reason for visiting the estate, however, is the idyllically-situated **hot water spring** and adjoin-ing camp site ($5 a person). Nothing beats an early morning dip in this wonderfully warm, clear pool sur-rounded by the indigenous bush.

Into Tanzania

Travel another 290 kilometres along the T2 to reach the Tanzanian border at **Tunduma**. The Zambian formalities

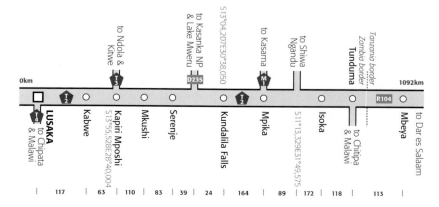

TANZANIA

Capital: Dodoma

Official languages:
English and Kiswahili

Area: 945 200 square kilometres

Population: 30 million

Visa requirements: Required by all

Time: UT +3

International dialling code: +255

Currency and rate:
Tanzanian Shilling TS900=$1

Climate: Hot and humid on coast; pleasant inland. Rains April, May and November

Highlights: Mount Kilimanjaro, Zanzibar and great game parks such as Ngorongoro and Serengeti

Driving: On the left. Main tarred roads are okay, others are poor

Accommodation: Backpackers and camp sites along all major routes, hotels (from cheap to luxury) in the main cities, and camp sites and lodges in the game parks

Food, shops and fuel: Spicy local dishes in restaurants, a few supermarkets and good fuel availability

Tourism info: Tanzania Tourist Board, tel: 022-211-3145, fax: 022-211-6420, email: md@ttb.ud.or.tz, website: www.tanzania-web.com

---

are swift and painless, but the Tanzanian side is chaotic and unpleasant. In addition to the normal custom and immigration requirements, you will have to pay $5 road tax, $20 for a temporary import permit and more insurance for the vehicle if your existing has expired or invalid.

Fuel is cheaper in Tanzania than in Zambia, but rather fill up in the relative calm of **Mbeya**, 113 kilometres along the **A7**, if you have enough fuel to get you there.

Accommodation in Mbeya includes the basic, but comfortable **Holiday Lodge**, which charges $9 for a self-contained double (tel: 065-2821), the more upmarket **Rift Valley Hotel** ($13/$16 single/double, tel 065-4429), and the **Mbeya Green View Inn and Camp Site** ($7/$12 single/double and $5 a site for camping). They are all in town and close to the intersection at S8°53.735 E33°26.892.

A far better place to stay, although a full 328 kilometres from Mbeya, is **Kisolanza Farm** (S8°08.348 E35°24.550) which has been in the Ghaui family for over 60 years. Situated between **Mafinga** and **Ifunda**, in the healthy **Southern Highlands**, the charming farmhouse and guest cottages are set in gardens, just off the main **A7** road. Clean, neat and very eco-friendly, they also have a camp site. Fresh vegetables, flowers and meat can be purchased at the farm stall. Camping costs $3 a person, bandas $15 double, and larger chalets are $50 a person for dinner, bed and breakfast. Contact Nicola Ghaui, e-mail kisolanza@bushlink.co.tz, website: www.kisolanza.com.

Passing **Iringa**, and the turnoff to the **Ruaha National Park**, another 12 kilometres takes you to **Riverside Camp** (S7°47.399 E35°47.779). Camping is $3 a person.

Continuing along the A7, the steep road down the escarpment is so well used by overloaded trucks, that the tarred surface has formed ruts deep enough to need a high clearance vehicle.

At about 135 kilometres past Iringa, you cross the **Ruaha River**. 16 kilometres past the bridge, is the turnoff to **Baobab Valley Camp** (S7°31.242 E36°35.874). Attractively situated on the banks of the Great Ruaha River in a valley thick with baobabs, the camp has a pool, bar and restaurant and offers accommodation in bandas ($40, sleeps three) or camping ($3,50 a person). Surrounded by national parks, they also offer three-day hikes into the mountains – speak to Darren Coetzee.

The road to **Morogoro** continues through deep gorges cut through mountains covered with baobab trees and then through the middle of the **Mikumi National Park**. Quite good sightings of game can be had, but watch out for the vicious speed humps. With the exception of upmarket lodges, the only accommodation is at the very basic community-run **Malela Camp** (S6°58.332 E37°16.881), which

costs $2,50 a person. Beyond Morogoro the road is being rebuilt, which means many rough deviations.

You enter **Dar es Salaam** along a wide double road which leads straight into the city centre. Dar es Salaam is of interest only for catching the ferry across to **Zanzibar**.

The best budget accommodation is near to the **Kisutu Bus Station**. **Jambo Inn** (tel: 051-11-4293, fax 051-11-3149) is on Libya Street and **Safari Hotel** (tel: 051-11-9104, fax: 051-11-6550) is close by, just off Libya Street. Self-contained rooms cost $11/$17 single/double. Air-conditioned rooms are a bit more and there is a good restaurant on the ground floor of Jambo Inn. Secure parking, however, is limited – especially if you want to leave your vehicle while across in Zanzibar.

Camping, and a place to store your vehicle while in Zanzibar, is available at **Silversands** (tel: 051-65-0231, fax: 051-65-0428, e-mail: silversands@africaonline.co.tz). Situated about an hour's drive up the crowded north coast road at **Kunduchi Beach**, it is grubby, crowded, difficult to find (first turnoff at S6°41.302 E39°12.225) and charges $3 a person.

In Dar you can rent a car or 4x4 at

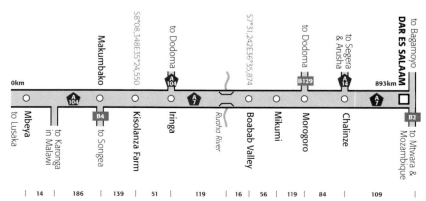

Avis, tel: 211-5381, e-mail: operations@skylinktanzania.com, website: www.skylinktanzania.com. To buy, sell or repair a vehicle, visit **DT Dobie & Co**, tel: 022-211-0704, fax: 022-286-5129, e-mail: dtdobie@twiga.com. The Land Rover dealer in Dar is **CMC Land Rover** in Maktaba Street, tel: 022-211-6398, fax: 022-211-3273, e-mail: antony@cmclandrover-tz.com

Sailing to Zanzibar

To reach Zanzibar by boat, it is best to go down to the port at Dar and enquire directly at the ferry offices there. Crossings cost about $30 to $40 depending on the speed of the boat (an average crossing takes about three hours) and are cheaper at night ($18). Hustlers will have attractive offers – avoid them and buy your ticket from the ferry office or tour operator recommended by your hotel or camp.

Zanzibar is a separate state within Tanzania and requires all visitors to have a passport and go through the formalities of customs and immigration. There is a very good tourist information service next door to the immigration office in Zanzibar port (tel: 024-23-3485, e-mail: zanzibartourism@zanzibartourism.net, website: www.zanzibartourism.net).

You will be hassled mercilessly by taxi drivers and, if you have made your choice of hotels, it is probably best to share a taxi with others wanting to go the same way – it will cost fractionally more than $1.

Walking through Stone Town for the first time is confusing and, with luggage, quite daunting. Addresses and communications are difficult and you will need a few days to really start finding your way around.

There is a large variety of accommodation available in Stone Town (the narrow-streeted maze that lies directly south of the harbour) from the magnificent **Serena Hotel** at $130 a person (tel: 024-223-1015) to backpackers joints at $7. I would recommend you try the **Jambo Inn** (tel: 024-223-3779) or **Florida Guesthouse** both of which are towards the southern end of town, near Vuga Road. They both charge about $12 a person sharing facilities, and have fans and mosquito nets.

For the adventurous, try eating at one of the many small local restaurants around town – a selection of small dishes to make up a filling dinner will cost less than $2. Another interesting option for food is to stroll around **Forodhani Gardens** in the evenings. Situated on the seafront opposite the **Arab Fort**, the place comes alive at night as stall owners prepare and sell tasty snacks of chipatis, kebabs of meat, prawns, tuna and calamari and freshly squeezed fruit juices. All you can eat for less than $5. The famous **Blues Restaurant** is there too. Built on a jetty over the water, this upmarket place is perfect for a sundowner and meal, with pizzas and seafood starting at around $10. Another great place to watch the sunset from is the roof-top bar at the **Africa House Hotel** (tel: 054-30708).

Wandering around Stone Town you will find the old Arab Fort, the Sultan's Palace next door and the bustling covered market. Spend some time hanging around the dhow harbour to the right as you enter the port gates. There is always activity, as cargoes and sails are manhandled and boats come and go according to the tides.

A spice tour is a 'must'. Everyone will offer you one, and they're all pretty good, but if you want to be sure, then join **Mr Mitu's Tours** which leave every morning from in front of the **Cine Afrique**, just outside the dock gates. You will be shown the amazing variety of plants and spices that grow on the island as well as some of the old historical ruins. The tour will end with a tasty meal incorporating many of these spices – all for $10 to $15, depending on how well you bargain.

Hotels will also be able to arrange the hire of a motor bike or scooter for around $15 to $20 a day if you want to explore the island .

If you don't get further out of Stone Town than on a spice tour, don't worry, the rest of the island is nothing to rave about. If you want to dive, then rather head north to Pemba Island.

Although most people refer to the island as Zanzibar, this is the name of the town, not the island, which is called Unguja.

To Zanzibar by dhow

There is another way to get to Zanzibar, and much more exciting and adventurous. Other guide books will tell you that it is dangerous and illegal, but a local dhow trip from **Bagamoyo** across to Zanzibar could just be the highlight of your trip (it will cost about $12, one way).

Take the north coast road from Dar es Salaam past Kundichi for 72 kilometres to Bagamoyo. Stay at the **Travellers Lodge**, where comfortable self-contained cottages right on the beach cost $35/$40 single/double including breakfast, and camping is only $3 a person (tel: 023-244-0077, mobile: 0744-85-5485, e-mail: travellers@baganet.com). There is a bar and restaurant overlooking the pretty gardens and sea and, most importantly, the staff are very helpful in finding dhows going across to Zanzibar.

The town is awash with history as it was the main port along this coast. Slaves, ivory and expeditions of discovery into the interior passed through here, as it is the closest point on the mainland to Zanzibar. The buildings are fascinating and crying out for restoration, but the attitude of the

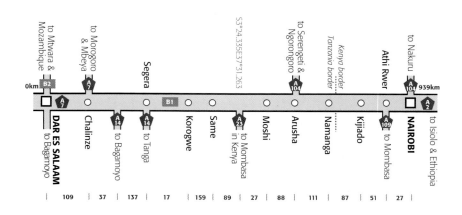

town's inhabitants is unfriendly, so tread lightly. The beach is particularly interesting and busy in the early morning with fishermen bringing in their catches to barter with the townsfolk.

When you've managed to organise a dhow, you will be told to be on the beach before low tide. While cargo is being carried out over the sand to the high-and-dry dhow, you will present your passport to the officer at the customs house. As the tide starts rising, passengers wade out, board and then wait for the boat to float off. This could happen in the middle of the night in pitch darkness – a very emotive experience. Hope for fair winds and the crossing could take as little as three hours.

It is best to arrange with the skipper for a return trip. Usually the dhow's turnaround time can be stretched to three or four days, so set a day and time to meet in the harbour for the return trip to the mainland.

The road to Kili and Kenya

If you've been staying in Dar, retrace your route back along the A7 for 110 kilometres to the turnoff north onto the **A14** at **Chalinze**. From Bagamoyo take the rough dirt road (avoid after heavy rain) directly inland (starts at a T-junction S6°26.539 E38°23.384), which runs for 64 kilometres to the A14 at **Msata** (S6°19.997 S38°23.384).

The road north is hectic with manic busses and corrupt traffic officials wielding radar speed-trapping devices that look suspiciously like hair driers. Before you reach **Segera**, there is a turnoff down to **Pangani** on the coast (about 70 kilometres). With a history

older than that of Bagamoyo, Pangani is a good place to soak up Swahili history and relax on the beach – let Jilly and Dennis Roberts of **Camp Paponi** look after you.

The junction town of Segera has a large truckstop with clean rest rooms and a traditionally clad Masai tribesman to clean your windscreen. There is also the **Segera Highway Motel** with a restaurant, rooms for $13/$19 single/double and camping for $4 a person, tel: 027-264-0815.

The good tarred surface continues as you turn north-west onto the **B1** and head for **Moshi** and **Arusha**. The road runs through little towns that are a haven for speed trapping cops, as the speed limits drop down to as low as 30 kilometres an hour sometimes. If caught, you can negotiate a 'discount' (usually half) for payment without an official receipt.

Turn left (west) at **Marangu junction** (S3°24.335 E37°31.263) and head for **Moshi** – hopefully, the sky will be clear and reward you with a view of **Kilimanjaro**. If you plan on climbing Africa's highest mountain, stay over in Moshi to organise things.

For accommodation try the area around Mawenzi Road where the **New Kindoroko Hotel** charges $8/$10 single/double with communal facilities and $10/$20 single/double for self-contained rooms, tel: 027-54054. **The Coffee Tree Hotel** is very centrally situated near the clock tower and is good value at $5 double (sharing facilities) and $7/$10 single/double (self-contained). Camping is available for $3 a person at the **Golden Shower Res-**

taurant out on the Marangu Road.

It is cheaper to arrange a Kili climb in Moshi than to pre-book one; an all-inclusive five-day trip along the Marangu route should cost $600 to $700 a person. You will be offered cheaper climbs, but be careful, not all operators are reputable. Try **Trans-Kibo Travels**, tel: 055-52017, fax: 055-54219, e-mail: transkibo@habari.co.tz or **Zara International**, tel: 055-54240; fax: 055-53105, e-mail: zara@form-net.co.

Arusha, the safari capital of East-Africa, is 88 kilometres east of Moshi and quite a large, bustling town. It is from here that you stock up for your visit to the game parks or organise a safari if you don't have your own wheels (see page 142).

It is also exactly halfway between Cape Town and Cairo and a fine place to celebrate with a few cold ones. Tanzania has a selection of at least 10 brands of beer, but be careful of the bottled Guinness – half a litre of beer at 7,5 per cent alcohol sure can kick!

If you have decided to skip the game parks to the west of Arusha or you have returned having already visited them, then your way north is the **A104**. Turn north just outside Arusha and drive 111 kilometres to the Kenyan border at

Namanga. Passing through this reasonably hassle-free post; Nairobi is 195 kilometres up a good tarred road.

What to do in Nairobi

Nairobi is a large city where you can stock up, fix up and live it up. But you can also be held up and roughed up, so be careful.

The most central camp site in Nairobi is the **Upper Hill Camp Site** situated in suburban Menegai Road (near Kenyatta National Hospital), S1°18.012 E36°48.703, tel: 02-272-0290, e-mail: upperhillcamp@africaonline.-co.ke, website: www.oja-services.nl/-kenya/. Camping is $3,50 a person, dorms $4 and double rooms $11. There is good security and parking.

Another option, a little way out of town, is the **Nairobi Park Services Camp Site** (S1°21.345 E36°45.718). Head along Uhuru Highway, past Wilson Airport (for local flights) and the Carnivore Restaurant, then turn off towards **Nairobi National Park** on the Langata Road. Situated next to a Mobil service station, it offers camping at $3 a person, dorms for $6 and double rooms cost $15. A popular pub and restaurant, as well as information and bookings for travel around the region, make this spot popular with overlanders and backpackers. Brendan Black is your host, tel: 02-89-0661, fax: 02-89-0325, e-mail: nps@swiftkenya.com.

There are many basic and cheap hotels in the Latema Road and Dubois Street area in dodgy, dangerous central Nairobi. The Iqbal (tel: 02-22-0914), Dolat (tel: 02-22-2797) or Danika hotels are worth a try and are cheap

---

Tips on Kilimanjaro

Go slow. Follow your guide's advice. Drink at least three litres of water a day. Keep a supply of energy food (chocolate) for the last day. Clothing left outside at night will freeze solid. Keep personal pack with valuables, water and snacks with you at all times.

KENYA

Capital: Nairobi

Official languages:
English and Kiswahili

Area: 582 650 square kilometres

Population: 28 million

Visa requirements: Required by almost all nationalities

Time: UT +3

International dialling code: +254

Currency and rate:
Kenyan Shilling KS78=$1

Climate: Tropical on coast, pleasant and mild inland. Rains from March to June and November to December

Highlights: Gameviewing in the Masai Mara Game Reserve and others, and climbing Mount Kenya

Driving: On the left. Good tarred main roads, quite well maintained. The gravel road north to Ethiopia is bad

Food, shops and fuel: Lots of meat in restaurants, also tasty chipatis. Nairobi has good shops and supermarkets. Obtaining fuel is a problem only for the long distances north

Accommodation: A wide variety to suit all tastes and budgets, but fewer camp sites than further down south

Tourism information: The best Kenya National Tourist Office is in Pretoria, tel: 012-362-2249, fax: 012-362-2252, website: www.kenyaweb.com

---

enough at $5 to $10 a person. Nairobi's most famous restaurant, **The Carnivore** (tel: 02-50-1709) is out on the Uhuru Highway, just past Wilson Airport. It's renowned for its all-you-can-eat $15 meat buffet, which includes a wide selection of game meat. The waiters will keep bringing more until you raise the little flag on your table as a sign of capitulation. More moderately priced dishes, including vegetarian meals, are available at the adjoining **Simba Grill**. With a bar and disco thrown in for less gluttonous good times, it's well worth an evening out.

The two big supermarket chains, Nakumatt and Uchumi, have branches all over town. The **Nakumatt Mega** is next-door to Toyota at the Lusaka Road circle on the way out to the interna-

tional airport and the **Uchumi Hyper** is just past Wilson airport and near to the Carnivore restaurant. Both stock a large range of goods and are ideal places to stock up for the imminent rigors of northern Kenya.

Land Rovers are looked after by **CMC Motors** in Lusaka Street (tel: 65-0235, fax: 53-6260, e-mail: lrservice@cmcmotors.com, website: www.cmcmotors.com). The Toyota agency is on the corner nearby and Mitsubishi on the left on the way out to the international airport.

Nairobi is a good place to get your **visa for Ethiopia**. The efficient and friendly embassy is situated in State House Avenue, tel: 02-72-3035, fax: 02-72-3401, and will issue one within 24 hours.

18

Arusha to Nairobi

via the safari route through Ngorongoro Crater,
Serengeti Game Reserve and the Masai Mara
Game Reserve 550 km

The safari route takes in the three best and most well-
known game parks in East Africa, which everyone
should try to visit. Lake Victoria is also en route. The
roads are poor and a 4x4 is essential, but this only
heightens the pleasure of visiting such wild, unspoilt
places. Long may the authorities keep the roads bad.

In Arusha, camp at the Masai Camp (S3°23.111
E36°43.205) two kilometres down the Old Moshi Road.

Right: Masai warriors
guarding their herds
on the rim of the
Ngorongoro Crater.
Below: The great
annual wildebeest
migration between
the Serengeti and
Masai Mara crosses
the Mara River.

It has good security, and a bar and restaurant that serves pizzas for $3, a burger and chips for $3,50 and beers at just over $1. Camping costs $3 a person and rooms $7 a person.

There are many local guesthouses around Levolosi Road behind the stadium, all offering basic accommodation for about $5. Your best option in the centre of Arusha is the Naaz Hotel near the clock tower where a self-contained double will set you back $25 (tel: 057-2087).

I will not attempt to recommend or list tour companies running safaris into the game parks of Tanzania – there are too many. Ask fellow travellers for recent recommendations or shop around, comparing prices and reputations. Your best plan is to visit only the two main parks, Ngorongoro and Serengeti, over a period of about five days. This will cost about $80 a person a day, four up in a Land Rover. If this sounds a lot, then remember that it covers everything including the costly park fees.

But anyway, you have your own vehicle, so head down Sokoine Road, past the Land Rover dealer (the Toyota dealer is in town, near to the clock tower) to the huge new Shoprite supermarket (S3°22.511 E36°40.744) to stock up. Keep heading west along Sokoine Road until you leave Arusha and pass through coffee plantations.

After 80 kilometres of reasonable tar, you will reach the turnoff to **Manyare** and **Ngorongoro** at S3°32.969 E36°06.071. A fine new tarred road whisks you along until deviations and construction slow you down closer to **Mto Wa Mbu**.

It is tempting to stay at the comfortable and friendly **Twiga Camp Site and Lodge** as it has an internet cafe, shop and shady trees (tel: 27-253-9101, e-mail: twigacampsite@hotmail.com). Camping is $5 a person, self-contained double rooms $25. They also rent out Land Rovers with driver for daytrips to Ngorongoro at $120 a day.

If you take the 26 kilometre, rough dirt road up the escarpment as far as **Karatu**, this leaves you only 15 kilometres to the park gate the next morning. The **Safari Junction** camp site is your best bet in Karatu (turn left at S3°20.343 E35°40.069 on your way out of town) and charges $5 a person for camping and $15 for a double room. The nearby **B&M Camp** is similar and the more upmarket **Ngorongoro Safari Resort** in town charges only $5 to

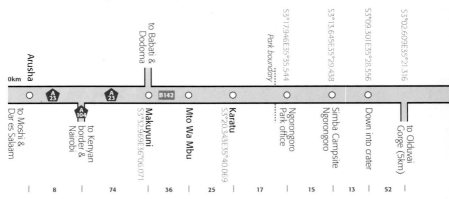

camp, but a hefty $65 a person bed and breakfast in a self-contained room. They also offer day trips into the crater in a Land Rover with a driver for $150 (takes up to six people, plus you pay your own $30 park fee).

Into Ngorongoro Crater

Wherever you overnight, you do not want to enter **Ngorongoro** (tel: 027-253-7019, fax: 027-253-7007, e-mail: ncaa-info@cybernet.co.tz, website: www.ngorongoro-crater-africa.org) much before 11h00, as your fees cover a 24-hour period from time of entry and you will want time to exit the park on your last day (this applies to Serengeti too).

Fill your fuel tanks at Karatu, as this is the last chance you will get for a while, and drive the 15 kilometres to the park gate (S3°17.946 E35°35.544).

You will be pleasantly attended to and charged the following fees: $30 a person for each 24 hour period ($5 under 16 years and free under 5), $30 a vehicle a day, $20 a person camping a night ($5 under 16 and free under 5) and $15 to drive your vehicle down into the crater. This adds up to a hefty $145 a day for two people in their own foreign-registered vehicle. Only 4x4

vehicles are allowed down into the crater and large trucks are banned from the park.

With your wallet still steaming from all the action, head into the park and drive through cool forests, up the crater rim to a viewpoint on the edge. The view of the entire crater encircled by a steep rim, with animals grazing on the plains, is quite breathtaking.

The park consists of a very basic camp site (S3°13.645 E35°29.438) and expensive lodges up on the rim, a rough, steep 'down' road (S3°09.301 E35°28.556) into the crater and an equally rough and steep 'up' road (S3°13.751 E35° 31.375) back out.

Masai live in the park and are allowed to graze their cattle there – the sight of a lone, red-blanketed herds-man leaning on his spear fits beautiful-ly into the park scenery.

You shouldn't get lost in the crater if you keep orienteering yourself with the up road, so meander around. There are waterholes, streams and a forest as well as a picnic area (S3°12.628 E35°36.052) where you can stop and use the toilet.

About 30 kilometres from Ngorongoro Crater, on the way to Serengeti, is the turnoff (S3°02.609 E35°21.316) to **Olduvai Gorge**. Drive five kilometres

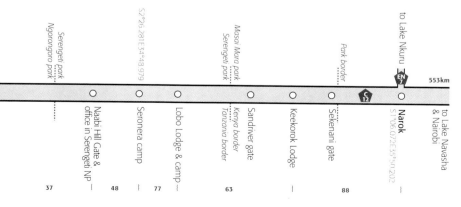

down to the viewsite where there is an interesting museum depicting the work done in the area and some of the ancient remains of early hominids found there (entry fee $3,50).

Into the Serengeti

The entrance gate to the **Serengeti National Park** is at **Naabi Hill** (S2°49.929 E34°59.888). The fees are the same as Ngorongoro, except that there is no crater fee to pay. **Seronera's Dik Dik Camp Site** (S2°25.277 E34°50.986) is 48 kilometres further on and, like the camp site Ngorongoro, does not even have a shower – for what you're paying, you'd expect a little more comfort. But, you're here to see the game, not wash. So, head out to an area called **Masai Kopjes**, where you're likely to see lion, leopard and cheetah.

There seems to be some confusion as to whether you can cross directly from Serengeti into Masai Mara in Kenya. The answer is "yes, you can" but I have never met anyone who has done it. Drive the 75 kilometres north to **Lobo Lodge** where there is a basic camp site and from there head up to the border at the **Sand River Gate**. The gate seems very low-key, but the necessary officials are there.

An alternative, especially if you want to visit Lake Victoria, is to exit the park in the west through **Ndabaka Gate**. The road to the gate from **Seronera** is difficult to find – take the road going north (across the bridge at the dam, don't turn left, keep straight) towards Lobo Lodge and at eight kilometres out of Seronera (S2°23.892 E34°48.655) turn left at a signpost to Serena Lodge

and Kirawira Camp. This section of the park is rather dull. Don't be tempted to turn left at about 105 kilometres, keep going until, at 145 kilometres from Seronera, you will reach Ndabaka Gate.

Once out of the park, head south for about 15 kilometres to the very smart and well-run **Speke Lodge** on the shores of **Lake Victoria**. Run by Jan and Melanie, it offers camping at $10 a person, furnished tents on a bed-and-breakfast basis for $25/$35 single/double and self-contained B&B bungalows on the water's edge for $65/$80 single/double (tel: 028-262-1236, fax: 028-262-1237, e-mail: spekebay@africaonline.co.tz, website: www.spekebay.com). There is a bar and restaurant and the camp's ablution block and filtered water is the best in East Africa.

Cheaper accommodation is available at the nearby **Serengeti Stop-over**. This locally run bar and restaurant offers camping at $5 a person and self-contained bungalows at $30/$40 single/double.

Kenya and the Masai Mara

From Speke Bay Lodge the **B6** is a good tarred road north, passing **Musoma** and **Tarime**, to the Kenyan border at **Isabania**. Fuel is difficult to find as you approach the border as it is cheaper across in the town of **Migori**.

Leaving Tanzania, you will have to produce your receipts for road tax and the vehicle's temporary import permit, both of which you bought at the border coming in. Immigration into Kenya is quick and easy, but you will have to pay for a Foreign Vehicle Authorisation Permit ($20 for engines of a capacity up to 2 000cc and $40 for above that), even if you have a carnet.

Refuel and change money in Migori (25 kilometres from border) and then double back to a turnoff just four kilometres south of town (S1°05.670 E34°27.373) signposted to **Kehancha**. This narrow, rough **C13** road will take you to the **Masai Mara Game Reserve** (e-mail: mara@triad.co.ke). At 28 kilometres from Migori there is a gate from where the road becomes a single 4x4 dirt track; at 39 kilometres (S1°12.216 E34°42.669) there is a bridge which is prone to washaways and at 53 kilometres you will reach the little village of **Lolgorien** (S1°13.680 E34°48.526). Turn south here (still on C13) and travel 35 kilometres to the **Oloololo Gate** (S1°15.520 E34°59.852).

Masai Mara Game Reserve fees are $27 a person, $6,50 a vehicle and $8 a person camping. This adds up to $76,50 for two people in their own vehicle for every 24 hours in the park.

Wildebeest congregate in herds of up to 10 000 in the Serengeti in April and May to migrate up into the Masai Mara during May and June. In October and November the process is reversed as they all head south again. The best viewing sites are along the Mara River where the wildebeest must run the gauntlet of huge crocodiles as they swim across. The park is not large and can be explored in a day.

The best camp site (S1°24.056 E35°01.143) is in the centre of the park, near to the ranger's headquarters and Mara Serena Lodge. Quite hidden off the road in a little thicket of trees, it has firewood and canvas toilets.

If you are planning on heading south into the Serengeti, then drive to the **Sand River Gate**. There is a camp site there and the officials on duty claim to be able to process you through. To continue north, exit through **Sekani Gate** and get onto the **C12**. This road is bad gravel which becomes bad tar (the **B3**) at **Narok** (S1°06.072 E35°50.202) and eventually joins the grand new **A104** highway which leads into Nairobi.

Not yet up to Nairobi?

If you are not yet ready for the chaos which is Nairobi, turn left before the **A104** and head north-west to **Elsemere** on **Lake Naivasha**. Three comfortable camps dot the shoreline. The first is **Crayfish Camp**, set among the hothouse of huge export rose farms, tel: 0311-20239. The second is **Fisherman Camp**, 17 kilometres from the turnoff and boasting shady, grassed sites, tel: 0311-30088.

The third is the nicest, **Fish Eagle Inn**, tel: 0311-30306, fax: 0311-21158, e-mail: fish@africaonline.co.ke, website: www.fish-eagle.com. They all charge around $2,50 a person camping and have dorms, rooms and bandas.

The road to **Hells Gate National Park** leads from here and around the western end of the lake is beautiful, flamingo-covered **Crater Lake**, which also offers rustic camping for $2 a person plus $1,25 entrance and $0,75 a vehicle.

But, you can't put off going to Nairobbery forever, so get onto the A104 highway and head south. The road climbs up the spectacular escarpment of the **Rift Valley** and there are great view sites along the way.

Routes in Northeast Africa

More than halfway now, the route becomes a serious, non-nonsense one, but is wonderfully rewarding as the rough road north of Nairobi carries you into glorious 'unexplored' Ethiopia, the attic of Africa. Memories of Southern and East Africa fade as the uniqueness of Ethiopia has you struggling to assimilate the attack on all your senses.

Don't miss

◆ Lalibela ◆ Axum
◆ Fasilidas castles ◆ Debre Damo
◆ Simien Mountains
◆ Source of the Blue Nile
◆ Blue Nile Falls
◆ Debre Birhan Selassie
◆ The birdwatching ◆ The food

NAIROBI TO GONDAR
via Moyale, Addis Ababa and Bahir Dar.
Total distance: 2 275 kilometres. Page 149.

The road north to the Ethiopian border at Moyale is one of the loneliest and roughest between Cape Town and Cairo. It's a hot, dusty track that can turn into an impassable mudbath during the rains. The remaining stretch to Addis is good tar all the way.

THE HISTORIC ROUTE
via Lalibela and Axum. Total distance: 1400 kilometres. Page 160.

The cream of all that Ethiopia has to offer is on this circuit. The rich historical and religious heritage is highlighted in places such as Lalibela, Axum and Gondar. The geographical splendour of the Rift Valley and the Blue Nile make this route a must.

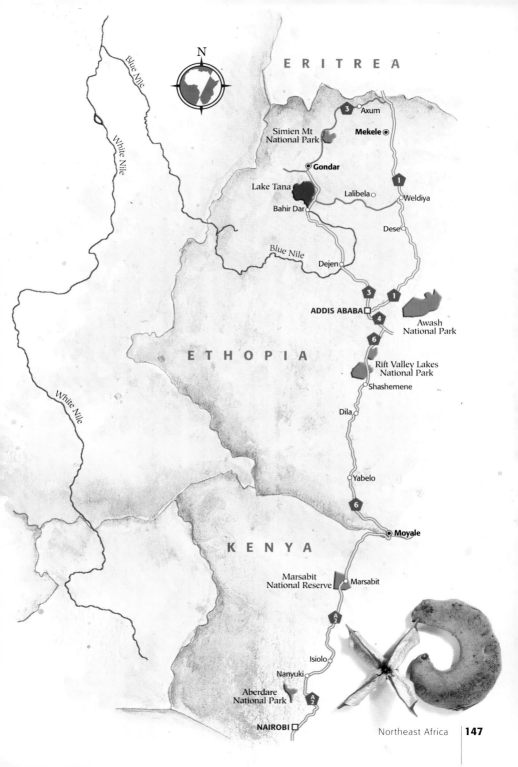

N

ERITREA

Blue Nile

White Nile

Simien Mt
National Park

3 Axum

Mekele ◉

◉ **Gondar**

Lake Tana

Lalibela ○ **1** Weldiya

Bahir Dar ○

Dese ○

Blue Nile

Dejen ○

3 **1**

ADDIS ABABA □

4

Awash
National Park

6

Rift Valley Lakes
National Park

ETHIOPIA

Shashemene ○

Dila ○

Yabelo ○

6

Moyale ◉

KENYA

Marsabit
National Reserve

Marsabit ○

A2

Isiolo ○

Nanyuki ○

Aberdare
National Park

A2

NAIROBI □

Nairobi to Gondar

via Moyale, Addis Ababa and Bahir Dar 2 275 km

I've always regarded Nairobi as halfway between Cape Town and Cairo. I know Arusha claims that honour and some like the romance of the equator at Nanyuki, but Nairobi is just so much more practical. So, when leaving Nairobi, turn your road music up high and sing along loudly – you're not almost there, but it's a lot closer than when you left Cape Town. Of course, the toughest part is yet to come, but let's not get into that just yet. There are two ways to tackle the long, hard 800 kilometres from Nairobi to Moyale, what the cartographers euphemistically call The Trans-East Africa Highway.

Above: A drum used by priests for religious ceremonies in the Ethiopian Orthodox Church. Right: Camel trains carry salt from the Danikil Depression to the markets in Mekele, Ethiopia. Left: Not all petrol pumps in Ethiopia look like this one in Adi Arkay.

You can do it in a two-day push or a three-day slog. For the push, leave Nairobi around eight in the morning and drive 280 kilometres along the A2 to **Isiolo**, refuel and then keep going for another 173 kilometres to the Catholic mission station at **Liasamis**. Then the next day, you have 100 kilometres to **Marsabit** where you can refuel again and drive the remaining 250 kilometres to the Ethiopian border at **Moyale**.

For the slog, you can leave Nairobi in the leisurely, late morning, after a last visit to the supermarket or waiting to pick up a visa. Drive to **Isiolo** (280 kays), sleep over, drive to **Marsabit** (275 kays), sleep over, and drive to **Moyale** (250 kays) – easy!

The A2 starts from the circle on Uhuru Highway at Museum Hill in central Nairobi. Keep your wits about you as the road winds through the suburbs – look out for signs to **Muranga** and **Thika**. The road will be busy, but is a good tarred dual carriageway. The countryside between Thika and **Nyeri** is green and hilly, but climbing out of Nyeri, the scenery becomes flatter and drier.

Look out for **Mount Kenya** on your right and stop for the obligatory photograph when you cross the **equator** on the outskirts of **Nanyuki** – quite a milestone. As most travellers stop here, there is a large curio village where you can bargain to your heart's content. The road remains fairly good tar, but make sure you keep left at 30 kilometres south of Isiolo, as the right fork branches off to **Meru**.

Isiolo, at 285 kilometres from Nairobi, is a frontier town. Roads lead north into the lawless deserts of Kenya and Somalia. Beautiful veiled women mingle with primly dressed convent schoolgirls and the warrior-like Somali and Samburu men are ever-present.

There is a lively market, a chance to refuel and the **Frontier Lodge** for a cold beer. Accommodation is basic but okay. Take your pick from the **Jamhuri Guesthouse**, **Madina Classic Lodge** and **Silent Inn** (no phones) all clustered behind Barclays Bank and charging around $4/$6 single/double.

For comfort, your only option is the **Bomen Hotel** (tel: 0165-2225). Spacious and comfortable self-contained rooms cost $16/$24 single/double. Safe parking is available.

Bus routes end here with the tar and the only way north for public transport travellers is to negotiate a ride on a

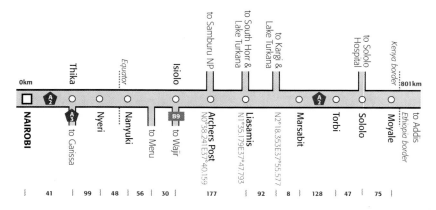

slow and heavily loaded truck.

The road surface now becomes rough gravel. At **Archer's Post** there is a turnoff (N0°38.241 E37°40.159) to the **Samburu** and **Buffalo Springs** national reserves – not really worth visiting as they charge full park fees. The impressive **Matthew's Mountains** flank the road on the left. The 140 kilometres to **Liasamis Mission** will take about another two-and-a-half hours – look out for the large Catholic church at N1°35.179 E37°47.793.

Ask Father Fernando's permission to camp at the mission station. There is no fixed charge, but make a donation equivalent to what a similar camp site would charge. They are not set up for receiving visitors and you will have to fiddle around organising water and toilets, but there is security at night. The mission also has a mechanical workshop and undertakes welding and other repairs.

It is important to know that all the mission stations in northern Kenya are willing to assist travellers in need – the mission at Sololo, right in the north, has a hospital that is a true lifesaver. But do not abuse their hospitality. They are not in the hotel business.

On the road north, look out for nomadic tribes on the move. Wrapped in traditional red patterned cloth, the women wear beautiful necklaces and beads, while the men carry long spears and wear feathers in their hair. They make a fascinating sight with all their belongings loaded onto trains of camels, but be careful, they don't like being photographed.

The road is very rough and, at times, made up of large sharp stones which can shred tyres. I hope you followed my earlier advice and fitted tyres with the highest ply-rating that you could find – especially the side-walls.

Although you will have to stop at a few police road-blocks, at time of writing it was not necessary to travel in convoy. If an opportunistic soldier or policeman suggests that you take him as a guard, he is probably trying to make some money or needing a lift to the next town – politely refuse him.

Approaching **Marsabit**, the harsh desert-like conditions soften, and greenery covers the hills. This small town is really 'out there' and, even though it has fuel and accommodation, most people pass through as fast as they can.

Although the surroundings are dry and desert like, it is amazing how often it rains here, turning the dusty roads into almost impassable muddy tracks. Steer clear of the area during April and May and, to a lesser extent, March, October and November.

If you are brave enough to want to head west via **Kargi** to **Lake Turkana**, fill up with fuel in Marsabit, then head back south out of town for one-and-a-half kilometres to the police check-point, continue on over two bridges, past the settlement and school of **Hula-Hula**, and at seven-and-a-half kilometres you should be at N2°18.353 E37°55.577 where you turn northwest towards Kargi. The road is long, lonely and rough – be totally self-sufficient and ready for anything.

Marsabit, for all it's lack of charm and downright scruffiness, has most of what you need. Reasonable accommodation is available at the **Jey Jey Centre**. Competently managed by Molu, it has hot showers, flush toilets and safe vehicle security (motorbikes park in the courtyard). A full breakfast costs $3 and a four-course meal $5. Self-contained rooms are $6 single and sharing facilities costs $4/$6 single/double.

A more upmarket alternative is the **Marsabit National Park** which, surprisingly for this dry area, includes some beautiful rainforests around an old volcanic crater. The rather run-down lodge is overpriced at $40/$60 single/double for bed and breakfast, as you have to pay an additional $15 a person and $3 a vehicle entrance fee to the park (accessible by 4x4 only).

However, the splendidly isolated camp site (N2°15.831 E37°55.883) in the park must be Kenyan's most beautiful, as it is situated in the crater, overlooking **Paradise Lake**, where elephants come to drink in the evenings. It costs only $2 a person plus normal park fees, but has no amenities.

A potential life-saver is the Shell garage in the centre of town – not only do they sell fuel, they also stock tyres, fix punctures, do mechanical repairs and undertake vehicle recovery. For a

fee, they will even drive you to Lake Turkana. Speak to Omar Salim, or his son Abdul Hakim, tel: 0183-2058, fax: 0183-2416.

Leaving Marsabit, you will pass through a police post at 12 kilometres where they will try and force an expensive armed guard onto you – resist the offer, as it is not necessary.

The road is very rough, stony and slow going as you pass the little settlement of **Bubisa** after 50 kilometres and a tall microwave tower at 100 kilometres. You will probably see nomadic tribesmen and their long camel trains but not much other traffic, as this is a very lonely road.

You will reach the halfway point of **Torbi** at 128 kilometres (N3°18.187 E38°22.668) where there is emergency food and very basic accommodation. The remaining 122 kilometres to the border is the section that can get very muddy after rain.

At 175 kilometres from Marsabit you will pass through another police checkpoint at the turnoff to **Sololo**. Eventually you will climb the hills leading into Moyale. Don't bother buying fuel on the Kenyan side, unless you have Kenyan shillings to use up – it's cheaper in Ethiopia.

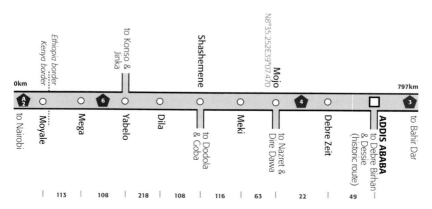

Getting into Ethiopia

After passing through the quick and efficient Kenyan border, you'll find yourself heading down across the bridge and into **Moyale, Ethiopia** – remember to swing over to driving on the right here. Park at customs on the left and walk across the road to immigration to complete the simple formalities.

Back at customs, prepare yourself for a lengthy process. Carnets are not recognised, but definitely facilitate the preparation of the quadruplicate documents that have to be prepared instead. They will want copies of the carnet and your international drivers licence – there is an inexpensive copy shop just up the road – and all this takes time. No need to lose your cool though, the authorities are pleasant and scrupulously honest.

Fill in a currency declaration form and list items such video cameras and laptop computers for re-exportation – strangely, no-one mentions or asks for insurance – and then after a thorough search of the vehicle, you're free to sally forth into exciting Ethiopia.

It's been said many times before – Ethiopia is different. But, I'll say it again, it is so unlike any other country, and nothing prepares you for your first visit. The ancient culture, undiluted by missionaries and colonists, embraces widely worn traditional dress, a highly unusual cuisine, an ancient Christian religion, the unique Amharic language, fantastic ruined castles and the proud, but warm and friendly, attitude of the handsome people.

Drive up the hill and, on the left, try the **Ysosadayo Moyala Borena Hotel** (N3°32.682 E39°02.902), tel: 06-44-0093, which has self-contained (cold shower) rooms for $3,50/$7 single/double, spaghetti and sauce for $1,50, beer $0,50 (yes, 50c), coffee $0,25 and tea $0,20! The manager, Anchinensh Seleshi is a good guy, the parking is secure and it's a pleasant introduction into travelling in Ethiopia – even though the power fails occasionally.

Heading north out of Moyale on **Route 6**, you have to show all your documents at the roadblock outside of town. The road is good tar and passes through thorny scrubland – the tallest termite mound I have ever seen is on the left of the road at N3°55.756 E38°26.728. After 113 kilometres., you will pass through the little town of **Mega** and another roadblock. Perched on a commanding hillside position just north of town, are the extensive ruins of an Italian fort dating back to their 1930s occupation.

Yabello – and a roadblock – is another 108 kilometres. The countryside becomes greener and you'll cross beautiful meadows surrounded by forest. The population density increases as you drive down the fertile escarpment to **Dila**, 440 kilometres from the border and a good place to overnight.

I recommend the **Lalibela Pension** (tel: 06-31-2300). It's situated five blocks down on the left from the 90-degree right-hand turn in the centre of town (N6°24.939 E38°18.469). Neat, quiet and comfortable it charges $2/$3 single/double, $4/$6 single/double self-contained and will throw in a traditional coffee ceremony if you're lucky. It doesn't serve food, but you'll find something if you take a stroll down the main street.

This is a coffee-growing region and the plantations and processing plants line the road. For bird lovers, you are now passing some of the most rewarding aquatic sites in Africa, the **Rift Valley Lakes**. For a very rewarding interlude of bird-watching, turn into **Awassa** and make your way to the **Awassa Wabe Shabelle No 2 Hotel** on the banks of Lake Awasa (N7º02.882 E38º27.624). From the hotel's well-wooded grounds on the banks of the lake, you can spot a huge variety of waders, woodland and aquatic birds. A single/double self-contained room is $9/$12, tel: 06-20-5397.

The road improves and is good tar all the way to **Addis Ababa**. Watch out for stray donkeys and heavily laden horse and carts. There is more good bird watching at **Lake Zwai** (sometimes spelt Ziway). Turn down to the jetty just north of the Agip garage in **Zwai** town. At **Mojo** (N8º35.252 E39º07.470) there is a T-junction where Highway 6 joins Highway 4 – turn left for Addis.

Right would take you on to **Awash** and **Djibouti** if you were adventurous, or **Dire Dawa**, **Harar** and down to **Somaliland** if you were very adventurous.

The road into Addis via **Debre Zeit** and **Nazret** becomes much busier with manic bus and truck drivers speeding and passing on blind rises.

Find your way in Addis Ababa

For years now, the Chinese have been building a ring road around Addis that will ease the traffic congestion. I hope they have finished by the time you read this. If so, get onto it at the circle coming into Addis and find your way into the city from any angle, without having to fight your way through the centre. The alternative is to keep heading deeper and deeper into the city until you reach **Meskal Square**. All roads lead off from here, so it is a good place to start exploring.

Addis, like so many African cities, lacks signposts. Street names have also changed regularly as successive regimes have imposed new names on the residents. With little town planning and roads that wind up and down the hills of the city, Addis is a difficult place to find your way around in. In listing places, I will try and describe how to get there from Meskal Square.

In Addis you are spoilt for choice in accommodation. From the extreme luxury of the **Sheraton** – one of the best

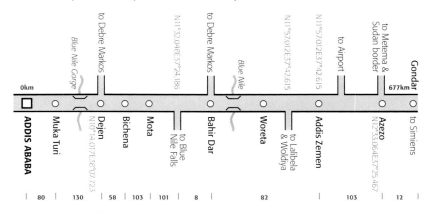

ETHIOPIA

Capital: Addis Ababa

Official languages: Amharigna and English

Area: 1 104 300 square kilometres

Population: 60 million

Visa requirements: Required by all

Time: UT +3

International dialling code: +251

Currency and rate: Ethiopian Birr B8,50=$1

Climate: Ranging from deserts at below sea level to lush mountain peaks up to 4 600 metres, Ethiopia has all climates. 'Big rains' fall from June to September and 'little rains' from February to April

Highlights: The monolithic churches of Lalibela, the stelae and ruins of Axum, castles of Gondar, Blue Nile Falls, walled city of Harar, birding in the Rift Valley and hiking in the Simien Mountains

Driving: On the right. Good system of main roads, some of which are tarred. Minor roads poor and very muddy in rainy season. Very mountainous with spectacular passes

Accommodation: Virtually no camping or backpackers. Larger towns have comfortable hotels, but small towns only very basic accomodation

Food, shops and fuel: Restaurants serve the hot, fiery local food and the best coffee in the world. No supermarkets and in rural areas only markets. Fuel widely available

Tourism info: Ethiopian Commission for Hotels and Tourism, tel: 01-51-7470, fax: 01-51-3899, e-mail: nto@telecom.net.et, website: www.tour.ethiopiaonline.com

hotels in the world and, at $2 800 for a chalet suite, really only for oil-rich millionaires and heads of state – to the dollar-a-night dumps around the market, Addis has it all. The **National Hotel**, just off Meskal Square, is reasonable value for $20/$24 single/double (tel: 01-51-5166, fax: 01-51-2417) as is the **Hotel Buffet la Gare** situated in pleasant grounds next to the railway station to the west of Meskal, which charges $11/$18 single/double, tel: 01-51-7888.

My favourite hotel in Addis though, is the **Finfine Adarash Hotel** (tel: 01-51-4711). This lovingly maintained old hotel in Johanis Road has hot spring water piped into the double rooms, which cost only $20, but is often full. The bar and restaurant is situated in one of Addis' finest old wooden buildings and serves some of the best traditional food at very reasonable prices.

Head for the **Piazza** area, just below **De Gaulle Square**, for budget backpackers accommodation (although not all will have security for your vehicle). Try the helpful **Wutma Hotel** on Muniyem Street (tel: 01-12-5360) for clean compact rooms at $7/$9 single/double. The **Baro Hotel**, just across the road, is also popular, tel 01-11-5590.

The Piazza area is also a good place

to eat, as is the Ras Desta Damtew Road area just up from Meskal Square.

A great little pub that is popular with locals as well as expats, especially on Fridays nights when there are free snacks and music, is **The Dutch Milkhouse** (turn up the first street left along Asmara Road, coming from Meskal Square). **My Pub** is further along on the left of Asmara Road near to the Plaza Hotel. A pool table, juke box and 'friendly ladies' make this a very popular spot. After midnight drift over to **Le Dome** nightclub at the Concorde Hotel or Memo's (**first** right down Bole Road) – the music is great and everyone dances.

The foyer of the **Hilton Hotel** up Menelik II Avenue (tel: 01-51-8400) is a useful place to visit, as it houses a forex bureau, Hertz car hire, DHL courier service, Ethiopian Airlines office (tel: 01-61222) and the National Tourist Organisation (tel: 01-51-4838, e-mail: nto@telecom.net.et).

The **Sudanese Embassy** (tel: 01-51-6477, fax: 01-51-8141) is off Mexico Square and will issue visas within 24 hours. You will need a letter of introduction from your own embassy, two photographs and $50.

The attraction of Addis lies not in the sights to see, but in the vibrancy of its culture and people. You should visit the **National Museum** (between Arat and Sidist Kilo) where the almost complete, 3.5-million-year-old hominid skeleton, Lucy, is displayed along with other relics of Ethiopia's past. The huge, sprawling **Merkato District** is also worth a visit as it claims to be the largest market in Africa, but take a guide – it's safer, and you could easily get lost.

If it's handicrafts and jewellery you're looking for, then head for **Haileselassie Alemayehu** at the top end of Churchill Avenue, on the right. The shop has secure parking, stocks everything that Ethiopia makes, is well

---

ETHIOPIA'S UNIQUE CUISINE

The basis of just about every meal in Ethiopia is *njera*, a large grey sponge-like pancake made from *tef*, a widely planted grain. A variety of sauces called *wat* is served on this slightly sour-tasting base. *Kai wat* is made fiery hot with an overdose of chilli pepper powder and usually contains red meat. *Alicha wat* is milder, and *doro wat* is made with chicken.

Wednesdays and Fridays are fasting days in the Ethiopian Orthodox Church, so vegetarian *wats*, called fasting food, are served on these days. *Tibs* is a tasty dish of little cubes of fried meat, while *kitfo* is not for the faint-hearted, being raw minced meat.

If all this sounds too much to handle right away, then order *inkolala* and *dabo*, egg and bread – or just ask for omelette.

Coffee – the best in the world – is called *buna*, mineral water is *ambo woha* and beer is fortunately easy to order as *birra*.

The correct procedure when walking into an Ethiopian restaurant is to first wash your hands at the washbasin, letting them drip-dry, then order, and when the food arrives without cutlery, use your hands to eat, washing them again afterwards.

displayed, and very reasonably priced – no hard-sell either.

You will search in vain for a decent supermarket in Addis (or in fact the whole of Ethiopia, Sudan and Egypt). But, for western-styled groceries try **Bambis** in Asmara Road or **Novis** in Bole Road.

The Merkato in Addis has a motor spares neighbourhood where spares, tyres and accessories for most vehicle models can be bought at small little shops. Major agencies include:

Moenco Toyota, tel: 01-61-3688, fax: 01-611-766, e-mail: moenco@tele-com.net.et. **Ultimate Motors** (Land Rover), tel: 01-655-350, fax: 01-65-3897, e-mail: ultimate-motors@tele-com.net.et. **Nyala Motors** (Nissan), tel: 01-61-3114, fax: 01-61-1888.

A final mention of Addis must be of its new **international airport** at the end of Bole Road. It serves as the head-quarters of the excellent Ethiopian Airlines, whose modern fleet of aircraft can fly you to almost any destination in Africa as well as many foreign ones.

Which way to Sudan?

From Addis you have to decide whether to take the **direct route** to Sudan via western Ethiopia and Gondar, or the more interesting **historic route**, a loop that takes you northeast and through most of the important sites of this ancient civilisation (see page 160).

To take the direct route north, head up Churchill Avenue, pass through De Gaulle Square, Menelik Square, Adwa Square and up into the hills behind Addis. Pass all the early morning joggers and enjoy the first 150 kilometres

> **Camping is really not an option in Ethiopia** – you will struggle to find a camp site and when you do, it will be no cheaper than a basic room in a hotel. Cooking your own food is also a waste of time as the ingredients you will be looking for are hard to find and expensive, and restaurant food is so cheap.

or so of this newly constructed road. You will have to negotiate many kilo-metres of bad deviations before hitting the pot-holed tarred surface of the old road, which takes you all the way to the **Blue Nile Gorge**.

A spectacular mountain pass winds down to the river and up again to **Dejen** at 210 kilometres on the other side. If you must stay here, avoid the flashy **Dejen Alem Hotel** and rather head for the **Ziman Hotel**.

About 10 kilometres north of Dejen at N10°14.017 E38°07.723, a well main-tained gravel road turns off right and offers a shorter (by 75 kilometres) and quicker alternative to the main road through **Debre Markos**.

Bahir Dar is 480 kays from Addis and getting through in one day is pushing it a bit, so I suggest staying over in what-ever little town takes your fancy when you start feeling like you just have to have a beer. Mota is the largest, but stop well before dusk, to avoid the live-stock rush hour as they crowd the roads, led home by their herders.

Some maps show the Dejen–Mota road ending in Bahir Dar town. In fact it joins the road down to the **Blue Nile**

Falls at a junction some eight kilometres short of Bahir Dar at N11°32.048 E37°24.186. Turn left to reach the town or turn right and drive another 22 kilometres to the village at the Blue Nile Falls, known locally as **Tis Abay**.

The road leads straight to the gates of the hydro-electric power station – stop here, the ticket office for the falls is directly on the left. Pay $2 a person and take the road down to the right, across a concrete canal to the parking area at the 'no trespassing' sign.

Walk down into the gorge and across the beautifully arched old **Portuguese Bridge**. Take the left path, up and over the hill, running the gauntlet of small children trying to guide you and sell cold drinks and woven cloth.

The wide-screen image of the falls hits you as you come over the hill and is impressive in all seasons, but keep going till you reach the last and best viewsite. To get to the base of the falls, a half hour hike each way, continue with the path. It follows a side stream up to a crossing point (good spot for a swim) and then doubles back downstream. Youngsters will accompany you, showing the way and offering to carry your equipment. Be compassionate and tip a few birr, as you'll probably also have to do for the 'car-minders' back in the car park.

Now head for **Bahir Dar**, entering the town past the **Commercial Bank of Ethiopia** at N11°35.269 E37°23.177 (an important waypoint if trying to find your way out of Bahir Dar and down to the falls). There is a traffic circle here and a Shell garage. Next door is the **Papyrus Hotel** – not the cheapest

> To make the history of Gondar come alive, read about the adventures of James Bruce in The Pale Abyssinian (by Miles Bredin) before you get there. Bruce made love and war with equal vigour. He left a legacy of battle tactics and a child with beautiful Queen Ester.

place in town at $12/$18 single/double, but smart and new, tel: 08-20-5100.

For cheap accommodation, drive up the palm-lined avenue towards the lake and explore the area around the bus station. The nicest hotel in town, as it is situated in large attractive gardens and in the best position on the lake, is the government-owned **Tana Hotel**. At $40/$50 single/double it's not bad value, especially if you're a bird lover, tel: 08-11-0603.

The **Ethio Star Hotel** is a rather soulless place along the main lakeside road, but not overpriced at $12/$14 single/double, tel: 08-20-2026.

The **monasteries** on the islands of **Lake Tana** are worth a visit, but not as impressive as Debre Birhan Selassie just up the road in Gondar. To organise a visit, speak to your hotel or try the **Ghion Hotel** on the lake front, tel: 08-20-0111.

A sight you cannot miss is the **source of the Blue Nile**, as it's just out of town on the road to Gondar. A bridge crosses the Nile at the point where it flows out of the lake – pause and consider that the next time you see the river will be at Wad Medani in the Sudan, just before it merges with its sibling, the White Nile, in Khartoum.

There are a few features along the good gravel road to Gondar. The first is 60 kilometres out, just after **Woreta** at N11°57.012 E37°42.615. The road that comes across from Lalibela and Weldiya enters here and is an important link between eastern and western Ethiopia. The second is a rather silly traffic circle in **Addis Zeman**, 90 kilometres out. Make sure you go around it and head up the mountain, passing a spectacular inselberg on the way up. Third, and most important, is the turnoff down to **Metema** at **Azezo** (N12°33.064 E37°25.467), which is only 12 kays before Gondar. Pass the turnoff and continue into Gondar as it is a pleasant town to stay in with lots to see.

Gondar and Africa's Camelot

Gondar is set among pretty hills and the road winds up into town to reach the central piazza. Facing you as you enter the square is the government-run **Quara Hotel** (tel: 08-11-0040) which is conveniently situated and reasonable value at $9/$11 single/double self-contained. Secure parking is available in a back courtyard.

On the opposite corner, is the very cheap **Ethiopia Hotel** which offers a basic room and bed for only $1,50. The **Belagez Pension** (tel: 08-11-4356, fax: 08-11-4347) is up the hill and behind the castles in a quiet area. Fairly new and clean, it has a large secure courtyard and charges $8 for a self-contained double and $6 for a plain double.

The top hotel, literally and figuratively, is the **Goha Hotel** (tel: 08-11-0634, fax: 08-11-1920). This government hotel is perched high on a hill on the northern outskirts of town and even if you don't want to spend $37/$50 for a comfortable, self-contained bed and breakfast room, drive up to enjoy a sundowner on the patio with views of the town and castles.

For budget food, head for the restaurant on the ground floor of the Ethiopia Hotel, and for good traditional food try the new **Habisha Kitfo** opposite the entrance to the castles where two local dishes and two beers will cost less than $5. A good place to sit and sip beer in the warm evening air, is the roof of the Quara Hotel.

But, you're not here just to guzzle beer (damn!). The imposing **Fasilidas castles** and the beautiful **Church of Debre Birhan Selassie** are two of the must-see sights of Ethiopia.

To visit the castles, take the right-hand road off the piazza – the royal enclosure is virtually in the centre of town and the entrance is off this road. The fee of $6 allows you multiple entrance for the day (opening times are 08h30 to 12h30 and 13h30 to 17h30) and the services of a guide, who will also expect a substantial tip. The impressive castles have been dubbed The Camelot of Africa and one half expects to see King Arthur and his Knights of the Round Table strolling around.

The Debre Birhan Selassie Church is on the north western outskirts of town and also has a nickname, The Sistine Chapel of Africa. It has a beautifully painted ceiling of colourful African angels smiling down on you. The walls are decorated with striking scenes from the bible, including one much-photographed image of the devil.

20
Addis Ababa to Gondar

via the historic route through Lalibela and Axum 1400 km

The previous chapter describes the shortest route to Gondar but, before you dash off down to the Sudanese border at Metema, let me tempt you into taking the Historic Route around Ethiopia, via the wonders of Lalibela, Debre Damo, Axum and the Simien Mountains.

Starting from Meskal Square, take the Asmara Road east out of Addis Ababa. Keep left at the fork just past the Central Shoa Hotel and don't get discouraged by the backstreet look about the road. The narrow, lumpy tar road winds through the hills and into the green patchwork quilt of high plains farming.

Above: Illuminated Bibles, written in ancient Géez, are preserved in Axum, Ethiopia. Left: A priest shows off ornate crosses in a church in Lalibela. Opposite: Underground tunnels link the carved churches of Lalibela.

At 129 kilometres, **Highway 1** passes through **Debre Birhan** and then climbs higher up to the pass above **Debre Sina**. Small villages cling to hilltops, as the road crosses old arched bridges, a legacy of the Italian occupation. At N9°50.794 E39°44.796 is a fabulous viewsite down the precipitous escarpment – herdboys will offer hand-spun woven woollen hats for sale. Through a dark, dripping tunnel, and then the road winds down to Debre Sina, a good stop for a meal and a rest. It is now warmer and drier and the road runs along a wide stony river. Some roadworks are in progress and a new wide road leads into **Kombolcha**, 375 kilometres from Addis and a good place to overnight.

The well-run **Tekele Hotel** is on the right as you enter town (N11°04.220 E39°44.591) and charges $6/$9 for a single/double self-contained room including good vehicle security, tel: 03-51-0056.

The **Hikma Hotel** (N11°04.833 E39°44.650) at the central traffic circle, next door to an Agip garage is cheaper at $3/$4 single/double, self-contained. It does not have very secure parking, but does have a nice terrace overlooking the street action.

As in all towns throughout Ethiopia, small bars and restaurants offer food, drink and a slice of local life at night.

Turn west towards **Dessie** at the circle when leaving **Kombolcha** (east will take you down into the **Danikil Desert** and on to Djibouti). The road is now a succession of spectacular mountain passes and green, fertile valleys. Go through Dessie, where the tar ends, and on to **Weldiya** (often spelt Woldia).

Lalibela's rock-hewn churches
You are now tantalisingly close to the rock-hewn churches of Lalibela, but unfortunately, they keep changing the road into this mountain-top World Heritage Site. Currently, the best option from the south is off the Weldiya/Werota road.

Make sure you refuel in Weldiya before turning west on the Gondar road, which winds over ever more spectacular mountain passes and eventually reaches **Gashena** (aka **Bet Hor**) at N11°41.303 E38°55.432. Turn north here.

The road starts out bad and then deteriorates. It is also subject to washaways, but after 49 kilometres you will cross a bridge and reach a tarred road at a T-junction on the other side

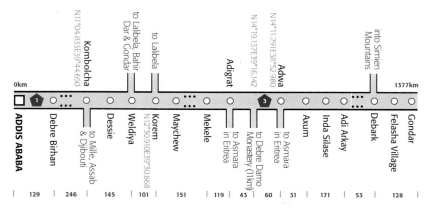

(N11°57.619 E39°00.693). Left will take you to the smart new **Lalibela Airport**, so turn right and follow the winding road up to the town that contains one of the wonders of the world. Set up in the mountains at nearly 3 000 metres, 13 churches have been carved deep into solid rock and are linked by underground tunnels.

You will be harassed by local guides and hotel touts as the road disgorges you into the centre of the little town. Directly up the hill to your left, is the **Seven Olives Hotel** where self-contained doubles cost a negotiable $20.

If you turn sharply back down the narrow lane to the right, you'll get to the **Asheton Hotel** (tel: 03-36-0030). It has a secure courtyard for vehicles, serves good food (foreign and local), and is reasonably priced at $8/$10 single/double, self-contained.

The best el-cheapo option is straight ahead at the **Kedempt Hotel** – a bit rough, but not bad for $2.

I will not attempt to guide you around the 10 magnificent rock-hewn churches that are the reason for making this arduous journey up to Lalibela – Philip Briggs in his *Bradt Guide to Ethiopia* describes them so well. But, I will guarantee you that they will knock your socks off.

Head down the hill to the right off the main square to the ticket office (open 06h00 to 12h00 and 14h00 and 17h00), where tickets sound expensive at $12, but are valid for the duration of your stay. Everybody wants to be your guide and it's best to have one, even if just to keep the others at bay, but set a fee beforehand, so as to avoid unpleas-

antness later. The official guides inside the complex are more knowledgeable and also better acquainted with the priests, but more expensive. Expect to pay a guide about $12 a day for one or two people.

You are required to remove your shoes when entering the churches, which means that a 'shoe-minder' will attach himself to you. It's unnecessary and irritating, but appoint one, chase the others away and give him a dollar at the end.

I would advise an early morning first visit, followed by a more leisurely afternoon visit. Sometimes you will hear about an all-night service, as these churches are in regular use. Go, the spiritual chanting by the large congregation, accompanied by the beating of the holy drums by the priests will be an experience you will never forget.

If all this traipsing around underground churches makes you hungry, I suggest you try an evening meal at **Chez Sophie** on the northern side of the square – spaghetti costs $1,20, pizza (without cheese!) is $1,50 and fasting food $1. Beer is $0,60.

The closest thing to a grocery store you will find in Lalibela is **My Supermarket**, a little place on the right on your way down to the churches.

If you are really desperate for fuel, they sell diesel by the jugful for $0,50 per litre from a little shop with a Shell sign on the square near to the Ethiopian Airline office.

If you're in Lalibela on a Saturday, head down the hill to the weekly market. Traditional clothing, handmade sandals, fruit and vegetables, metalware, coffee beans, honey and honey wine, blocks of salt, baskets, earthenware pots, lots of dried chillies and a full livestock market will keep you fascinated for hours.

Getting out of Lalibela

The way north out of Lalibela is just as confusing as coming in from the south and is not yet shown correctly on any map I have seen. You have two options, both via **Sekota**. Drive west out of Lalibela's main square, past the Kedempt Hotel. A reasonably good gravel road leads up and down many mountain passes – each one worthy of a name and fame in any country other than Ethiopia, where there are so many that no-one notices them any more. It is the most spectacular and pleasing mountain road I have driven.

Isolated little towns billow past with the dust until you reach a junction at 110 kilometres (N12°37.512 E39°02.109). Turn right to get back to the main **Asmara** road at **Korem**. Turning left would take you another 20 kilometres to **Sekota** and then on via this spectacular and quite good gravel road straight up to **Adwa**. But you would miss the cliff-side churches of eastern **Tigray** and the mountain-top monastery of **Debre Damo**.

So turn right and enjoy the ultimate 'Roof of Africa' drive on a good gravel road. You will hardly see another vehicle on the 75 kilometres to Korem (N12°30.910 E39°30.868). Turn left here and drive another 41 kilometres to **Maychew**, where you will thankfully find your first fuel station since Weldiya, more than 1 000 kilometres back.

Continuing north, there is not one single stretch of level road as you yo-yo between 2 000 and 3 000 metres. The roads are being upgraded, which causes some disruption, until you get onto a new tar road which leads you into **Mekele**.

There are a number of good hotels in the just-under-$10 range situated around the main square, where you will also find banks, an Ethiopian Airline's office and a Total garage. If you want to spoil yourself a bit, head for the impressive **Abreha Castle Hotel**, built on a hill on the south side of town. Shaped like a castle and set in attractive gardens, it charges $20/$25 single/double, self-contained. Book through the head office in Addis, tel: 01-51-3222.

The **Tigray Tourist Bureau** (tel: 03-40-0769) is upstairs above the **Commercial Bank of Ethiopia** at the southern end of Alula Road. The staff are knowledgeable and helpful, and distribute a selection of useful pamphlets on the rock-hewn churches and monasteries of the region. Good ice cream, grills and pizzas ($3) are served at the **Yordanis Resaurant**, situated just beyond the circle at the southern end of Alula Road.

Mekele has a market for the salt which is mined in the **Danikil Depression**. Slabs of this essential commodity are transported through the desert on the backs of camels – keep an eye out for the caravans plodding along as you approach or leave the town. The salt market is not part of the main market, but on the way out of town, heading north. From the main circle, take the Wukro/Adigrat road

past the Telecom building to the old
Agip garage on the right. You should
spot the camels and piles of salt blocks
across the road and down a lane at
N13°30.279 E39°28.941.

There are some deviations on the
way to **Wukro**. The countryside is lit-
tered with stones – ideal for building
solid houses, but difficult to farm in.
Ten kilometres north of Wukro lies the
little town of **Negash**, interesting
because of its importance in Muslim
history. During the early 7th century,
Mohammed and his followers, who
were being persecuted, were offered a
safe refuge in Christian Ethiopia.
Altogether 116 Muslims, including the
Prophet's daughter and two of his
future wives settled in Negash. The
graves of some of them can still be
seen, but the mosque which now
stands on the site is modern.

A little further is a cluster of three
rock-hewn churches in the **Tsaeda
Imba (White Cliff)**. To reach these
churches, also known as the **Teka
Tesfai** cluster, turn right at the
Shwadini school, 10 kilometres from
Negash. You will know you're at the
right place if youngsters crowd around
offering to guide you. You will need
one, who will also find the priest with
the keys for the churches. The tracks
are very rough and you might decide to
rather walk between the churches.

To visit all three entails quite a lot of
climbing, but if you're in a hurry, lazy or
just plain 'churched-out', at least try
and get to **Medhane Alem Adi Kesho**
(park at N13°57.176 E39°36.796). Set
into the cliff face with four massive
columns in front, the vaulted interior is
covered with beautiful carvings of
crosses and circular designs. The
entrance fee is $3 a person plus a tip for
the key-carrying priest and, of course, a
tip for your young guide.

Less than 50 kilometres further on is
the town of **Adigrat** where I recommend the **Woldu Sibagadis Modern
Hotel** at N14°16.853 E39°27.667.
Modern, clean and spacious, the self-
contained double rooms cost $7 or,
sharing facilities, $4, tel: 04-45-2346, e-
mail: helenzz2002@yahoo.com. Good
food is served in a neat dining room
and there's a secure courtyard for your
vehicle. The budget dollar-a-night
hotels are east of the town's main
intersection, near the bus station.

Men-only mountain top

The next stop on the round Ethiopia
Historic Route is the mountain-top
monastery of **Debre Damo**. Only men
are allowed to visit this 6th-century
Axumite church – not because the cliff
climb is too dangerous, but because the
monks have banished everything
female from their domain, even hens
and nanny-goats.

Drive 37 kilometres to **Biset** and
after another six kilometres turn right
(N14°19.137 E39°16.142) at the signpost
to Debre Damo. Although the track is
narrow, rough and steep, it has been
quite well constructed. After 11 kilo-

metres (keep right at the top) you will reach a few houses and a church near to the Debre Damo cliffs (N14°22.586 E39°17.481). Walk to the cliff base and start negotiations (which should end around $6 a person) for the rope and assistance to get to the top. One leather thong is tied around your waist and another is used to climb, monkey-style, up the 15-metre sheer cliff.

The top is flat with a little village of picturesque stone houses. The main church, reputed to be the oldest surviving church in Ethiopia and renovated in 1955, is a large solid stone structure which glows in the sunlight. Richly decorated with paintings and carpets, it contains ancient Geez Bibles – ask the head priest to open up the church up for you. Also climb the nearby bell tower to see the old bells and church drums.

Onwards to Adwa and Axum

The road on to Adwa is through fantastically shaped inselbergs. At the circle in **Adwa** (N14°11.291 E38°52.980) turn west towards **Axum** (north will take you up to the Eritrean border, closed at time of writing). Another 20-odd kilometres of dust finds you driving past the smart new airport and into Axum.

The **Yeha Hotel** is the best in town and is centrally situated on a hill overlooking all the main sights, but expensive at $40/$50 single/double, tel: 04-75-0605. The **Axum Touring Hotel** is good value at $9/$12, tel: 04-75-0205, while the best of the cheaper places seems to be the friendly **Atse Kaleb Hotel** which charges $6 for a double room, tel: 04-75-0222. All the above places are self-contained and have safe parking.

The **Mini Pastry** (next door to the Atse Kaleb Hotel) serves good hamburgers and omelettes for around $1.

To visit all the historic sights around Axum, you will first have to buy a ticket at the **Axum Museum**, which is in the main church complex on the left going to the stelae field. This $6 ticket gives you multiple entry into all the sights (except the Tsion Maryam Church) for the duration of your stay.

Explore the museum first for some interesting artefacts and history before heading up the road to the main stelae field. The **Queen of Sheba's Pool** is across the road on the right. To get to the **Trilingual Tablet** and **Kaleb's Palace** drive up through the trees between the stelae and the pool.

The compound of churches opposite the stelae contains the **Tsion Maryam Church** with its paintings and interesting musical instruments, as well as a rather ordinary building which is supposed to house the most important of all Christian religious relics, the **Ark of the Covenant**. There is also a collection of beautifully bejewelled crowns and illustrated Bibles. Entrance to all this costs an extra $7.

The **Dongar Palace** is just out of town to the west and is also known as the **Queen of Sheba's Palace**. The Queen of Sheba is an important figure in Ethiopian history, as she was supposed to have come back pregnant from a visit to King Solomon in Jerusalem, thereby starting the royal Solomonic line of emperors. Although the dates don't always tie in, it makes a wonderful story and is typical of the epic nature of the country's history.

Bombed-out tanks in the passes of Ethiopia remind travellers of the conflict with Eritrea.

Into the Simien Mountains

Fill up with fuel before heading west out of town towards the **Simien Mountains**. Don't dawdle and leave late, as it will take you seven hours of solid driving to do the 260 kilometres to Debark. The road is rough, rocky and very mountainous and you will pass the wrecks of countless tanks, armed personnel carriers and army trucks, as this is the battleground when Ethiopia and Eritrea go to war.

Debark is not a pleasant town and you will be forced to stay at the **Simien Park Hotel** which charges $3/$5,50 single/double and $7 self-contained double a night.

Of course Debarks *raison d'etre* is organising climbs in the mighty Simien Mountains. This can be done at the **National Park Office**, which is just up the road from your hotel. Official guides there will assist you – a typical five-day hike inclusive of park fees, guide and mules will cost about $140. Trips can also be arranged from Gondar; try Bedassa Jota, tel: 08-11-5073, e-mail: bejgobena@yahoo.com, website: www.geocities.com/bedassajote/.

Heading south, the road improves somewhat and passes some fantastic viewsites (N12°45.248 E37°32.450). One last stop before reaching Gondar is **Woleka**, the so-called **Felasha Village**, actually just a few roadside curio stalls (N12°38.563 E37°28.626). This is where Ethiopia's last ancient community of Jews lived before emigrating to Israel in 1991.

All that remains is four kilometres into Gondar, and you're back on track for our crossing into Sudan.

Routes in North Africa

The game parks and tropical islands of South and East Africa are behind you now as you tackle the deserts of North Africa. Cultural flavours change too, as Arab and Muslim influences predominate. The people, particularly in Sudan, are wonderful; warm and friendly, they compensate for the inhospitable nature of the route.

Don't miss
- ◆ Pyramids of Giza ◆ Desert oases
- ◆ Sphinx ◆ Valley of the Kings
- ◆ Camping along the Nile
- ◆ Luxor temples ◆ Desert driving
- ◆ Whirling Dervishes
- ◆ Omdurman souk
- ◆ Confluence of the Niles

GONDAR TO CAIRO DIRECT ROUTE
via Khartoum, Wadi Halfa, Aswan and Luxor. Total distance: 2 400 kilometres. Page 170.

The final leg of your Cape to Cairo odyssey is a tough one. You will have to deal with kilometres of red tape and some very sandy tracks in the north of Sudan. Accommodation is also sometimes difficult to find.

WESTERN DESERT OASES ROUTE
via El Khanga, Dakhla, Mut, Al Qasr and Farafra. Total distance: 1 330 kilometres. Page 184.

This route is an interesting alternative to the rather dreary run down the Nile between Luxor and Cairo. It also allows you a glimpse of Bedouin life at unspoilt desert oases, far from the hustle and hard-sell of touristic Egypt.

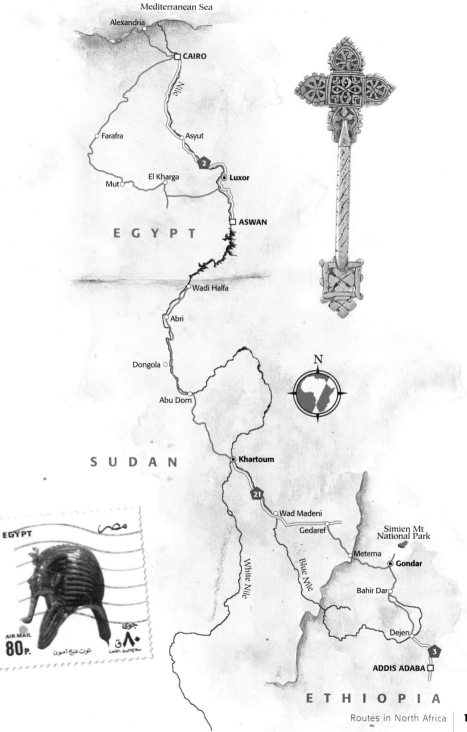

Mediterranean Sea

Alexandria

CAIRO

Nile

Farafra

Asyut

Mut

El Kharga

2

Luxor

ASWAN

E G Y P T

Wadi Halfa

Abri

Dongola

Abu Dom

N

S U D A N

Khartoum

21

Wad Madeni

Gedaref

Simien Mt
National Park

Metema

Gondar

Bahir Dar

White Nile

Blue Nile

Dejen

3

ADDIS ADABA

E T H I O P I A

EGYPT

مصر

AIR MAIL
80 P.

جوى

٨٠ق

توت عنخ آمون

21

Gondar to Cairo
via Khartoum, Wadi Halfa, Aswan and Luxor 2400 km

This section separates the sheep from the goats. The border crossings are nerve-racking and the roads are bone-jarring. There are cultural and language difficulties and the climate is dry and harsh. But nothing beats camping in the desert under date palms on the banks of the Nile, except, of course, the emotional entry into your final destination, Cairo.

It is sadly prophetic that you pass the Dashen Brewery as you leave Gondar and drive south to Azezo.

Right: The Colossus of Memnon guards the road to the Theban Necropolis on the west bank at Luxor.
Below: Small villages along the bank of the Nile in northern Sudan welcome travellers.

This is the last you will be seeing of beer (or any other alcohol) until your arrival in Aswan, Egypt. It is also the last you will be seeing of fuel until Gedaref, 387 kilometres away, so make sure your tanks are full.

Drive through little town of Azezo, and, at 12,5 kilometres from the piazza in Gondar, turn right (N12°33.065 E37°25.466) towards **Metema**.

Although a gravel road, it is newly made and in good condition. **Aykel** is passed at 50 kilometres from the turnoff and at 62 kilometres you say goodbye to the healthy highlands of Ethiopia and head down the escarpment into malaria country.

At 154 kilometres you will reach **Shehedi**, the last Ethiopian town with amenities. Check whether you still have to clear customs and immigration here (N12°46.600 E36°24.457) or whether the new border post in Metema has finally been completed.

Accommodation choices in Shehedi are limited and you will be forced to stay the night at the very basic but friendly **Sak Besak Hotel** (single rooms $2 and meals $1).

The next morning it is 36 kilometres to the border town of Metema, which has been totally disrupted by the new road slicing through the middle of it. Show your passport and papers at the border huts before getting the okay to cross the smart new bridge into the little Sudanese town of **Gallabat** (border opens at 08h00).

Into Sudan and on to Gedaref
You notice the difference in the official attitude immediately – in Sudan you don't have rights, you are granted favours. A new customs and immigration office is under construction here too, so look out for the right one. The processing of documents is slow, but carnets are recognised and temporary import permits issued for cameras, videos and laptops.

Make sure you have finished with everyone and had all your documents stamped, including your passport, before heading out northwest for 155 kilometres to **Gedaref**.

The road has been vastly improved and it is now possible to drive to Gedaref and on to **Wad Medani** in a day. Look out for camels as the countryside becomes more arid.

Approaching Gedaref, the road degenerates into a series of tracks. Head for a large tin shed at N14°00.590 E35°23.864 where the Gallabat road

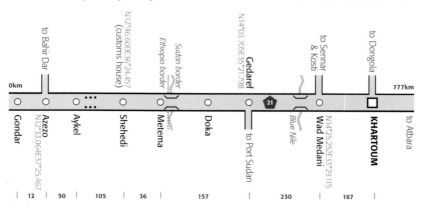

SUDAN

Capital: Khartoum

Official languages: Arabic

Area: 2 505 800 square kilometres

Population: 28 million

Visa requirements: Required by all. Also an Aliens Movement Permit to travel within the country, obtainable at border or first large town (Gedaref if coming from Ethiopia)

Time: UT +2

International dialling code: +249

Currency and rate: Dinar SD250=$1

Climate: Summer is very hot, winter is pleasant. Avoid the rains around the Ethiopian border during July, August and September

Driving: On the right. The main tarred roads can be quite potholed, the rest are sandy or stony tracks

Highlights: The confluence of the Niles at Khartoum, pyramids of Meroe, and driving through the desert along the Nile

Accommodation: Adequate in Khartoum, scarce in other large towns and lacking in villages. Local people very hospitable, though

Food and shops: Restaurants only serve local food (tasty and similar to Egyptian). No supermarkets and few shops – buy basics in markets.

Fuel: Cheap and available, but long distances between stops

Tourism information: Sudanese Tourist Information Office, tel: 011-74664. Alternatively, try the good private tourist organisation, Globtours, tel: 011-79-8111, e-mail: globtours_sudan@yahoo.com website: www.arab.net/sudan

---

disgorges itself onto a tar road and turn left. You might have to go into Gedaref to register at the foreigner's office (N14°01.915 E35°23.092), but try and leave this for later in Khartoum (check latest requirements when crossing border). If you have to stay over in Gedaref, the **Amir Hotel** is for tight budgets and the **Elmotwakil Hotel** for a bit more luxury.

Get onto the main **Port Sudan to Khartoum road** at the circle (N14°03.705 E35°21.798) outside Gedaref and head west.

The tar road is badly potholed in places and you'll have to get used to being overtaken again as huge inter-city busses sweep past at breakneck speed – truck and trailer rigs coming up from the coast are another hazard. The flat, black, cottonsoil plains are monotonous but it's at least easy to eat up the kilometres.

If you want to eat anything else, or have a cooldrink or cup of tea, stop at one of the clusters of huts that pass as truckstops around here.

At **Wad Medani** you are reunited with your old friend, the **Blue Nile**. Together with the White Nile at Khartoum, it will be your constant companion all the way on to Cairo.

Turn into this pleasant town at the circle just across the bridge and drive down to and along the cornice on the banks of the river. There are two hotels:

The Continental Hotel at $15 for a double, self-contained rooms and the better Nile Hotel (tel: 0511-45739) at $23. Food is available from the many stalls and restaurants on the banks of the slow-flowing Nile. There is also a large garage in town that can repair punctures. Many of the gold merchants in the souk (market) will change money at a good rate.

What to do in Khartoum

Keep right (north) for Khartoum at the circle (N14°25.252 E33°29.115) just north of Wad Medani – left would take you south to Sannar and Damazine – and drive the fairly good, but crowded, road into the capital.

As it is only 187 kilometres, you will arrive in Khartoum with lots of time to find your way around. Keep right at a fork (N15°31.984 E32°33.807) in the dual-carriage road which will bring you in past the airport on your right. Cross the railway line into a circle, head straight across and through Khartoum.

You will run straight into the Nile at the Blue Nile Sailing Club. This wonderfully situated spot on the river is the only practical place to camp in Khartoum and charges $3 a person plus $5 a car (speak to William). The

ablution block is reasonable (although it only has cold showers) and there is a snack bar and kiosk. (The German Club, opposite the airport, sometimes also allows camping in its car park). A focal point at the club is Kitchener's old gunboat, the *Malik*, with which he subdued the Mahdi and recaptured Khartoum. Although this historic craft now lies high and dry on the riverbank, for many years it served as the floating club house.

For cheap hotels, try the Safa (tel: 011-79985) or Asia on Sharia al-Baladaya, just off UN Square in the centre of town. Rooms, double or single, cost around $5 but there is unfortunately no secure parking.

The best place to stay in town, if a little pricy at $43/$62 single/double, is the Acropole Hotel on Sharia Babika Badri, tel: 011-72860. Always filled with expats, aid workers and overlanders, it also serves good food (no chance of a beer though) and has secure parking.

The local Land Rover agent is Nefeidi Motors, Al-Parlaman Street; tel: 011-78-0500, fax: 011-77-1532, e-mail: nefeidimotor@hotmail.com.

To taste a selection of local food, head to Souk Arabi in the centre of town (within walking distance of the

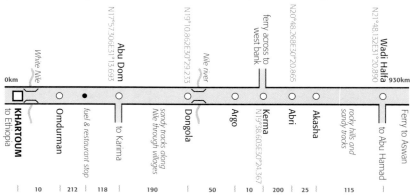

yacht club) where a meal of soup, meat, fish and salad for four can cost as little as $6. A slightly more expensive option, but smarter and more comfortable, is to visit the garden restaurants along the banks of the Nile in the cool of the evening. There is a cluster of them opposite the museum.

Downstream, along the **Sharia el-Nil**, is the **National Museum** ($4) which is worth visiting for its reconstructed temples of Buhen and Semna as well as a great selection of artefacts and antiquities from Sudan's long and interesting history.

Cross the White Nile at the point where it joins the Blue Nile to explore **Omdurman**. There is an old and a new bridge which are sometimes turned into one-ways. Follow the diversions to the correct one if necessary.

In Omdurman you should visit the old **Khalifa's house** ($4) which is steeped in the history of the struggle for Sudan. Across the road (N15°38.356 E32°29.295) is the impressive **Tomb of the Mahdi**, but be careful of photographing it.

Other places of interest in Omdurman are the mud fortifications built by the Mahdi on the banks of the Nile, just downstream from the confluence. Further downstream is a spot on the banks where boat builders chip and hammer away at their ancient craft.

You might also want to brave the Omdurman souk. Safe, but huge and chaotic, you can find anything there.

Of course, if it's Friday, the **Dervishes** must be whirling. This Sufi sect gathers during the late afternoon every Friday in front of the **Hamed an-**

EATING IN SUDAN

Sudan has a limited local cuisine based on the humble brown bean, usually stewed. Good salad is always available, as is bread, in the form of flat, grey unleavened loaves. *Ta'amiyya*, little balls of deep-fried ground chickpeas and similar to Egyptian *felafel*, is a tasty addition to any meal.

Meat is served as kebab and fish is often available from the Nile.

Shai saada, sweet tea without milk, is the national drink and is often deliciously spiced with cloves, mint or cinnamon. An even more tasty drink is the freshly liquidised fruit juice on sale everywhere.

As in many other parts of Africa, you will have to eat with your hands – just remember to wash first and only use the right hand.

Nil Mosque and, dressed in colourful jalabijjas and gowns, they dance, chant and beat drums while whirling themselves into a detached state of mind. Don't miss it.

The most knowledgeable person in Khartoum with information on the **Wadi Halfa ferry** is Midhat Mahir of **Globtours**, whose office is on the ground floor of the Safari Palace Hotel in Abdul Rahman Street, tel: 011-79-8111, e-mail: globtours_sudan@-yahoo.com. He is in contact with Kamal Osman in Wadi Halfa, the local Mr Fixit, and claims to be able to make bookings for you.

There is a **Tourist Information Office** in Sharia al-Baladya near to UN

Square. Tthe **office for security registration and travel permits** is on
Sharia Othman Diqna, four blocks up
from the Blue Nile Sailing Club.

The desert road to the border

The only way through to Egypt from
Sudan at the moment is via Wadi
Halfa, and the only way from there to
Aswan is on an expensive ferry. There
are, however, two routes north out of
Khartoum. The one I favour is directly
north across the desert to Abu Dom
and then down the Nile via Dongola to
Abri and on to Wadi Halfa. The alterna-
tive is to stick with the Nile north to
Abu Hamed via Atbara and then follow
the railway line across the desert to
Wadi Halfa.

Leave Khartoum across the **old
White Nile Bridge** and at the circle
(N15°38.392 E32°29.149) in Omdurman, turn left to Souk Libya. Travel
down a long dual road, filling up with
fuel along the way (the Shell garage
towards the end is a good place).

The road becomes a chaotic single
lane through the souk to the outskirts,
where at N15°38.841 E32°25.145 you
turn right. This brings you up to the
main road north through the desert.

This road really ought to start more

impressively, but at the moment, it can
only be reached via this circuitous
route. It is a fairly new tarred road in
good condition and once you have
shown your papers at the roadblocks, it
is a very lonely and monotonous route.
Be sure to take lots of water.

There is a truckstop with food and
fuel at 222 kilometres. The few thorn
trees that dot the landscape outside
Khartoum soon fade away and the
desert becomes a hot, dry and barren
wasteland. At 340 kilometres you will
reach a small cluster of foodstalls and a
fuel station which in 2003 marked the
end of the tar.

The circle (N17°57.306 E31°13.693)
will one day have new roads leading
left and right to Dongola and Karima
respectively, but for now it is better to
head straight across and continue
north to where you will bisect the **old
Dongola/Karima road**. Turn left to the
village of **Abu Dom**.

Navigation is difficult in these parts,
but easier if you remember to never
stray too far from the Nile – just relax
and take the most well-used track and
try to bypass the little villages. Another
useful navigation aid is the telephone
and power lines – stay close to these
and you won't go wrong.

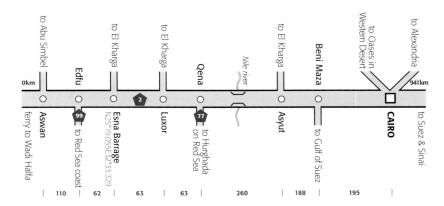

The sand is deep and soft (especially around **Al Ghaba**) and the dust creeps in everywhere. Villages such as **Al Goled Bahri** are fairly self-sufficient, with a souk where you can buy fruit, vegetables and bread, and sometimes even fuel. Look out for wires which crisscross the sandy village streets, carrying the feeble power of put-put generators.

Accommodation is a bit of a problem. Of course you will find a place to sleep, the hospitality of the northern Sudanese people being legendary, but you will struggle to find anything resembling a hotel anywhere outside larger towns such as Karima and Dongola.

Camping, on the other hand, is a pleasure. The countryside along the Nile is green and fertile and, although you won't always be able to camp right alongside the river, the irrigated fields and palm trees make wonderful camp sites. Farmers head back to their villages at night leaving you in blissful isolation – hordes of mosquitoes will keep you company though, so take precautions. You will drift off to sleep with the soft sounds of a chug-chug pump over on the Nile, the call from a distant mosque and faraway dogs barking – pure bliss. In the morning the harsh braying of a donkey will be your alarm clock as the sun filters through the palm fronds.

About 30 kilometres before **Dongola** you will encounter roadworks and then, oh joy, tar. A T-junction at N19°09.296 E30°26.374 leads left to the airport and right into Dongola. The town is pleasant and has one of the best little souks in Sudan, but you are given the run-around when trying to book into a hotel. It is quite common in Sudan that you will not be allowed to register until some snooty official at the police station has pawed incomprehensibly over your papers and eventually scribbled on a scrap of paper that it's okay. The **Ola Hotel** is as good as any in Dongola and charges $2 a person in rooms with overhead fans. Food is served in a shady courtyard.

Up the eastern bank of the Nile

You can keep to the western bank and cross by ferry 60 kilometres north of Dongola at **Kerma en Nuzl**, but then you would miss the most attractive villages along this stretch of the Nile, which are situated on the eastern bank. So, fill up with fuel and head for the busy **ferry** just outside Dongola (N19°10.862 E30°29.233) that carries busses, trucks, *boksis* (passenger-carrying light trucks) and assorted livestock back and forth across the mighty, sluggish Nile. Pedestrians travel free, but vehicles cost $3.

The road up the eastern bank from here is through well-maintained and prosperous villages. Lovely big trees give welcome shade and the people are very friendly and outward going.

At 50 kilometres, **Argo** has fuel and a well-stocked souk, and 10 kilometres further you will pass the ferry at Kerma en Nuzl (N19º38.603 E30º24.367). The rocky outcrops of the **Third Cataract** are just beyond this – look out for the traditional boat builders around here.

At about 95 kilometres from Dongola, the road swings east and away from the river – at one point you are even travelling south. Don't panic, just stick to the most obvious of tracks as the road swings back to a more northerly direction and passes through some rocky hills. The track is sometimes so corrugated that you will be forced to abandon it and drive through the desert. It rejoins the Nile eventually at two attractive nipple-shaped hills. You will probably have to camp along this section of the river as the villages are very small with no amenities.

Heading further north, the corrugations become worse, but you are able to travel a bit faster as the road bypasses most of the villages.

The largest village along this stretch, **Abri**, is reached at 260 kilometres (N20º48.268 E30º20.865). There is a decent market and a very basic guesthouse. The corrugations now become the worst in the whole wide world. At 320 kilometres (N21º04.510 E30º42.469) you drive through **Kosha**. The road turns inland through the stony desert, leaving the river and any sign of water until the shock of the blue waters of **Lake Nasser** at **Wadi Halfa**.

When you first spot Lake Nasser, you can't believe that so much fresh water can be just sitting there in the middle of the desert with no vegetation – there is not even a blade of grass down at the water's edge. So don't expect an attractive leafy little town – Wadi Halfa is a hole.

You will arrive at a circle (N21º46.869 E31º23.016) and have to work your way around towards the left to a couple of hills in the distance. The original little town was laid out in front of the railway station, but due to some cock-eyed calculations, it flooded and all fell down. Now Wadi Halfa is a shambles, with different sections of town spread all over the desert. Many buildings are make-shift shacks and everything is rather expensive.

There are two very shabby hotels close to each other, the **Wadi el Neil** and the slightly better **Nile Hotel** (N21º48.132 E31º20.890). Prices are inflated when the ferry arrives, but are negotiable for the rest of the time, especially if you are prepared to sleep outside. Three dollars a person seemed an average rate – a bit much for a tin shack with sand floors and buckets for washing in. There is an open-air restaurant across the road which serves local dishes.

Getting out of Sudan

At the time of writing there was definitely no chance of crossing from Sudan into Egypt overland by driving up along the **Aswan Dam**. There is a track up the western bank of the Nile which crosses into Egypt and links up with the tarred road at **Abu Simbel**, but it is blocked by barbed wire and mine fields as you approach the border – you have to use the ferry.

Give yourself a day to deal with the formalities required to leave Sudan. All the officials, especially customs, want

Huts on the outskirts of Gedaref in Sudan.

you to use the local Mr Fixit, Kamal Osman, as it makes their job easier. Now Mr Kamal is a nice guy, speaks English and is very efficient, but why pay a man money for something that you can do yourself?

The quick and efficient **Aswan Ferry** ticket office (N21°48.010 E31°21.048) is in a small prefab shack behind the Immigration office. The ferry leaves Wadi Halfa on Wednesdays around 17h00, takes about 18 hours to Aswan and costs $30 a person (it runs in the opposite direction on a Monday, arriving in Wadi Halfa on a Tuesday). For this you get a bench seat in a crowded below-deck area plus a meal and a cup of tea (if you don't want the meal and tea, it's a bit cheaper). Many travellers prefer to sleep up on deck to avoid the stuffiness and overcrowding.

Cars of up to Land Rover size cost $600 and motor bikes $50. Vehicles are not loaded onto the passenger ferry, but onto a pontoon which is lashed to the side of the ferry. There is an occasional cargo-only ferry which costs $300 a vehicle, but only allows one passenger a vehicle.

The smart, new, white customs office (N21°48.317 E31°19.997) is situated halfway between the railway station and the port. They will encourage you to use Mr Kamal, but if you go it alone, they are surprisingly efficient and conclude the formalities of the vehicle and other valuables, such as videos and laptops, quite quickly.

The immigration office is crowded, disorganised and chaotic. First you pay $7,50 a person for port tax, then $0,50 exit tax and then finally you will be given an exit form to fill in and must have your passport stamped. Each one of these steps has to be done at a different window.

The final part of this saga is to drive to the port, where there is another $3,50 port tax to pay for the vehicle before reversing onto the pontoon (which could probably take eight vehicles at a push).

You now wait in a smart departure lounge until your passport and all receipts are double-checked. Customs check your hand luggage and three security goons check you and your papers again. Out on the jetty there is more waiting until the immigration check your papers for one final time, and then the ferry officials check your ticket again and you board.

Currency is a bit of a juggling act, as all payments in Wadi Halfa are made in Sudanese dinar, except for the ferry office which will take dollars. There is a bank opposite the immigration office, but try to use up all your dinars before boarding the ferry, as only Egyptian pounds are acceptable on board. With nowhere to change money legally on the ferry, this is a problem.

The faithful kneel in prayer as the ferry cuts swiftly through the waters of the lake. Nobody will stop you if you want to climb down onto the pontoon to cook or sleep in your car. Late at night, if you are awake, look out for the floodlit temples of **Abu Simbel** on the western shore.

Getting into Egypt

The next morning, the view is unimpressive as you pass barren outcrops and islands. Around midday the tower at the **Aswan High Dam** comes into view and you dock around 13h00.

You can be held up for hours on the ferry as everyone's papers are thoroughly checked, but eventually with much shoving and pushing, you will be free of the ferry. Drive the vehicle off the pontoon and up to the customs office. It is imperative that your carnet is issued in the names of the owner and the driver of the vehicle, if the driver is not the owner. It must also be endorsed to validate it for Egypt, otherwise you will not pass the dreaded Mr Hammam Yassar at customs. You will instead be forced to travel by train to Cairo to sort out your carnet with the Automobile Club of Egypt while your vehicle waits for you in Aswan customs (N23°58.654 E32°53.880).

If you did not have a carnet, it was suggested to me by someone in the Aswan customs that you could employ a customs official (at $67 a day plus expenses) to escort you through Egypt to your exiting border – I would most definitely not take that chance!

If all your documentation is fine, you pay Mr Hammam a hefty $225 (in Egyptian pounds) for one month's vehicle tax and proceed into town to the traffic department (N24°05.066 E32°54.503). This crowded and chaotic place is where they issue new Egyptian number plates for your vehicle ($8), but not before the vehicle has been inspected (another $8). Of course, all this takes time – it will probably take up the afternoon of your arrival and most of the next morning. If you are heading south and need to book the ferry, the offices of the **Nile Valley Navigation Company** (tel: 097-30-3348) are next to the tourist office outside the main railway station in Aswan.

Fortunately, **Aswan** is a lovely town. Smart hotels and restaurants line the cornice above the Nile, sails of feluccas billow in the soft breeze, and everywhere there is opulence. Coming from the austerity of Sudan, it's quite overwhelming. ATMs spew money, scantily-clad tourists offend the locals and Stella beer is freely available.

Spoil yourself by staying in a room with a view of the Nile. The **El-Salaam Hotel**, 101 Cornice el Nil is good value at $8/$12 single/double for self-contained rooms with air-con; tel: 097-30-2651. The **Hathor Hotel** next door costs slightly less, tel: 097-31-4580. In either place, request a Nile-facing room. For cheaper options ($2/$3), delve into the souk, just behind these hotels. The **Abu Shelib, Orabi**, and **Keylany** hotels are worth a try. The **municipal camp site**, between the **Fatimid Cemetery** and the **Unfinished Obelisk**, has poor ablutions but grassy sites and good security and costs $1 a person plus $1 a vehicle.

A very pleasant few hours can be spent drifting around the islands off Aswan in a felucca. You don't have to look for one, the touts will find you and, as with everything in Egypt, it is necessary to bargain hard for a good price.

Another worthwhile excursion is a visit to the complex of **Isis** on the **island of Philae**. Head for **Shellal**, just south of the old Aswan Dam, from where you will have to take a short boat ride ($0,50 a person if in a group) across to the island temple (entrance fee $5 a person). Although there is a fine road to the great **Temple of Abu Simbel**, check first with the tourist police, as it is often closed for security reasons.

Driving in convoy to Luxor

Security is tight in Egypt and the authorities will do anything to avoid attacks on tourists. This is great for your safety as there are security forces on every corner, but very restrictive if you are travelling independently in your own vehicle. Roadblocks are everywhere and, as a tourist, many routes can be travelled only in convoy under police escort.

Convoys leave Aswan for the south at 09h00 and 14h00. The police are very strict and will sometimes force you to empty jerry cans of fuel and even the gas from your cooking stove.

Head down the Cornice to the southern end to join the convoy of tourist busses. The hotshot security forces, bristling with automatic weapons and designer sunglasses, will marshal you into line before racing off with sirens screaming. It would be quite fun, if it were not so dangerous.

Travelling at 110 kilometres an hour plus, your escorts sweep everything off the road ahead of you – donkey carts lurch aside, pedestrians dive for cover and other motorists cower in the gutters as you race past. If you try and slow down out of a concern for safety or because you just might want to see some of this country you have come so far to see, a siren from behind will blast you forward again.

The 235 kilometres flash by and soon you reach the outskirts of **Luxor**. Pass the new bridge that has been constructed across the Nile to the West Bank and the **Valley of the Kings** and negotiate the inevitable roadblock. Keep left and drive to the traffic circle at the Novotel Hotel. Many of the town's budget hotels are off to the right near here – the best is **Happy Land Hotel** in El Kamar Street; tel: 05-37-1828, fax: 05,37-1140; e-mail: happylandluxor@hotmail.com. A good breakfast is included in the rates of $2 for a dorm and $5 a person in a self-contained room with overhead fan. However, it is not easy to find and situated down some very narrow and busy streets, making it difficult to drive there in a heavily laden 4x4 (N25°41.526 E32°38.212).

For a bit more luxury, try the **Karnak Hotel** which is out of the hustle and bustle of town, past the Temple of Karnak and opposite the Hilton Hotel. With a garden and pool, they charge $40/$50 single/double, tel: 05-37-4155. If you want to camp, there is the **Rezeiki Camp** (N15°42.607 E32°38.905) near to the Karnak Temple which charges $2,50 a person plus $2,50 a vehicle.

Luxor has temples and tombs like nowhere else in Egypt and you are

Recommended reading:
Lovers on the Nile
by Richard Hall on the adventurer
Samuel Baker and his exploration
of the sources of the Nile with
his slave/wife Florence.

A Nile-side restaurant in northern Sudan. Cuisine in Sudan is limited, but salad always available.

going to have to visit the **Luxor Temple** and **Karnak** on the East Bank, and the **Temple of Hatshepsut** and the **Valley of the Kings** on the West Bank.

Luxor Temple is on the banks of the Nile in the centre of town, and is open from 06h00 to 21h00. The ticket office is on the Cornice and entry is $5 a person. Early evening is a good time to visit, as it is cooler and the temple is floodlit.

Karnak is about two kilometres north of town along the cornice. Open from 06h00 to 17h30. Tickets cost $5 a person.

To get across to the West Bank, head south and cross the Nile at the new bridge. Turn right at the T-junction, heading north again to the signposted left turn to the ticket office at the end of the road (N25°43.374 E32°36.277). West

Bank sites are open from 07h00 to 17h00 and cost $3 for the Temple of Hatshepsut and $5 to visit any three tombs in the Valley of the Kings. Parking at each of these places cost $0,25.

The last leg to Cairo

Travelling north to Cairo (see page 187) along the Nile is 700 kilometres of fairly ordinary Egyptian driving – dodging carts, trucks and busses, the probability of convoys and only the fine temple at **Abydos** to distract you.

If you have the time, rather swing out into the **Western Desert** and visit the string of oases there. Not all fit the image of the stereotyped oasis, but driving through the desert is still a great experience.

22

Luxor to Cairo

via the oases of the Western Desert 1 330 km

Although a fairly lengthy detour on your way to Cairo, this loop through the Western Desert is on a good tarred road and gives you a glimpse of another side of the country, away from the lush fields of the Nile. You will experience the vast emptiness of the desert and explore well-preserved Bedouin villages. This is unspoilt Egypt.

The Egyptian authorities don't want you driving into the desert; in fact, they don't want to let you out of their sight. So, to dodge the roadblocks, drive south out of Luxor towards Aswan for about 55 kilometres.

Left: One camel that did not make it.
Right: The Sphinx and pyramids at your destination, Cairo.

At N25°19.055 E32°33.329 turn west and cross the Nile at the Esna Barrage. Turn right and drive north again, parallel to the Nile, to N25°34.893 E32°27.233, where a signposted road turns west into the desert to **El Kharga**.

Make sure you have enough fuel and water, the desert is empty and harsh, and although the road is a good tarred surface, there is hardly any traffic. This newish road does not appear on all maps, but is a good alternative to going all the way around via Asyut.

At 37 kilometres from the Nile (N25°26.143 E32°11.416) do not turn right, but keep straight ahead. The surroundings are flat and sandy with rocky hills and mountains in the distance. The only features that break the monotony are absurd concrete bus shelters and the occasional first-aid station in the middle of nowhere.

At 240 kilometres you encounter your first roadblock. The guys that they send out to do roadblock duty in the desert are not the brightest dudes, but they can still hold you up, so agree with everything they suggest. If they would prefer you to be from Germany because they've never heard of South Africa, then let them write Germany in their tatty old logbook. What does it matter, as long as you get through as quickly as possible?

Four kilometres further you pass the unimpressive little oasis of **Baris**. Turn right at N24°48.777 E30°34.857 and travel 70 kilometres through a green belt of mini oases to **Kharga**. Kharga is a large and unattractive town with most amenities and doesn't make you want to stop over.

These Western Desert towns fall under the New Valley Governorate and the authorities are moving people into the area, hoping to develop it as an economic and agricultural alternative to the Nile Valley.

At the circle in Kharga (N25°26.877 E30°32.550), turn left to take the road to **Dakhla**, refueling on the right on the way out. Back in the desert, the road has had to be rebuilt in many places to bypass huge dunes that have drifted across it. You've also got to laugh at the hundreds of road signs, many indicating steep uphills and downhills in a desert that is as flat as a pool table. You will pass fantastically shaped rocky outcrops which offer good opportunities for camping.

Dakhla Oasis, about 580 kilometres from Luxor, might be a bit far to travel in one day, but the roads are good.

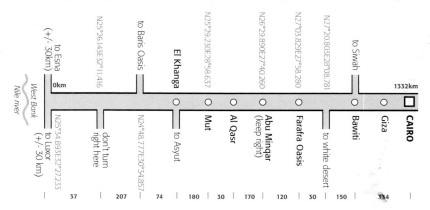

Mut, the largest town in this oasis area, is a good place to overnight and explore. The new **Al Forsan Hotel** (N25°29.230 E28°58.637) in Mut is in Sharia al-Wadi near to the old city square of Midan al-Gamaa.

Here you will find **Magdi Atia**, a very knowledgeable local guide who speaks English and French. Contact him for camel treks, jeep trips and camping in the desert on mobile 1002010564-1129 or magdimohamed@yahoo.fr.

The hill behind the hotel is an old burial ground and you can still see human remains sticking out of some of the exposed tombs. From the hill you have a great view of the **Old City** – well worth spending a few hours exploring the labyrinth of winding lanes and mud-brick houses that surround the **Old Citadel**.

Thirty kilometres past Mut, and still part of the Dakhla Oasis, is the medieval town of **Al Qasr**. One of the best examples of old desert architecture in Egypt, Al-Qasr is officially protected and slowly being renovated. A guide will lead you through the narrow covered streets, showing you the mosque, olive press, flour mill, blacksmiths bellows, pottery works and Madrassa (school of Islamic law). Make a point of climbing the mosque's tall minaret for a spectacular view of the earthy-toned town.

The next oasis, **Farafra**, is 290 kilometres away. To get there, turn right at **Abu Minqar** (N26°29.890 E27°40.260) and climb a surprisingly steep escarpment – watch out for speed humps in the road 25 kilometres before **Farafra**.

The big attraction here is **Bir Sitta**, a

hot spring that is oh-so relaxing after a long drive through the desert. Turn west in town, just past the fuel station at N27°03.829 E27°58.280 and follow the signs to **Aqua Sun Hotel** for six kilometres, keep left of the hotel and at N27°04.841 E27°55.300 you will see a small concrete reservoir. Hot sulphurous water gushes in from a pipe, creating a rough and ready spa bath – perfect on a chilly moonlit night. But, beware of the brown muck that clings to the walls of the pools, it stains.

The best place to stay in Farafra is the **Al Badawiya Hotel**, attractively built and decorated in Bedouin style. Rates are $2 a person for camping, $5 a person for a room and $10 a person for a self-contained room. It has a good restaurant, can organise desert expeditions and sometimes presents performances by local Bedouin musicians.

Another overnight option is to head for the **White Desert**. About 30 kilometres north of Farafra you will pass through an area of white rock formations, eroded into fantastically weird shapes by the wind. If you turn off at N27°20.803 E28°08.781 you can drive to a particularly good spot. Overnight camping among these other-worldly outcrops is unforgettable.

The chaos that is Cairo

You're now left with just 515 kilometres of good tarred road through the dullest, deadest and most featureless grey desert before reaching your ultimate goal, **Cairo**. The outskirts of this big city greet you with modern housing estates, shopping malls, amusement parks and chaotic city traffic.

You will be in sight of the mighty **pyramids of Giza** when the road forms a T-junction at N29°56.818 E31°05.972. South goes to Al-Fayoum and north to Cairo or on to Alexandria. It is a confusing intersection, as you can only turn south and then cross over to the northbound lane a little further down.

In Giza, get onto **Al Haram** (Pyramids Road) and follow signs to **Gezira** and **Doqqi**. Around **Midan Giza**, you will drive up over the chaos on an elevated road, keep left when on top and carry on straight past the zoo and university. At the circle just past the **Cairo Sheraton**, turn right and cross a side channel of the **Nile** onto **Gezira Island**. Keep going along **Sharia Tahrir** to the bridge that takes you across the main channel of the Nile. No time to stop and greet your old river friend now as you're approaching the heart of the beast. Two blocks further, and there it is, **Midan Tahrir** – the central square of the 'Mother of the World', Cairo. Congratulations, you made it!

Where to stay in Cairo

My favourite place to stay in Cairo is **Ismailia House Hotel**, although it is not ideal if you need to park a car, its position overlooking Tahrir Square is the most central in the city. Ashraf and Mustapha run a secure, no-nonsense little operation and can arrange inexpensive excursions around Cairo and the rest of Egypt. It is on the eighth floor under the big Sanyo neon sign – look for the dodgy old antique lifts behind the news stand next to the Ali Baba Cafeteria.

Dorms cost $3,50, rooms $4,50/$9 single/double and self-contained doubles $11 all inclusive of breakfast, tel: 02-796-3122, e-mail: ismahouse@hotmail.com. Try for room 805, as it has a huge wrap-around balcony that overlooks the Egyptian Museum and at night has a fabulous view of the animated neon Coke sign.

A five-day pre-booked and guided tour to Aswan and Luxor, including feluccas, trains, hotels and meals, can be organised through Ismailia for a very reasonable $120 a person.

The two or three blocks behind Ismailia are well stocked with restaurants and food stalls, including (if you really must) a KFC, Pizza Hut and MacDonalds.

A good option if you are worried about the safety of your vehicle and want to avoid the hustle of the city is to head out along the airport road to the suburb of **Heliopolis**. The **Hotel Beirut** (tel: 02-291-6048) and the **Baron Hotel** (tel: 02-291-5757) both charge in the $30/$60 range.

Camping in Cairo is available only at **Motel Salma** (tel: 02-384-9152, fax: 02-385-1010). Situated a bit far out of town (N29°58.283 E31°10.766) – take the road to Abu Sir from Giza – it costs $1,50 a person.

What to see in Cairo

The two must-see sights of Cairo are the **Egyptian Museum** and the **Pyramids of Giza**. The museum is centrally situated on **Tahrir Square**, costs $4,50 (cameras $2,50) and is open daily from 09h00 to 16h45. You could spend months exploring this vast collection of ancient

You can hire a camel (or an Arab horse) to ride round the pyramids at Giza in Cairo.

Egyptian art, or just home in on the two main exhibits, the royal mummy room (a whopping extra $9) and the golden treasures of Tutankhamen.

To get to the **Pyramids of Giza** from Tahrir Square, take Sharia Tahrir across the bridge onto Gezira Island, over the next bridge to Al-Galaa Square, past the Sheraton Hotel and along Sharia Al-Giza. You will be running parallel with the Nile, but one block back. Go past the **Cairo Zoo** and at Midan Giza bear right and onto Sharia Al-Haram (Pyramids Road). Keep going for about eight kilometres and you will run straight into the main gates of the pyramids, opposite the famous **Oberoi Mena House Hotel**.

To get to the more southern entrance, with a better view of the Sphinx and the pyramids in the background, turn left at the last intersection and then right where the tourist shops thicken. There is a $4,50 general entrance fee, $4,50 for entry into each of the pyramids plus the usual $2,50 for a camera.

Useful contacts in Cairo

A very important address in Cairo is that of the **Automobile Touring Club of Egypt**, tel: 574-3191, fax: 574-3348. It is situated in Qasr el-Nil Street between the museum and Talib Harb Square, on the second floor of a building with Tamimi written on it.

Head down the arcade on the right to the entrance next to the **Nile SAT Travel Agency**. Mrs Mohamed Rashad is particularly helpful.

If you need your vehicle serviced or repaired, **Land Rover** are represented in Cairo by **Ahmed El Gharib** of **Jaguar Egypt**, tel: 02-401-7329, fax: 02-263-4614, e-mail: agharib@mm-group-eg.com. There is a service centre at Joseph Tito Road, Heliopolis (next to Cairo airport).

23 Where next?

Africa is the cradle of humanity and has been crisscrossed by us since the dawn of time. These routes were followed by traders, conquerors, slavers and pilgrims, and they are still being used. This book has not covered the Sahara routes nor western Africa, but when the political situation in these regions improves, I will be able to include them in future editions.

You could disagree with and disregard everything in this book and still have a fabulous time. My hope is that reading this book has convinced you to travel through Africa and that I have been able to enthuse you with the same love and wonder that I have for this vast, beautiful continent. Be self-sufficient, keep an open mind and go. It just might change your life.

I welcome any constructive suggestions, current information or just a note telling me of your experiences at mcopeland@telkomsa.net.

Index Bold indicates a box

PHOTOGRAPH CREDITS: (l=left r=right t=top b=bottom br=bottom right)
David Bristow: 88l, 93, 119. **Robyn Daly:** 16r, 28t, 32, 48b, 58, 59b, 71, 75b, 88r, 89, 190. **Cameron Ewart-Smith:** 10, 47, 48t, 59t, 111, 114, 127, 130, 131b, 140. **Justin Fox:** 1, 8t, 31, 34t, 74, 100b, 101, 123t, 148, 149, 150, 151, 167. **Cathy Lanz:** 117, 122. **Don Pinnock:** 3, 6, 8b, 11, 16l, 19, 20, 28b, 28br, 33, 34b, 38, 40, 42, 45, 50, 55, 75t, 100t, 118, 121, 123b, 129, 170, 171, 179, 183, 184. **David Rogers:** 15, 95. **Patrick Wagner:** 97, 115, 131t, 141, 185, 189.